***Family Process* (ISSN: 0014-7370)** Published quarterly by Family Process Institute, Inc. www.FamilyProcess.org
Administrative Office: P.O. Box 23980, Rochester, NY 14692-3980, USA; Tel: 585-482-7390; info@FamilyProcess.org
Editor: UPMS Health System, 3811 O'Hara St., Rm. 441, Pittsburgh, PA 15213; Tel: 412-624-0804; editor@FamilyProcess.org
Copyright © 2002, Family Process Institute, Inc. Periodicals postage paid at Rochester, NY and at additional mailing offices.
**Postmaster:** Send address changes to Family Process Institute, Inc., P.O. Box 23980, Rochester, NY, 14692-3980.

## NOTICE TO SUBSCRIBERS

*Family Process* is a multidisciplinary journal that publishes clinical research, training, and theoretical contributions in the broad area of family therapy.

*Family Process* is indexed and abstracted (in whole or in part) in: *Abstracts of Research in Pastoral Care and Counseling, Abstracts for Social Workers, Care and Counseling, Family Research Database, Index Medicus, Psychological Abstracts, Sage Publications Family Studies Abstract, Social Work Research Abstracts, Sociological Abstracts, Social Services Abstracts* and the *International Bibliography of Periodical Literature on the Humanities and Social Sciences.*

*Family Process* is published quarterly, appearing in March, June, September, and December and is also available online. Subscription rate, which includes online access, for North America are $54 (individual), $24 (student) or $108 (institutions); for other countries are $66 (individual), $32 (student), or $120 (institutions). Prices include delivery. Single-issue prices are $18 (North America) and $38 (other countries) plus shipping & handling. Online only prices are available through our web site. All rates are in US dollars and checks must be drawn on a US bank. Checks should be made payable to *Family Process* Institute and sent to *Family Process*, P.O. Box 23980, Rochester, NY 14602-0838, USA. For additional information and online ordering visit our web site at www.FamilyProcess.org

**Change of Address:** Subscribers are requested to notify the Subscription Office, *Family Process*, P.O. Box 23980, Rochester, NY 14692-3980, Tel: 585-482-7390; Fax: 585-482-2902 of changes in address as promptly as possible. Failure to do so will delay receipt of the Journal. To insure uninterrupted delivery, provide your name, old and new addresses, and zip codes.

## NOTICE TO CONTRIBUTORS

### Submission of Manuscripts

*General requirements.* Manuscripts should be sent to Carol M. Anderson, Ph.D., Editor, *Family Process*, UPMC Health System, 3811 O'Hara Street, Room 441, Pittsburgh, PA 15213 USA. In a cover letter, please include the word count of the article, and the address, phone number, fax and e-mail address of the principal author. Authors will be notified about the status of their manuscripts as rapidly as possible. Manuscripts are received with the understanding that they are not being submitted simultaneously to another publication.

Authors are requested to prepare their articles in conformity with *Family Process* Style. Papers should be written clearly and concisely, using gender-neutral language and a minimum of jargon. Brevity is also desirable. All case reports should protect patient confidentiality.

*Typing:* Manuscripts (original and 4 copies) should be on white bond paper, double-spaced throughout, and with 1-1/2 inch margins. A copy of the manuscript on an IBM compatible disk in text only format (.txt) should be included with initial submission. Files submitted in Wordperfect or MS Word format are encouraged. In either case, the author is advised to keep a copy for checking against galley proofs. Upon acceptance, authors will be expected to provide the final manuscript on disk.

**Authors:** Because *Family Process* uses a blind review system, a separate cover page should be used to provide the identifying information about the authors. The authors' names should not be included on subsequent pages. For each author, give professional degrees/title, and name and location of the principal institutional affiliation, and complete mailing address of the principal author; the latter information will appear in a footnote on page 1 of the article if accepted. Specify the address for reprint orders.

**Acknowledgments:** Any listing of grant support or special appreciation that the authors wish to include should be included on the cover page. If the article is accepted for publication, this information will appear in another footnote on page 1.

**Opening Summary:** For full-length articles, the author should include an abstract of approximately 200–250 words. Research articles should use the standard categories of introduction, methods, results and discussion. In articles describing theory, training or clinical interventions, the abstract should make it possible for the reader to have a brief overview of all relevant aspects of the work, including the intent, scope, general procedures, and principal conclusions. For brief reports, these summaries should be similar in content, but limited to 100 words.

**References:** An important responsibility of the author is the preparation of a correct reference list, double spaced and located at the end of the article. References should be checked against original sources.

**References in text:** First citation may include up to 4 names (NB: et al. = "and others"); more than 4, cite first 3, et al., date. Subsequent citations: include dual authors; more than 2, cite first surname et al., date. Serial listings: alphabetize by surname of first author.

**Reference list:** Alphabetize by surname; list *all* authors; spell out journal names: abbreviations for journals and shortcuts (*ibid., op. cit.*) are not acceptable. (See following examples.)

> *Articles:* Ackerman, N.W. (1971). The growing edge of family therapy. *Family Process 10:* 143–156.//Smith, N., Smith, A., & Jones, P. (1988). . . . .

> *Chapters:* Goldstein, M.J., & Strachan, A.M. (1987). The family and schizophrenia (pp. 481–509). In T. Jacob (ed.), *Family interaction and psychopathology: Theories, methods, and findings.* New York: Plenum Press.

> *Edited books:* Wynne, L.C., McDaniel, S.H., & Weber, T.T. (eds.). (1986). *Systems consultation: A new perspective for family therapy.* New York: Guilford Press.

**Quotations:** Page number(s) must be provided.

**Footnotes:** The appearance of a footnote should be indicated by a superior number at the appropriate place in the text. The numbered list of footnotes, typed double space, should be located after the reference listing.

**Headings:** The journal uses a bicolumn format; headings must be short. Within the text, three levels of headings are used: major heads are centered, boldface capitals, thus:

## METHOD

Major subheads are flushed left, boldface, with initial capitals, thus:

### Family Constellation

Minor subheads are flushed left, italicized, with initial capitals, thus:

### *Case Example*

**Tables:** Use a separate sheet of paper for each Table.

**Figures:** High-contrast glossy prints or camera-ready copies must be supplied by the author; legends are typed on a separate page. See current issues of the Journal for models. Indicate in the text where tables/figures are to be placed, thus:

/Table (Figure) 1 about here/

**Copy Editing, Proofs, and Reprint Orders:** After an article has been accepted for publication, it is copy-edited for literary style, conformity to the style of this journal, clarity of presentation, coherence, punctuation, standard usage of terms, spelling, etc. After the article is typeset authors may be charged for any changes they wish to make. The author will receive page-proofs from the printer, together with a reprint order that must be returned within 10 days of receipt.

Occasionally, and with the author's permission, an article that has been accepted will be followed by an invited commentary to which the author may submit a rejoinder. The author's unwillingness to participate in this process will in no way affect the publication of an accepted article.

**Books for listing or review,** as well as articles on professional publications in the field, should be sent to Carol M. Anderson, Ph.D., Editor, *Family Process,* UPMC Health System, 3811 O'Hara Street, Room 441, Pittsburgh, PA 15213 USA

## NOTICE TO ADVERTISERS

*Family Process* accepts paid advertising relating to matters of interest and concern to the family therapy and wider psychological and psychiatric communities. Advertising about new publications, forthcoming conferences, and professional events is particularly welcomed. Our rates are deliberately set low to help contribute to the widest possible dissemination of information to the research and therapeutic communities we serve. **Mechanical specifications:** Full page—5-1/2″ wide by 8″ high; Half page—5-1/2″ wide x 4″ high; black & white. **Rates:** Full page—$300.00; Half page–$175.00. **Deadline:** Space reservation and artwork must be made within 60 days of publication. Contact: Business Manager, Family Process Institute, Inc., P.O. Box 23980, Rochester, NY 14692-3980; Tel: 585-482-7390; Fax: 585-482-2902; E-mail: info@FamilyProcess.org. *Family Process* reserves the right to reject any copy deemed unsuitable.

## PHOTOCOPY REPRINT & REPUBLISH REQUESTS

Authorization to photocopy items for internal or personal use, or the internal or personal use of specific clients, is granted by *Family Process,* ISSN: 0014-7370, provided that the appropriate fee is paid directly to Copyright Clearance Center, 222 Rosewood Drive, Danvers, MA 01923, USA, 978-750-8400. Prior to photocopying items for educational classroom use, please contact Copyright Clearance Center, Inc. directly. For additional information available online, contact http://www.copyright.com/

# FAMiLY PROCESS

SUMMER 2002                                                    VOLUME 41 • NUMBER 2

# Introduction to the Special Issue on Marriage in the 20th Century in Western Civilization: Trends, Research, Therapy, and Perspectives

WILLIAM M. PINSOF, Ph.D.†

T HE purpose of this Special Issue of *Family Process* is to focus on what happened to marriage in Western Civilization in the 20th century. This has been a time of immense transformation in virtually every aspect of human life in the West, including the human family. A core tenet of early family systems theory and family therapy concerned the centrality of the marital dyad to the health and well-being of the family and its members. During the 20th century this dyad was also transformed.

In the first article, I address the major marital changes or trends, focusing primarily on the fact that during the last half of the 20th century, for the first time in history, divorce replaced death as the endpoint of the majority of marriages. I explore the causes or correlates of this death-to-divorce transition, reflect on what it might mean about the human capacity and inclination to pair-bond permanently, offer a set of precepts for building a new paradigm of pair-bonding that better fits the relational realities of today, and explore the implications of these precepts for social policy, family law, marital research, and couple therapy.

In the 20th century, for the first time, marriage and intimate relations in general also became the objects of scientific study. In the second article, John Gottman and Clifford Notarius delineate the process whereby marriage progressively moved into the purview of science. They explore the application of various research strategies to marriage, including self-report, observational and, most recently, psychophysiological

---

† Guest Editor.

methodologies. They also review the major findings from these research strategies and provide recommendations for marital research in the 21$^{st}$ century.

Along with the dramatic increase in divorce and its new status as an object of scientific study, in the 20$^{th}$ century, marriage also became, for the first time, an object of psychotherapeutic intervention. Alan Gurman and Peter Fraenkel describe and explain the process by which marriage and intimate relations increasingly moved into the consultation room. After exploring the early stages of "marriage counseling," they delineate the proliferation of couples therapies, as well as some of the major influences on the development of specific approaches and the field as a whole. They conclude with recommendations and predictions for the conduct of couples therapy in the 21$^{st}$ century.

It would be impossible to talk about what happened to marriage in the 20$^{th}$ century without addressing the rise of feminism and the fundamental changes in the biopsychosocial roles of women. As detailed in the first three articles, feminism has been one of the most influential factors in the redefinition of marriage and the increase in divorce, as well as the study and treatment of marriage in the 20$^{th}$ century. In addition to commenting upon and extending the discussions of feminism in each of the three initial articles, Cheryl Rampage identifies different stages in the impact of feminist beliefs and values on marriage, research, and treatment, and argues for the more complete integration of these values and beliefs in the future.

Lastly, no discussion of what happened to marriage in the 20$^{th}$ century would be complete without addressing the dramatic changes in marriage that occurred within the African American community. In certain ways these changes mirrored what happened to European-American couples, but in important ways they differed. Extending the discussions on this subject in the first three articles, Elaine Pinderhughes focuses on the extraordinary decrease in the marriage rate among African Americans in the last half of the 20$^{th}$ century and some of the major factors associated with that change. She attends particularly to the impact of the legacy of slavery and pervasive racism on African American marriage and gender roles, as well as the influence of contemporary social and economic factors. She argues for more thorough integration of historical and contextual factors into the theory, research, and treatment of African American couples.

Although none of the articles in this Special Issue explicitly make this point, they collectively and implicitly challenge the idea articulated above that the marital dyad is the central and, to some extent, the most important dyad in the family. As these articles reflect, the place of marriage within today's single parent, bi-nuclear and remarried families has gotten more ambiguous and complex. These articles clarify and explain many of the changes in marriage, marital research, and couples therapy in the 20$^{th}$ century in the West, emphasizing the need for new theory, research, and practice to take a more complex, multifaceted and diverse perspective on marriage, divorce, and human pair-bonding in general into the 21$^{st}$ century.

# The Death of "Till Death Us Do Part": The Transformation of Pair-Bonding in the 20th Century*

WILLIAM M. PINSOF, Ph.D.†

*During the last half of the 20th century within Western civilization, for the first time in human history, divorce replaced death as the most common endpoint of marriage. In this article I explore the history of this death-to-divorce transition, the forces associated with the transition, and what the transition may have revealed about the human capacity for monogamous, lifelong pair-bonding. The impact and consequences of the transition for the generations that came of age during it and immediately afterwards are examined, with particular attention to the emergence of new, alternative pair-bonding structures such as cohabitation and nonmarital co-parenting. The article highlights the inability of the dichotomous marriage-versus-being-single paradigm to encompass the new pair-bonding structures and the normalizing of divorce. Precepts for a new, more encompassing, veridical and humane pair-bonding paradigm are presented, and some of their implications for social policy, family law, social science, and couple and family therapy are elaborated.*

*Fam Proc 41:135–157, 2002*

To have and to hold
from this day forward,
for better or worse,
for richer or poorer,
in sickness and in health,
to love and to cherish,
till death us do part.

*Solemnization of Matrimony*
*The Book of Common Prayer* (p. 301)

---

* I thank the following friends, colleagues, and relatives for their editorial feedback on this article: Carol Anderson, Douglas Breunlin, Lindsay Chase-Landsdale, James Feldman, John Gottman, Jay Lebow, Penny and Michael Mesic, Arthur C. Nielsen III, Suzan Pinsof, Laura Pinsof, Cheryl Rampage, and Rick Zinbarg. I particularly thank Catherine Barcy for her enthusiasm and energy in helping me find the facts, and Jean Goldsmith for helping me develop many of the ideas in this article.

† President of the Family Institute at Northwestern University and Director of Northwestern's Center for Applied Psychological and Family Studies, 618 Library Place, Evanston IL 60201; e-mail: w-pinsof@northwestern.edu.

DURING the 20th century, human life was transformed in a number of substantial ways. These transformations pertained primarily to human life in the West, but also to certain industrially developed parts of Asia, South America, and Africa. In regard to the family, perhaps the most fundamental transformation concerned marriage. Prior to the 20th century, the most common endpoint of marriage was death. During the 20th century, the most common endpoint of marriage became divorce. In 1900, two-thirds of all marriages ended as a result of partner death within 40 years; by 1976 that figure had gone down to just over one-third (Uhlenberg, 1980). Nineteen seventy-four marked the point at which more marriages ended as a result of divorce rather than death (Hagestad, 1988). In 1867, less than 10% of all marriages in the U.S. ended in divorce; by 1985 that figure had grown to over 50% (Cherlin, 1992). By the end of the 20th century in the West, divorce replaced death as the "normal"[1] endpoint of most marriages.

This transformation in the way the majority of marriages end has had numerous consequences for families and society. Two consequences, or at least correlates of this transition, were that during the last half of the 20th century marriage became an object of therapeutic intervention (Gurman & Fraenkel, 2002) and scientific inquiry (Gottman & Notarius, 2002). Additionally, in the last 30 years, divorce became a major topic of social and political discourse. In almost all of these contexts, and with few exceptions (Ahrons, 1994; Goldsmith, 1982), divorce has been defined as an undesirable end to marriage. Many studies have documented the deleterious short- and long-term effects of divorce on children and adults (Bray & Hetherington, 1993), and divorce has been viewed as a "social disorder" whose frequency approaches "epidemic" proportions and urgently needs to be reduced.

At the beginning of the 21st century, when divorce has become the statistically, if not culturally "normal" endpoint of marriage, the time has come to examine the shift from death-to-divorce from a

_____

[1] I am using "normal" in this specific context in the statistical sense—meaning "most common" or the highest (most frequent) point in a normal distribution. For a comprehensive examination of normality and families see Froma Walsh's *Normal Family Processes* (1982, 1993).

more historical, evolutionary, and ethological perspective. It is time to move beyond thinking about the divorce rate as an indicator of a social disorder that must be reduced, to thinking about it more neutrally and inquisitively. The trend, initiated with Goldsmith's (1982) pioneering efforts to define the postdivorce family as a "normal unit," needs to be intensified and expanded.

New questions need to be asked, such as, what does this death-to-divorce shift mean? What may it reveal about human beings' capacities and inclinations for permanent pair-bonding? What does it imply for expectations about the permanence of marriage and the theories that are needed to encompass these expectations? What are the implications of this shift in regard to the kind of social and legal structures and procedures that could and should be created to support couples living the new "marital reality?" From a clinical perspective, what does this shift imply for the kinds of theories and practices that should be developed by mental health practitioners to deal with the new realities of human pair-bonding? What kind of research questions need to be asked and pursued in light of this shift. Lastly, and most fundamentally, does this shift require a new paradigm for marriage in the 21st century and beyond? This article represents an initial attempt to address these questions.

## MONOGAMOUS MARRIAGE WITHIN WESTERN CIVILIZATION

This article conceptualizes, contextualizes, and defines marriage in specific ways. Marriage is conceptualized from an interspecies perspective as a form of pair-bonding. Pair-bonding is a concept from ethology (Eibl-Eibesfeldt, 1989) that refers to a species' establishment and maintenance of mutually exclusive and enduring dyadic relationships. Pair-bonding typically implies the existence of a sexual relationship between the partners, which defines the couple as potentially procreative. Pair-bonding has been typically thought of as a heterosexual phenomenon, although heterosexuality is not a necessary or inherent part of the concept as used in this article. Some species apparently pair-bond for life, whereas others pair-bond more flexibly (Barash & Lipton, 2001).

From an intraspecies or human perspective, this article locates marriage within a specific systemic context—"Western civilization."[2] It includes Europe, North America, Australia, and New Zealand and is essentially European-American civilization. The concept of marriage targeted in this article does not include marriage as generally defined and practiced within the non-Western civilizations—the Islamic, Hindu, Sinic (Chinese), African, Japanese, and Latin American.[3] This is not to deny that there may be certain Westernized groups within these civilizations to which this definition of marriage applies.

In addition to contextualizing, permanent pair-bonding within Western civilization, this article addresses marriage as a relationship that is predicated on a mutual and voluntary commitment to a lifelong, monogamous partnership. "Monogamy" refers to sexual exclusivity (Laumann, Gagnon, Michael, & Michaels, 1994) and means that the partners in a marriage pledge sexual fidelity as part of their commitment. Additionally, they commit to stay married for life—"till-death-us do part." That many partners fail to honor

these pledges and commitments does not deny their role in defining the type of relationship to which the partners originally committed themselves.

In conclusion, the type of marriage addressed in this article can be thought of as romantic or love-based marriage: from this perspective, marriage is primarily love-driven. Secondarily it may be economically, politically, or socially-driven. This type of marriage primarily expresses the desires, goals, and interests of the partners, as opposed to their families or others. In this kind of Western marriage, the partners marry primarily because they want to, and they do it primarily for love and for life.

## TRANSITION FROM DEATH-TO-DIVORCE

To contextualize the death-to-divorce transition adequately, it is necessary to understand what marriage was like historically, when the endpoint of death predominated.

### Pre-Modern Marital Experience

Beatrice Gottlieb, the historian, has written extensively about the family in the Western world from 1400 to 1800—from the end of the Black Death Plague to the dawn of industrialization. During this period,

> most marriages broke up after about ten or twenty years, not because of desertion or legal action, but because of death . . . The fragility of life was something no one could be unaware of . . . The fragility of marriage was also something deeply embedded in the consciousness of all, not least because hardly anyone grew up with a full set of parents or grandparents. From the point of view of the married couple, this meant that however fond they were of each other they were likely to feel it necessary to make provisions for a future without each other. Marriage contracts were primarily provisions for widowhood. For couples who were not particularly fond of each other, it was not unrealistic to dream of deliverance by death. [1993, p. 108]

---

[2] For a detailed discussion and definition of the term "civilization," see Huntington, S. (1996, pp. 40–44).

[3] Whether or not Latin American civilization actually differs sufficiently from Western civilization to warrant designation as a separate civilization is a legitimately debatable subject and beyond the scope of this article.

Marriages were viewed as permanent, but relatively unstable and short-lived. "In the past when a couple got married they could not help but have ambivalent expectations about the durability of their relationship. They were tightly locked into it and could not easily get out of it by legal means, but they knew very well that the time was probably not far off when death was going to part them" (p. 105).

Along the same lines, writing about pre-industrial, Catholic Poland, Kuklo (1990) reports 15 years as the average duration of marriage in most towns. Once again, most of these marriages ended as a result of death. Furthermore, in normal years in pre-industrial Warsaw, two-thirds of all marriages were first marriages. However, in years of natural calamities, spousal mortality decreased this proportion to 50%.

### The Modern Marital Experience

Some form of divorce or formal marital dissolution has always been part of the human species. The divorce rate has varied depending on the era and restrictions placed on divorce; but even under the most divorce-restricting regimes (e.g., the Catholic Church in Europe before the Reformation) people found ingenious and even bizarre ways to annul marriages and essentially divorce (Gies and Gies, 1987). Prior to the dawn of industrialization, in the middle of the 19th century, the probability that a marriage would end in divorce (or annulment) hovered below 10% (Cherlin, 1992). In the U.S., the proportion of marriages begun in each year that will end in divorce has steadily increased from less than 10% for 1867 to over 55% for 1985 (Cherlin, 1992). The statistics for Western Europe have shown a similar trend. However, by the mid-1980s that 115 year trend stopped. The divorce rate in the U.S. and Europe leveled off and even decreased slightly through the rest of the 20th century.

The divorce rate is a complex and somewhat contentious statistic that can be defined and derived in a variety of ways (Peck, 1999). A very crude measure is to look at the number of marriages and divorces occurring within a particular locale annually. For instance, according to the Centers for Disease Control, in the United States in 1994, 2,362,000 couples married and 1,191,000 divorced. Another method considers the number of divorces in a given year for a certain number of people. A standard statistic is the divorce rate per year per 1000 people, which in modern times has ranged from a high of 5.3 in 1981 to a low of 2.0 in 1940. It has generally hovered around 5.0 since 1981 (Peck, 1999).

Another common statistic that is used to characterize marital duration is the divorce median—the number of years by which half of all divorces will occur. Numerous studies have revealed that half of all divorces occur within the first seven years of marriage and that the rate of divorce slows down after that point. The implication of this seven-year median, is that, if half of all contemporary marriages will eventually end in divorce, *one-quarter of all marriages last less than seven years.*

A related statistic that is linked to what is called life-table analysis is the cumulative proportion of marriages disrupted through divorce or formal separation by a specified point in time, typically some number of years. Using this statistic and the derivative probability of disruption statistic, Bramlett and Mosher (2001) present preliminary conclusions from a very large, federally planned and funded, national U.S. survey that was conducted in 1995.[4] Consistent with Gottlieb's (1993)

---

[4] The conclusions from the Bramlett and Mosher (2001) study are based on data from the 1995 National Survey of Family Growth, Cycle 5, conducted

historical observation that "most marriages broke up after ten or twenty years . . . because of death," Bramlett and Mosher report that, for first marriages, the probability that the marriage will end in divorce or separation by its 20$^{th}$ year is .48 for whites; .63 for blacks; and .52 for Hispanics. This means that for these three groups, more than half of their marriages (.54 specifically) will end in divorce or separation by their 20$^{th}$ year.

Bramlett and Mosher's data for second marriages are more limited (they only go out to ten years as opposed to 20 for first marriages), but reflect an accelerated trend for whites: .39 of second marriages will divorce, versus .32 for first marriages, by the ten-year point. This means that almost 40% of white second marriages will end in separation or divorce within ten years. Extrapolating from this finding, it is not unreasonable to conclude that the proportion of white marriages (first, second, and beyond) dissolving before their 20$^{th}$ year will be greater than 50%.

Recent state statistics reflect similar trends. In New York in 1995, 1996, and 1997, 83% of all divorces occurred before the 20$^{th}$ year of marriage. In the state of Florida, in 1998, 87% of all divorces occurred before the 20$^{th}$ year. These statistics are conservative estimates of the rate of marital dissolution based exclusively on legal marriage and divorce records. They do not include separations or annulments.

Integrating the data that have emerged in the last quarter of the 20th century about the divorce rate and the longevity of marriages, it is reasonable to conclude

_____

by the Centers for Disease Control and Prevention's National Center for Health Statistics. It involved in-home computer-assisted interviews with 10,847 women—1553 were Hispanic, 6483 were white non-Hispanic, 2446 were black non-Hispanic, and 365 were of other races/ethnicity.

that one-quarter of all marriages will dissolve by their seventh year, and approximately half of all marriages will end before their 20$^{th}$ year as a result of divorce or separation. The remaining 50% of marriages will end primarily as a result of death over the next 40 to 50 years.

## FACTORS BEHIND THE DEATH-TO-DIVORCE TRANSITION

The shift from death-to-divorce as the most common endpoint of marriage in the 20th century was associated with and perhaps driven by three major factors: the increased lifespan in Western civilization; the shift in the biopsychosocial roles of women; and legal and social value changes. The extent to which these factors can be viewed as causally related to the death-to-divorce transition varies across the factors and different studies.

### Increased Lifespan

A fundamental and unprecedented transformation in the lives of people in the West in the 20th century was the increase in the human lifespan. From 1900 to 2000, the average human lifespan for white Americans increased over 25 years (for men from 48 to 74; for women from 51 to 80); for non-white Americans, who started with a shorter average lifespan in 1900, it increased over 30 years (Caplow, Hicks, & Wittenberg, 2001). Western Europeans experienced a similar lifespan increase (Hall, 1993). "The mortality decline in this century is greater than the total mortality decline that occurred during the 250 years preceding 1900" (Uhlenberg, 1980).

If the most common endpoint of marriage is death, an increased lifespan should result in longer marriages. The assumption is that as people live longer, they will stay married longer. However, this has not been the case. As people in the West came to live longer, it appears that the average duration of their marriages did not substantially increase. Instead, people dramatically increased their use of divorce. The average or median duration of marriage did not change but, rather, the factors that maintain that average or median changed. Along these lines, Robinson and McVey (1985), citing Davis (1972), write:

> . . . for over a century (1860–1970) the overall marital dissolution rate in the United States remained relatively unchanged. Although some short-term and minor variations were apparent, no sizeable or significant differences had occurred in the yearly rate and therefore, it was concluded that marital stability was maintained over the general time period. The relative contributions of death and divorce to marital dissolution, however, had changed. Specifically, the proportional contribution of divorce had increased "drastically." Death still dissolved more marriages each year than did divorce throughout the entire time period. [p. 98]

### Biopsychosocial Roles of Women

Michael (1988), an economist and disciple of Gary Becker (1981), the first economist to focus primarily on family systems, used statistics systematically to examine the contributions of various factors to the doubling of the divorce rate in the U.S. between 1960 and 1980. Michael ruled out U.S.-specific phenomena because of the comparable (if slightly smaller) rise in the divorce rate in Western Europe. Furthermore, his analyses led him to dismiss arguments attributing the rise to the increased aging of the U.S. population, the increasing rate of second and third marriages, and geographical location within the U.S.

Employing a complex regression analysis, Michael found evidence to support the impact of the reduced fertility rate in the U.S. (which decreased from 3.42 in 1961 to 1.63, below replacement, in 1974) and Western Europe on the divorce rate. In his and Becker's analyses, having one

child reduced the likelihood of divorce approximately 30% between the fifth and fifteenth year of marriage; having two children reduced the rate another 30%. The reduced fertility rate directly links to Michael's finding that the diffusion of modern contraceptive technology accounts for approximately 50% of the variance in the rise in the divorce rate into the late 1970s. Additionally, Michael unequivocally concludes that "the rise in women's income is a dominant force affecting the divorce rate" (1988, p. 392). The power of the findings on women's income in almost all analyses of the rise of divorce from the early 1960s to 1978 is particularly intriguing because it emerges in the face of the rise in men's income during this period, a variable that has been consistently associated with a diminished likelihood of divorce.

The two variables that account most consistently for the rise of the divorce rate in Michael's analysis are women's income and the diffusion of contraceptive technology.[5] The impact of the latter variable was further substantiated, in Michael's opinion, by the much slower rise in the divorce rate in Japan during the same period, and Japan's reluctance to adopt the contraceptive pill through the early 1970s. What is most striking about these two variables is that they greatly increased women's choice. The income variable provided women with economic opportunity and choice. It reduced women's economic dependence on men and provided them with opportunities to support

-----

[5] He also identifies two other strong predictors of divorce—the rise in public assistance payments (linked to women's income), and the coming of age of the postwar baby-boom generation (the percentage of women in their twenties, compared to in their thirties, forties, and fifties, increased from one-third in 1960 to one-half by 1975). The coming-of-age variable placed a disproportionately large number of people in the early years of marriage, the time of greatest risk for divorce.

themselves that had not existed prior to the last half of the 20th century. The contraceptive variable provided women with choice about when and if to become pregnant. It opened biological options that did not exist heretofore. The radically reduced fertility rate in the entire Western world reflects the impact of this contraceptive breakthrough and the elective options it offered women (and men).

## Social Value and Legal Changes

Undoubtedly, one of the most debated factors in the effort to explain and account for the increase in divorce in the 20th century is the transformation of divorce laws, specifically the implementation of no-fault divorce laws. Michael dismissed the often-cited explanation tying the rate rise from 1960 to 1980 to the easing of divorce laws within the U.S. "Many states exhibited rising divorce rates several years before a change in the law occurred" (Michael, 1988, p. 369). Going beyond Michael's analysis, Marvell (1989) studied the impact of different types of divorce laws on divorce rates in 38 states to challenge the results of at least ten studies which "explored the impact of no-fault divorce laws on divorce rates, with most concluding that there is none" (p. 546). He found that different types of laws had different effects, some of which were significant. However, he concluded that his "findings only mildly contradict the earlier studies finding no such impact" (p. 564).

The extent to which changes in divorce laws drove or were driven by the rising divorce rate up to 1980 is probably impossible to determine. However, it is clear that the change in divorce laws in the last half of the 20th century reflected a change in social values—a change that simultaneously attempted to: 1) make divorces easier to obtain; 2) reduce the social and legal stigma associated with divorce; and 3) reduce the psychosocial trauma (blame and character assassination) associated with divorce.

It is impossible to understand the transition to divorce in the last half of the 20th century without considering the value shift associated with the rise of feminism. As cited above, the role of women changed dramatically in the course of the 20th century, economically and reproductively. However, these changes were closely associated with dramatic and profound shifts in the roles women took on in the family, in marriage, and in society in general. These shifts also began a transformation in men's roles within the family and marriage, as well as a general reduction in patriarchy within the broader society. They also led to a sustained series of critiques of marriage as an institution. Rampage (2002) explores the impact of this feminist and ultimately gender-role revolution in the 20th century on marriage and divorce.

## AFRICAN AMERICAN EXPERIENCE

In general, African Americans experienced the same trends as white and Hispanic Americans, but only more so. The divorce rate per 1000 women in the African American community increased from 78 in 1960 to 358 in 1990, whereas the rate for whites changed from 38 to 153 (Tucker & Mitchell-Kernan, 1995). However, the greatest change in the African American community during this period was in the marriage rate. As of 1992, "fewer than three of four black women overall can expect to marry compared to nine of ten white women" (1995, p. 12).

The increasing divorce rate and the huge reduction in the marriage rate in the African American community can be partially attributed to the factors that have influenced these rates in the white community (lifespan; women's economic and reproductive choice; and social/legal values), but there are significant additional factors. The two primary additional factors that have emerged in the analysis of these trends in the African American community are changes in the demographic sex ratio and male employment.

In regard to sex ratios, over the last half of the 20th century the male/female sex ratio has changed dramatically, such that there are substantially more women than men in the appropriate age cohorts. This gender disparity has been attributed to relatively high (compared to white) adolescent homicide/suicide rates (gang violence and drug overdoses), and the high rate of adolescent and young adult incarceration. Secondly, the disappearance of blue-collar jobs in the industrial Northeast and Midwest had a devastating impact on male employment and income in African American communities (Wilson, 1996). Simply stated, in the last 20 years of the 20th century, in the African American community, there have not been enough men for the available women, and many of the men who have been available as potential marriage partners, have been unattractive as providers because of unemployment or relative (to female) underemployment (Patterson, 1998). Pinderhughes (2002) explores the African American marital experience in the 20th century in greater detail.

## LEVELING OF DIVORCE RATE AFTER 1980

Along with the skyrocketing divorce rate between 1960 and 1980, many social demographers have noted another dramatic trend: the divorce rate dropped slightly after its 1981-high and stayed around 22 divorces per 1000 married women (50% lifetime probability of divorce) through the rest of the 20th century (Caplow et al., 2001). The same leveling of the divorce rate also occurred in Western Europe after the early 1980s (Hall, 1993).

Goldstein (1999) statistically examined various predictors to test their capacity to explain this leveling off in the United States. First of all, his analysis suggests that the leveling trend is sufficiently robust that it can be viewed as a "real" phenomenon as opposed to a temporary depression in the century-long increase. Secondly his compositional analysis failed to explain the leveling as a result of any of the following variables: age structure of the population, age at marriage, marriage order (first, second, etc.), educational attainment, number of children, and the timing of childbearing. Lastly, his analysis suggests that "any increased selectivity of marriage linked to cohabitation appears to be only a small part of the story behind the leveling of marital instability" (p. 414). He concludes that the current divorce rate will continue at its present level and that "new theories are needed to explain the determinants of divorce rates at the population level" (p. 409).

A possible explanation may reside in the hypothesis that the overall level of marital stability has not changed, but rather the means by which that level is maintained have changed. If this is true, that the level of marital stability has remained the same, it may well be that, from a population perspective, the increasing divorce rate over the last century maintained the 20-year average or median duration of marriage in the face of the largest human lifespan increase in recorded history. The divorce rate increased until the median duration of marriage returned to the 20-year level and then it stopped.

It is puzzling that the divorce rate stopped growing after 1980, despite the continuing increase in women's income and employment, the primary statistical predictors (and correlates) of the rise in divorce rates between 1960 and 1980. From 1980 to 1997 the percentage of married women in the work force in the U.S. increased from 50% to 65% and women's earnings as a percentage of men's earnings increased from 60% to 74% (Caplow et al., 2001). In other words, the primary "drivers" of the rise in divorce rates continued increasing after the rise in the divorce rate stopped, a finding that is statistically counterintuitive. Based on these data, it is not unreasonable to hypothesize that as long as the increased lifespan, the increase in women's income and employment, the availability of effective and cheap contraceptive technology, and divorce-friendly laws and values remain facts of life, the 50% divorce rate is here to stay. It fits the evolved human level of monogamous marital stability.

## HUMAN PAIR-BONDING

The data on the death-to-divorce transition raise important questions about the extent to which human beings, at least human beings in the West, have evolved to be permanent, monogamous pair-bonders. In the context of a 50-year lifespan, no economic independence or reproductive choice for women, and divorce-hostile social and legal values, marrying till death us do part was realistic. However, these changes in the 20th century have created a new context in which the majority of couples will not sustain marriage until death. Why? What, if anything, have the increased lifespan and the other biopsychosocial changes associated with death-to-divorce transition revealed about the human capacity and inclination to pair-bond permanently and monogamously?

### Capacity to Pair-bond as a Set of Individual Factors

A major issue that emerges from this question is whether it would be useful to view the capacity for permanent, monogamous pair-bonding as a complex set of factors located within an individual? This individual capacity may be normally distributed, with certain individuals having a lot of it, others (the majority) having a moderate amount, and others having very

little. This capacity might include the following set of factors: the ability to select an appropriate partner; the ability to commit to an intimate relationship; the ability to attach to another human being; the ability to maintain a certain level of personal integrity, morality, and responsibility; the ability to regulate emotion (particularly anger) and impulses (particularly sexuality); the ability to get along with another person over an extended period of time; and the ability to love another person.

Undoubtedly, like all individual abilities, the capacity to pair-bond permanently and monogamously would be influenced by genetic and environmental factors. Viewed as an individual capacity, a substantial amount of the variance in this set of factors could be accounted for by personality variables. McAdams (1995) has proposed a three-level model of personality that goes from the deepest and most genetically influenced trait level to the highest and most environmentally impacted "narrative" level. The deepest level of personality embodies *dispositional traits*—"relatively nonconditional, relatively decontextualized, generally linear, and implicitly comparative dimensions of personality" (p. 371).

Over the last 20 years, personality researchers (Digman, 1990; McCrae & Costa, 1996) have settled on a set of traits called the Five-Factor Model of Personality. The "Big Five" are Openness to Experience, Conscientiousness, Extraversion, Agreeableness, and Neuroticism. The Big Five are influenced by heredity, with Extraversion generally considered the most genetically determined. It may well be that individuals with high scores on Neuroticism and low scores on Agreeableness and Conscientiousness have higher rates of divorce than individuals low on Neuroticism and high on Agreeableness and Conscientiousness. To state the obvious— people who are highly anxious, contentious, and unreliable probably do not make very good mates.

Within McAdams' model of personality, the second level of personality is a psychological smorgasbord that contains *personal concerns*—motives, values, defense mechanisms, coping styles, developmental issues and concerns, personal strivings, attachment styles, and strategies and tactics for getting what one wants and avoiding what one does not want in particular contexts (1995, p. 376). Personal concerns are less influenced by genetics than dispositional traits, and more influenced by individuals' early experience in their families of origin.

The second level encompasses what psychopathologists refer to as personality disorders, the Axis-II disorders of DSM-IV. On this level, it makes sense that individuals with major personality disorders and substantial psychopathology within their families of origin are more likely to have troubled marriages and higher rates of divorce. To state the obvious, adults with interpersonally disruptive personality disorders, such as paranoid, antisocial, borderline, and narcissistic, tend to have troubled social relations in general and probably have difficulty sustaining marital relationships over long periods of time.

The third and top level of personality pertains to *identity,* which McAdams defines as "an internalized and evolving life story, or personal myth" (1995, p. 382). These stories or narratives are primarily determined by environmental factors, with family-of-origin and general life experience playing the major role. These personal narratives give meaning, purpose, and coherence to people's lives. They are the primary psychological vehicle for integrating one's sense of self (who one is) from the past to the present and into the future. Sternberg (1998) has taken narrative theory into the domain of couple and marital relations, theorizing that people in relationships have at least three multilevel domains of narratives—mine, yours, and ours. He has hypothesized that "relationships are more likely to succeed when common stories generate shared worldviews, assumptions about relationships, and interpretation of events . . ." (p. 10). It is the compatibility of couple's stories, their fit, that predicts marital success.

## Capacity to Pair-Bond as a Set of Couple Factors

Sternberg's theory begins to bridge individual and systemic perspectives. It is not sufficient to think about the capacity for pair-bonding as solely a set of individual factors. It denies the systemic nature of marriage. From a systemic perspective, it is less the characteristics of the individuals in the marriage that predict whether or not they will get divorced, but rather the characteristics of the couple, including the characteristics of the individuals in relationship to each other. A step in this direction is the homophily hypothesis, which states that individuals who are more alike demographically (age, religion, socioeconomic status, etc.) and attitudinally (beliefs and values) have a higher probability of staying married than individuals who differ on these dimensions (Laumann et al., 1994). The homophilic couple characteristic is demographic similarity, whereas the narrative couple characteristic is compatibility.

However, systems theorists would argue that the homophilic and narrative approaches are still additive—for them, the whole never becomes greater than the sum of the parts. To do that, theorists need to move to a level of description of the couple that is not based on individual attributes. In four studies over 25 years, Gottman (1993; Gottman & Notarius, 2002) found that married couples with a set of specific interactional characteristics have almost a 100% probability of getting divorced within four years. The characteristics of these couples, which emerge in a relatively brief face-to-face interaction in Gottman's laboratory, are criticism, defensiveness, contempt, and stonewalling—a quartet of factors called the "Four Horsemen of the Apocalypse."

The identification of this highly at-risk group of couples constitutes a major step forward in the study of divorce. However, family psychology is still far away from being able to predict over longer (than four years) periods of time which couples will and which couples will not divorce. What is clear at this point, however, is that the capacity to pair-bond is a product of capacities of the individuals in a relationship as well as capacities of the couple. There is emerging evidence that suggests that whether or not a couple will divorce is not just a function of their individual upbringing or their history and current functioning as a couple, but also of their genetic heritages (McGue & Lykken, 1992; Reiss, Neiderhiser, Hetherington & Plomin, 2000). Thus, the capacity to pair-bond monogamously for life is a complex set of biopsychosocial factors that science has just begun to differentiate and study (Gottman & Notarius, 2002).

### Inclination to Stay Married/ Capacity to Divorce

In the preceding examination of the psychosocial factors that influence whether or not a couple will stay married, staying married is viewed as a capacity. The capacity perspective on marriage typically assumes that the capacity to stay married is a good thing and that having more of it is better than having less of it. This perspective takes a deficit view of divorce. However, it is possible to take a different perspective that considers the capacity to divorce as a characteristic of an individual and/or a couple. This perspective does not just view divorce as a failure of the capacity to stay married, but as a potential positive event or outcome. Any marital therapist who has treated a wide variety of couples over a number of years, knows that in certain circumstances, getting a divorce is a courageous and positive act. In such circumstances, staying married may reflect an inability to pursue what may be in the best interests of oneself, one's partner, and even one's children.

In this regard, Becker's (1981) and Michael's (1988) economically based theory views individuals as decision-makers who are constantly evaluating the benefits and costs of marriage. The decision to divorce, from their perspective, derives from one or both individuals in a couple concluding that the benefits of divorce outweigh the benefits of staying married. In essence, they define people as rational decision makers, and the decision to divorce as a rational act that is perceived by the individual making that decision as a beneficial step in his or her life.

No discussion of marital stability would be complete however without considering the inclination of a person to get divorced. The inclination to divorce is another complex phenomenon that contains a variety of individually anchored factors that collectively determine the extent to which an individual is disposed or inclined to consider divorce as a realistic and positive option. Although linked to factors like reproductive choice and socioeconomic opportunity, the inclination to divorce is distinct. It targets what might be thought as a person's unencumbered attitude toward divorce. Some of the factors that comprise this phenomenon are an individual's: degree of religious conviction; beliefs about the sacrosanctity of marriage and relational commitment; sense of entitlement to relational happiness; family history of divorce; social context; and perception of the damage that a divorce will inflict on loved ones.

## Adult Development and Marital Stability

Another factor behind the death-to-divorce transition is the human capacity for growth over the life course. It is not coincidental that developmental psychology expanded beyond childhood and adolescence in the second half of the 20th century as the human lifespan lengthened and a healthy and vigorous life became a reality for many people into their eighties. The capacity for adult development in the context of an expanded lifespan means that people are changing and evolving values, goals, and beliefs as they age. People are not the same people at 40 that they were at 20, nor will they be the same at 60 and 80. Since most people now marry between 25 and 35, in all probability, they will have changed (grown) substantially by the time they reach 40.

The findings that half of all divorces occur by the seventh year of marriage and that the vast majority of divorces will have occurred by the 20th year of marriage do not support the idea that as people age and differentiate the likelihood increases that they will become incompatible and divorce.[6] An alternative life-course explanation is that people's sense of their relational future at 35 and 40 is very different now than the sense of the future 35- and 40-year-olds had before the 20th century. The prospect of another forty to fifty years with decent health and possibilities for individual growth in an unhappy relationship is very different than the prospect of another 10 to 15 years under the same conditions.

---

[6] These findings and the lack of a resurgence of divorce in later life may be artifacts of the relatively early state of divorce research. It will be interesting to see the extent to which these findings hold up as the generations that married in the last quarter of the 20th century move into the later years of their marriages in the first quarter of the 21st century.

## Evolution of the Capacity to Pair-bond Flexibly

The capacity to divorce and remarry may also derive in part from human beings' evolutionary heritage. The human capacity for serial monogamy and pair-bonding is an essential characteristic of the human species. With death as the primary terminator of marriage, human beings were left with basically two options after the loss of a spouse—remain single the rest of one's life or remarry. The capacity to bond, lose a spouse, and bond again is critical to the survival of the human species, particularly after events like the Black Plague, famines, and wars. Natural selection favored the survival of people with the capacity for flexible and serial pair-bonding. The result of this selection process over millennia is that human beings have the capacity to lose a spouse through divorce or death and to find another partner to marry. If human beings did not have this capacity, it would make marriage more secure, but it might jeopardize the survival of the species.

## THE IMPACT OF THE DEATH-TO-DIVORCE TRANSITION

A secondary hypothesis of this article is that the death-to-divorce transition in the last half of the 20th century, and in particular the doubling of the divorce rate between 1960 and 1980 had a profound, if not traumatic impact on the children of parents who divorced during the rate rise (up to 1980). Furthermore, that impact resulted in a variety of new pair-bonding patterns that clearly emerged in the last 25 years of the 20th century and that will probably endure as long as men and women enjoy an increased lifespan, have economic and contraceptive choice, and live in a society that defines divorce as an acceptable option.

Approximately half of the children born after 1960 in the Western world experienced parental divorce. This experience occurred within societies in North American and Europe that were not equipped legally, socially, and emotionally to deal with this experience. In fact, divorce did not become an object of serious scientific study until the last quarter of the 20th century (Goldsmith, 1982; Gottman & Notarius, 2002). These children felt shame, isolation (despite their numbers), and a lack of social and emotional support. They were told that their families were "broken," and many of these children felt emotionally responsible for the breakdown. There were no models for bi-nuclear families (Ahrons, 1994). Only after this period did research begin to reveal the critical role of a good co-parental relationship between divorced ex-spouses and the importance of sustained and significant involvement by the nonresidential parent. In other words, these children experienced divorce at a time when there were no psychosocial road maps, social facilitators, or societal supports. Traumatology since the Vietnam War has revealed that negative posttraumatic sequelae are greater when the traumatized individual feels socially isolated, lacks social support, and feels ashamed and/or embarrassed about the trauma. These children of the escalating divorce rate, were a psychologically traumatized generation, traumatized by their parents' divorces *and* their own sense of social isolation and shame.

This traumatic experience created great suspicion about marriage. If half of that generation's parents made life-long commitments to each other which they eventually abrogated, what did that say about marriage? Was it really forever, if the majority of people who pledged forever did not stick to the agreement? This suspicion has led that generation, and to a significant extent following generations, to question the meaning of marriage and the pathways that historically led to it. In doing so, they began experimenting with a variety of pair-bonding alternatives and alternative perspectives on pair-bonding that were in full bloom by the dawn of the 21st century.

However, it would be a mistake to reduce the new perspectives on pair-bonding that emerged from the generation that came of age after 1970 to the traumatic effects of their parents' divorces and society's failure to support and integrate them and their experience. The changes in values, beliefs, and behavior in regard to marriage, divorce, and pair-bonding alternatives that occurred in the last forty years of the 20th century also derived from broader and nontraumatic factors like the rise of feminist values (Rampage, 2002), beliefs about individuals' right to personal happiness and fulfillment, and heightened expectations for intimate relationships.

## REDEFINING MARRIAGE, COHABITATION, AND CO-PARENTING

As the divorce rate soared after 1960, three other major trends started to emerge that were part of the 20th century's transformation in pair-bonding in the Western world: the rate of marriage decreased, while the rates of cohabitation without marriage and nonmarital births increased. In the U.S., the marriage rate (per 1000 unmarried women per year) decreased from approximately 80 in 1970 to a low of 50 in 1996. "The marriage rate generally rose and fell with the business cycle. The 1990s, with conspicuously low marriage rates in years of unprecedented prosperity, were exceptional" (Caplow et al., 2001, p. 68). A slightly greater drop occurred in the marriage rate in Western Europe. The percentage of cohabiting, unmarried couples in the U.S. increased from less than one percent in 1960 to over seven percent of all couples by 1998. The rates for Western Europe were higher, e.g., 19% in the U.K. (Hall, 1993). In the U.S., the percentage of nonmarital births for white women increased from around 2% in 1960 to 26% by 1997, and from 24% to 69% for black women over the same period (Caplow et al., 2001). Across Europe, the nonmarital birthrate in 1960 was 5% or less, depending on the country. In 1988, over 25% of the births in the U.K. and France were nonmarital, whereas in Denmark and Sweden the rates were 48% and 52% respectively (Hall, 1993). This nonmarital birthrate increase is particularly impressive because it occurred at the same time that women in the West had more contraceptive choice than ever before in the history of the human species.

These three trends represent what might be thought of as a collective deconstruction of marriage by the generations that came of age in the last quarter of the 20th century. Historically, cohabitation, marriage, and childbearing were all part of one inseparable package. Marriage and cohabitation were usually co-occurring, and both were typically followed by the birth of children. These three trends reflect an unprecedented separation of cohabitation, marriage, and childbearing.

Data from the National Survey of Family Growth in 1995 found that over half of the women between the ages of thirty to thirty-four were either cohabiting at the time of the survey or had cohabited before they got married (Caplow et al., 2001). These data suggest that for most of the women in this age cohort, cohabitation and marriage were distinct events. However, distinct does not mean unrelated. For many, if not most cohabiting couples, cohabitation represented a major step toward marriage, as opposed to an end in itself.

The fact that in 1997, over one-quarter of the Caucasian babies and over two-thirds of the African American babies in the U.S., and almost half of the babies in Scandinavia were born to unmarried women suggests that for many women (and couples), the decision to have a baby

had become distinct from the decision to marry. Once again, being distinct does not mean unrelated. Caplow et al. noted that the white "parents of a considerable number of these infants eventually married" (2001, p. 86).

These trends reflect the emergence of a new, nondeviant pair-bonding sequence in the last twenty years of the 20th century. This sequence typically began with cohabitation. For the majority of couples this was followed by marriage, but for a very substantial minority in the white community and for many in the African American community, cohabitation was followed by the birth of children. Subsequently, many of these couples married. What emerged was a pattern in which the three events began to represent three somewhat independent choices. Initially, a couple committed to live together—to share property, expenses, and space. Then many couples decided to have children—to commit to being co-parents. A substantial number of these couples then decided to marry—to commit to being life partners. For many couples that followed this pattern, cohabitation represented an opportunity to check each other out, to get to know the other person and the relationship better before making the decision to have children and/or marry.

Many African American families did not follow this alternative pattern. For many families, cohabitation did not precede or follow nonmarital childbirth. Due to the paucity of good statistical data and the flexibility and unofficial nature of many cohabitating arrangements, it is hard to estimate the exact numbers of families in which the unmarried parents did not live together before or after the birth of their child. Official statistics report that in 1998, 57% of black families with children under 18 were headed by a single female parent (Caplow et al., 2001). This distinct trend of nonmarital and noncohabiting childbirth and childrearing within the African American community still supports the hypothesis that African Americans, along with white North Americans and Europeans, in the last half of the 20th century, engaged in a process of disaggregating cohabitation, childbirth, and marriage.

It will be very interesting in the coming years to see whether the marriages that occur after cohabitation and childbearing are more enduring than those that are not preceded by cohabitation and/or childbearing. There is currently a widespread debate (addressed below) as to the meaning of recent findings that couples that cohabit before marriage appear to have a higher incidence of divorce than couples that do not cohabit before marriage (Axinn & Thornton, 1992; Bumpass & Sweet, 1989). It will also be interesting to see the extent to which the trends of the last twenty years of the 20th century continue into the 21$^{st}$. Were the decrease in the rate of marriage and the increase in the rates of nonmarital cohabitation and childbearing primarily characteristics of a psychologically traumatized generation that came of age between 1960 and 1980, or in the case of the African American community, characteristics of an economically and socially traumatized generation, or will these trends characterize subsequent generations that experienced divorce in a more normalized and supportive context?

## IMPLICATIONS OF THE DEATH-TO-DIVORCE TRANSITION

The emergence of the death-to-divorce transition and many people's subsequent redefinition of pair-bonding in the latter half of the 20th century, present numerous challenges to social policy and law makers, social scientists, and mental health practitioners. Despite the fact that the death-to-divorce transition was apparent for at least the last twenty-five years of the 20th century, the currently predominant social policies, laws, research practices, and clinical intervention models pertaining to marriage are predicated upon the life-long, till-death-us-do-part traditional model of marriage. As a result, they are and will continue to be unsynchronized with the new emerging normal realities of pair-bonding in the West. They have been tweaked somewhat in order to accommodate the increase in divorce and the realities of single-parent and bi-nuclear families, but by and large they are still based on a normative and traditional life-long marriage model.

## Toward a New Pair-bonding Paradigm for Western Civilization

For social policies, laws, research practices, and clinical interventions to incorporate the new marital realities of the 21$^{st}$ century in Western civilization, they need to be based on a new pair-bonding paradigm that integrates the implications of the death-to-divorce transition. It is probably presumptuous to attempt to articulate a new pair-bonding paradigm at this early stage, before it is possible to determine the enduring nature of the pair-bond changes that occurred in the 20th century. Instead, the following represent an initial set of precepts that could constitute part of the foundation of a new pair-bonding paradigm.

1. *Marital theory needs to become pair-bonding theory:* The theory of intimate relations that has guided most policies, research, and intervention in the 20th century has been a dichotomous model that looks at people as married or unmarried: the only serious pair-bonding state is marriage. Many couples in the last half of the 20th century defined four serious pair-bonding states—cohabitation without children, cohabitation with children, marriage, and a relatively new phenomenon that might be called *elder pair-bond-*

*ing.*[7] Replacing dichotomous marital theory with a pluralistic theory of human pair-bonding lays a theoretical foundation for identifying, acknowledging, and addressing the multiplicity of serious pair-bonding structures that have evolved over the last 30 years.

2. *The existence and viability of a multiplicity of pair-bonding arrangements need to be acknowledged and addressed:* This precept derives from and extends the first. At a minimum, the four arrangements listed above need to be recognized as legitimate pair-bond structures that fulfill important functions for their participants.

3. *Entering into any particular pair-bond structure entails a distinct and legitimate decision-making process:* This precept disaggregates the one-decision model of traditional marriage in which the commitment to cohabit, have children, and marry, are all part of the same package.

4. *Young adults, contemplating pair-bonding, need to be able to consider a variety of pair-bond options that fit their cultural beliefs, personal preferences, and relational goals:* As young adults consider pair-bonding, they need to be freely able to choose the pair-bond that best fits who they are and where they want to go. They also need to be able to understand that there is a multiplicity of structures that can be entered into sequentially, as their needs and objectives change.

5. *Marriage should continue to be defined as the lifelong, monogamous pair-bond:* Marriage should continue to function as an objective for those who desire such a bond, representing the most committed and enduring pair-bond.

---

[7] A number of elderly, usually widowed individuals live together as intimate couples without formally marrying. In all likelihood this phenomenon will become more common as the baby-boom generation comes of age.

6. *Marriage, as a life-long, monogamous committed relationship, should be available to all mentally competent adults who desire to enter into such a legal and formal relationship.* This precept pertains particularly to gays and lesbians, but also potentially to other groups whose right to marry has been or could be restricted.

7. *Co-parenting without marriage needs to be recognized as a legitimate and life-long, nonmonogamous pair-bond:* Once couples who are not married have children, they are co-parents for the rest of their lives. Their commitment as co-parents needs to be recognized and legitimated.

8. *Co-habitation without children or marriage needs to be viewed not only as a legitimate end-state in itself, but also as a legitimate form of pre-marriage:* Premarital cohabitation is clearly being used by many couples in the West to determine compatibility and the potential for co-parenting and marriage. In 1981–82, in a national survey or 18–34 year olds in Australia, "55% of females and 62% of males agreed that "it is good to have a trial marriage," by which they meant cohabitation (Carmichael, 1985, pp. 98–100). These findings clearly reflect the way in which many Western young adults use and view premarital cohabitation. As of 1988, approximately 60% of all first cohabitations in the U.S. ended in marriage (Bumpass & Sweet, 1989).

9. *Divorce and relational dissolution need to be viewed and treated as normal social events in the life course of modern families:* Public societal discourses on divorce, and relational dissolution in general, need to acknowledge the normality of these events in the life course of families.

10. *The decision to divorce needs to be viewed with greater complexity, thoughtfulness, and neutrality:* Rather than viewing divorce as a failure, it needs to be treated as a complex relational process

that can have good and poor outcomes. It is not inherently good or bad (Hetherington & Kelly, 2002). In fact, under certain circumstances, it can be a positive and even courageous act.

These ten precepts represent an initial foray into the task of articulating a new pair-bonding paradigm. That paradigm remains to be fully articulated. Nevertheless, these ten precepts offer a pre-paradigmatic foundation that can inform subsequent examinations of the implications of the death-to-divorce transition for social policy, law, social science research, and intervention.

## Social Policy

In the last half of the 20th century, people in the Western world began to make new choices about how they wanted to live with each other and create families. Specifically, in about half of the married couples at least one of the partners decided that he or she wanted to divorce. Subsequently, over half of all couples in certain age cohorts decided that they wanted to live together, particularly as a prelude to marriage. Lastly, despite available contraceptive and abortive technology, about a quarter of white women and over two-thirds of black women in the U.S., and almost half of the women in Scandinavia decided to have children out of wedlock.

These new choices and behaviors confronted social policy makers with a core dilemma. They could either attempt to direct human behavior in the direction of favored political and moral agendas or support the choices that people make to improve their lives and express their values. They could define nonmarital cohabitation as "the enemy of marriage" (Popenoe & Dafoe Whitehead, 1999) and encourage social policies that would discourage nonmarital cohabitation. Alternatively, they could attempt to create policies to support and help people in what-

ever type of social structures they create, giving equal credence and respect to divorced and married people, cohabiting and married couples, to children born out of wedlock and children born to married couples, and to married and unmarried parents.

From a psychological perspective, it is hard to imagine the value of defining any major social group that is not physically or emotionally harming itself or others as deviant or undesirable. In Scandinavia, the general trend has been to develop and implement social policies that support the choices people make, as opposed to using such policies as tools to shape those choices. In contrast, the U.S. has been far more ambivalent about supporting choices that deviate from the standard script of get married, live together, and have children. The implications of the emerging pair-bonding paradigm for social policy makers is that social policies need to support people as they enter into, reside within, and move to whatever pair-bond structures fit their needs and goals. People living in a particular pair-bond structure should not be advantaged, nor should their offspring. Social policies must be based on respect for people's right to choose—to live alone or to live within any particular pair-bond structure.

## Law

Law pertaining to marriage and family has struggled to catch up with the new realities of human pair-bonding at the beginning of the 21st century. Attempts have been made to determine and enforce the rights and mutual obligations of nonmarital partners, the legal obligations and rights of unmarried fathers to their children, the access rights of the parents and siblings of divorced or never-married parents to their grandchildren and nieces or nephews, and the rights of gays and lesbians to marry (Morrissey, 2002). The courts increasingly came to understand the value of the divorced co-parental relationship in regard to healthy child development as well as the value of divorce mediation as an alternative to the normal adversarial divorce procedure. However, the legal system is still out of step with the new marital realities and the emerging pair-bonding paradigm. The legal community has responded to the new pair-bonding structures with ambivalence. "These new family structures are reshaping traditional views and reweaving the fundamental fabric of society, prompting some legal experts to call for sweeping change . . . But rethinking domestic relations law is likely to be a lengthy, contentious process" (Morrissey, 2002, p. 38).

At the core of this process is a basic redefinition of family from a unit defined exclusively by blood and procreation, to a unit increasingly defined by intentionality—what the participants intend. Family rights, particularly the right to marry, for gay and lesbian couples, has become the central and to some extent polarizing issue. Currently, Vermont is the only state that allows gay and lesbian civil unions—almost marriages. However, it is hopefully just a matter of time before society and the legal system recognize the legitimacy of homosexual marriages. Consistent with the sixth pre-paradigmatic precept, partners, regardless of their sexual orientation, should be able to marry—to make a public, legal, and life-long monogamous commitment to each other.

A new system of laws needs to be created that recognizes the appropriate rights and responsibilities of partners, their families of origin, and their offspring in all of the four major pair-bond structures (married, divorced, unmarried cohabiting, unmarried co-parents), their major permutations, and gay-lesbian marriage. This system must transcend the dichotomous marriage versus everything-

else model by legally recognizing and appropriately protecting nonmarital cohabiting, nonmarital childbearing and childrearing, as well as marriage. A key word in this regard is "appropriately," which refers to the fact that the rights and obligations of people in the different pair-bonding structures need not and in all probability will not be the same. The challenge is to determine what set of rights and obligations makes the most sense for each of the structures in regard to the mental health and socioeconomic well-being of the participants, their children, and their families.

Despite the improvements that have occurred in many jurisdictions to diminish the trauma of the divorce process to the participants, their children, and their families, the adversarial legal process is still traumatic and humiliating for most participants. A major challenge that is central to the destigmatization and cultural normalization of divorce is the creation of nontraumatic legal processes that do not become party to and inflame the acrimony and alienation that most families bring to the divorce process.

### Social Science

Social science, particularly research on marriage (Gottman, 1993; Gottman & Notarius, 2002), has tended to view divorce as an undesirable outcome whose probability needs to be reduced. Premarital training programs like PREP (Markman, Resnick, Floyd et al., 1993) treat the reduction of the probability of divorce for people going through the program as a primary outcome criterion. Gottman's research on the predictors of divorce is predicated on reducing its incidence. Most social science research on divorce and couples at-risk of divorce conceptualizes divorce as a bad outcome.

Social scientists need to confront the implications of the death-to-divorce transition and the emerging new pair-bonding paradigm. Divorce is here to stay, and about half of all people who marry will probably experience it at some point in their lives. Social science researchers need to move beyond a judgmental attitude toward divorce. Divorce needs to be viewed as a normal outcome that may be desirable or undesirable. Researchers need to stop comparing children of divorce to children of happy marriages, determining through such research that divorce is emotionally and physically bad for children. That is the wrong comparison.

Children of divorce, if they are to be compared to anyone, should be compared to children in families with unhappy and deeply troubled marriages. People who divorce do not divorce because they are happy with each other. A substantial number of couples who divorce had miserable marriages with high rates of addiction, depression, and/or conflict. It is the rare social scientist who would assert that such deeply troubled family contexts are better for childrearing than a divorced couple that can co-parent collaboratively. The emerging data will probably confirm the hypothesis that, in most situations, a good divorce is better for all concerned than a bad marriage.

Similarly, gross, simplistic, and politically driven characterizations of nonmarital cohabitation as the enemy of marriage (Popenoe & Dafoe Whitehead, 1999) obscure the complexity of nonmarital cohabitation. Research indicates that people who elect to live together before marriage have a higher eventual divorce rate than those who elect to marry without prior cohabitation. As Axinn and Thornton (1992) have pointed out, the problem with this research is that it does not adequately account for selection—people who chose to live together before marriage are not the same people who chose to marry directly. They comprise at least two groups with different attitudes toward marriage, religion, and relationships in general. Furthermore, nonmarital cohabitors contain various subgroups that need to be differentiated. More importantly, the attitudes, beliefs, values, and life histories of the couples in these groups need to be understood in much greater detail before causal conclusions can be drawn about cohabitation. To attribute premarital cohabitors' higher subsequent divorce rate and non-premarital-cohabitors' lower subsequent divorce rate to the fact that they did and did not cohabit before they married is unwarranted and bad science.

The sequential pathways of different couples need to be investigated, along with their outcomes. For instance, how many couples follow each of the four following pathways: 1) marriage, simultaneous cohabitation, subsequent childbearing; 2) cohabitation, marriage, and subsequent childbearing; 3) cohabitation, childbearing, and subsequent marriage; 4) cohabitation and subsequent childbearing without marriage? Are there healthy and pathological variants within each type, and, if so, what factors determine which outcomes? What are the effects of each pathway on the adults and the children? Other pathways that involve additional steps and decisions after a divorce, like remarriage, or cohabitation, and/or nonmarital childbearing, also need to be investigated.

Similarly, returning to the overall distribution of marital duration discussed above, what are the different subgroups that make up that distribution? Who are the people who divorce a lot? Who are the people who never divorce, and what do their marriages look like over the life course? Who are the early divorcers and who are the late life divorcers? Are there personality differences between the groups? Are there couples at high risk for divorce, but who might be helped by intervention? Are there couples for whom intervention would not and/or should not help them stay together?

Just as plane-based radar and satellites can help see over the horizon to better predict weather and other events, social science needs to develop better technologies and knowledge to predict the future behavior of partners and relationships. Research has just started to look at the early relational behaviors that predict what couples will be like after ten to fifteen years (Gottman, Coan, Carrère, & Swanson, 1998). Answers to these questions can help couples make better choices in selecting partners and in responding to relational behaviors that might be risk-markers for later problems (Pinsof & Hambright, 2001).

## Mental Health Services

The treatment of marriages and couples has emerged as a distinct form of mental health intervention in the 20th century (Gurman & Fraenkel, 2002). The development of this treatment initiative has coincided, by and large, with the death-to-divorce transition in the last half of the 20th century. Now is the time for mental health practitioners consciously to integrate the implications of the death-to-divorce transition and the emerging pair-bonding paradigm into their theories and interventions. How can modern societies provide appropriate mental health services that are consistent with the pre-paradigmatic precepts?

Family and marital therapists help couples stay together and dissolve their marriages every day. However, most if not all forms of couple therapy are designed to strengthen marriage. Given that 50% of all couples in the Western world will probably divorce, it seems appropriate that mental health professionals develop services to help couples divorce as well as to help couples stay together. Most family and marital therapy training programs do not teach therapists when and how to help couples dissolve their marriages. In medicine, this would be equivalent to not

training obstetricians to do nonvaginal deliveries, or not training oncologists how to treat patients who do not respond to chemotherapy. To do so in medicine would be irresponsible and unethical. The time has arrived to develop more explicit theories and practices to help couples exit from their existing pair-bond structures with minimal damage to both parties (and their children). Concomitantly, these theories and practices need to be formally integrated into couple and family therapy training programs so that subsequent generations of therapists can help people enter into, enjoy, and if necessary leave the multiplicity of family structures in which they actually live.

Since most couples in certain age cohorts appear to use cohabitation as an opportunity to check out and get to know their partner better before making a life-long commitment, what has prevented mental health practitioners from helping couples learn to use cohabitation more consciously and constructively to that end? At least one answer is the lack of scientific knowledge about what to look for as reliable predictors of future behavior. However, most marital and family therapists have some fairly strong ideas about what these couples should look for in order to decide whether to marry or not. In general, these ideas have not been explicitly formulated, published, and/or put into educational curricula.

Mental health practitioners in all probability will become the primary social educators about the various types of pair-bond structures derived from the new paradigm. Increasingly they will need to think about themselves as offering a set of services to couples and potential couples that will range from educating them about alternative pair-bond structures and helping them select the one that is most appropriate for them at this particular point in their lives, to intervening therapeutically to repair damaged relationships, or to facilitate their constructive dissolution.

Despite the fact that so many white and even more black children in the U.S. will be born to unmarried parents, what has prevented mental health practitioners from developing programs to support and help these children feel normal and just as valuable to society as children born to married parents? Only recently, have practitioners begun to develop programs to support children of divorce. *We must develop services to help all children and families in times of need.*

## CONCLUSION

The lengthening of the human lifespan; the biological, psychological, social, and economic improvement of women's lives; and the emergence of new relationship or family values and laws within Western civilization in the 20th century have been associated with, and perhaps have driven, a fundamental transformation in pairbonding. Divorce has replaced death as the primary terminator of marriage. It has become a "normal" marital endpoint. This death-to-divorce transition reveals heretofore obscured aspects or potentials of the human capacity and inclination to pair-bond. The implications of these revelations and the transition warrant the elaboration of a new pair-bonding paradigm. This paradigm needs more fully to inform emerging social policies, family laws, social science research, and last but not least, the mental health services offered to families and couples. This article begins to articulate this new paradigm and to illuminate some of its implications.

Beyond presenting a set of findings, conclusions, and recommendations, the purpose of this article is to stimulate family science and practice to integrate what can be learned about human pair-bonding from the events of the 20th century into a new paradigm and set of practices for the 21st century. The twin hopes of this article are that the paradigm and set of practices will better fit the new pair-bond structures that have evolved and will help facilitate the development of healthy human beings within those structures.

## REFERENCES

Ahrons, C. (1994). *The good divorce: Keeping your family together when your marriage comes apart.* New York: Harper Collins.

Axinn, W.G., & Thornton, A. (1992). The relationship between cohabitation and divorce: Selectivity or causal influence. *Demography* 29: 357–374.

Barash, D.P., & Lipton, J.E. (2001). *The myth of monogamy. Fidelity and infidelity in animals and people.* New York: W.H. Freeman.

Becker, G.S. (1981). *A treatise on the family.* Cambridge: Harvard University Press.

Bramlett, M.D., & Mosher, W.D. (2001). First marriage dissolution, divorce and remarriage: United States. *Advance data from vital and health statistics;* (no. 323). Hyattsville MD: National Center for Health Statistics.

Bray, J., & Hetherington, E.M. (1993). Families in transition: Introduction and overview. *Journal of Family Psychology* 7: 3–9.

Bumpass, L.L., & Sweet, J.A. (1989). National estimates of cohabitation. *Demography* 26 (4): 615–625.

Caplow, T., Hicks, L., & Wattenberg, B.J. (2001). *The first measured century: An illustrated guide to trends in America, 1900–2000.* Washington DC: American Enterprise Institute (AEI) Press.

Carmichael, G.A. (1985). The changing structure of Australian families. *The Australian Quarterly,* Autumn/Winter: 95–104.

Cherlin, A.J. (1992). *Marriage, divorce and remarriage.* Cambridge: Harvard University Press.

Davis, K. (1972). The American family in relation to demographic change (pp. 239–265). In C.F. Westoff & R. Parke (eds.), *Demographic and social aspects of population growth: United States Commission on population growth and the American future.* Washington DC: Government Printing Office.

Digman, J.M. (1990). Personality structure:

Emergence of the five-factor model (pp. 417–440). In M.R. Rosenzweig & L.W. Porter (eds.), *Annual review of psychology* (Vol. 41). Palo Alto CA: Annual Reviews.

Eibl-Eibesfeldt, I. (1989). *Human ethology.* New York: Aldine de Gruyter.

Gies, F., & Gies, J. (1987). *Marriage and the family in the middle ages.* New York: Harper & Row.

Goldsmith, J. (1982). The postdivorce family system (pp. 297–330). In F. Walsh (ed.), *Normal Family Processes.* New York: Guilford Press.

Goldstein, J.R. (1999). The leveling of divorce in the United States. *Demography 36* (3): 409–414.

Gottlieb, B. (1993). *The family in the Western world: From the Black Death to the industrial revolution.* New York: Oxford University Press.

Gottman, J.M. (1993). A theory of marital dissolution and stability. *Journal of Family Psychology 7:* 57–75.

Gottman, J.M., Coan, J., Carrère, S., & Swanson, C. (1998). Predicting marital happiness and stability from newlywed interactions. *Journal of Marriage and the Family 60:* 5–22.

Gottman, J.M., & Notarius, C.I. (2002). Marital research in the 20th century and a research agenda for the 21st century. *Family Process 41:* 159–197.

Gurman, A.S., & Fraenkel, P. (2002). The history of couple therapy: A millennial review. *Family Process 41:* 199–260.

Hagestad, G.O. (1988). Demographic change and the life course: Some emerging trends in the family realm. *Family Relations 37:* 405–410.

Hall, R. (1993). Europe's changing population. *Geography 78:* 3–15.

Hetherington, E.M., & Kelly, J. (2002). *For better or for worse: Divorce reconsidered.* New York: W.W. Norton.

Huntington, S. (1996). *The clash of civilizations and the remaking of world order.* New York: Simon and Schuster (Touchstone).

Kuklo, C. (1990). Marriage in pre-industrial Warsaw in the light of demographic studies. *Journal of Family History 15* (3): 239–259.

Laumann, E.O., Gagnon, J.H., Michael, R.T., & Michaels, S. (1994). *The social organization of sexuality: Sexual practices in the United States.* Chicago: University of Chicago Press.

Markman, H., Resnick, M., Floyd, F., Stanley, S., & Clements, M. (1993). Preventing marital distress through communication and conflict management training: A 4- and 5-year follow up. *Journal of Consulting and Clinical Psychology 61:* 70–77.

Marvell, T.B. (1989). Divorce rates and the fault requirement. *Law and Society Review 23* (4): 543–567.

McAdams, D.P. (1995). What do we know when we know a person. *Journal of Personality 63:* 365–396.

McCrae, R.R., & Costa, P.T. (1996). Toward a new generation of personality theories: Theoretical contexts for the five-factor model (pp. 51–87). In J.S. Wiggins (ed.), *The five-factor model of personality: Theoretical perspectives.* New York: Guilford Press.

McGue, M., & Lykken, D.T. (1992). Genetic influence on risk of divorce. *Psychological Science 3* (6): 368–373.

Michael, R.T. (1988). Why did the U.S. divorce rate double within a decade? *Research in Population Economics 6:* 367–399.

Morrissey, S. (2002). The new neighbors. Domestic relations law struggles to catch up with changes in family life. *American Bar Association Journal 88:* 37–41.

Patterson, O. (1998). *Rituals of blood. Consequences of slavery in two American centuries.* New York: Basic Civitas Books.

Peck, D. (1999). The fifty percent divorce rate: Deconstructing a myth. *Journal of Sociology and Social Welfare 20* (3): 135–144.

Pinderhughes, E.B. (2002). African American marriage in the 20th century. *Family Process 41:* 1269–282.

Pinsof, W., & Hambright, A. (2001). Toward prevention and clinical relevance: A preventive intervention model for family therapy research and practice (pp. 177–196). In H.A. Liddle, D. Sanisteban, R. Levant, & J. Bray (eds.), *Family psychology: Science based interventions.* Washington DC: American Psychological Association.

Popenoe, D., & Dafoe Whitehead, B. (1999). *Should we live together?: What young adults need to know about cohabitation before marriage: A comprehensive review of recent re-*

*search*. Piscataway NJ: National Marriage Project.

Rampage, C. (2002). Marriage in the 20th century: A feminist perspective. *Family Process* 41: 261–268.

Reiss, D., Neiderhiser, J.M., Hetherington, E.M., & Plomin, R. (2000). *The relationship code: Deciphering genetic and social influences on adolescent development*. Cambridge: Harvard University Press.

Robinson, B.W., & McVey, W.W., Jr. (1985). The relative contributions of death and divorce to marital dissolution in Canada and the United States. *Journal of Comparative Family Studies 16:* 93–109.

Sternberg, R.J. (1998). *Love is a story: A new theory of relationships*. New York: Oxford University Press.

Tucker, M., & Mitchell-Kernan, C. (1995). Trends in African American family formation: A theoretical and statistical overview (pp. 3–27). In M. Tucker & C. Mitchell-Kernan (eds.), *The decline in marriage among African Americans*. New York: Russell Sage Foundation.

Uhlenberg, P. (1980). Death and the family. *Journal of Family History 5:* 313–320.

Walsh, F. (ed.). (1982). *Normal family processes*. New York: Guilford Press.

Walsh, F. (ed.). (1993). *Normal family processes* (2nd ed.). New York: Guilford Press.

Wilson, W.J. (1996). *When work disappears*. New York: Random House (Vintage).

Manuscript received September 4, 2001; final revision submitted and accepted March 19, 2002.

# Marital Research in the 20th Century and a Research Agenda for the 21st Century

JOHN M. GOTTMAN, Ph.D.†
CLIFFORD I. NOTARIUS, Ph.D.‡

*In this article we review the advances made in the 20$^{th}$ century in studying marriages. Progress moved from a self-report, personality-based approach to the study of interaction in the 1950s, following the advent of general systems theory. This shift led, beginning in the 1970s, to the rapid development of marital research using a multimethod approach. The development of more sophisticated observational measures in the 1970s followed theorizing about family process that was begun in the decade of the 1950s. New techniques for observation, particularly the study of affect and the merging of synchronized data streams using observational and self-report perceptual data, and the use of sequential and time-series analyses produced new understandings of process and power. Research in the decades of the 1980s and 1990s witnessed the realization of many secular changes in the American family, including the changing role of women, social science's discovery of violence and incest in the family, the beginning of the study of cultural variation in marriages, the expansion of the measurement of marital outcomes to include longevity, health, and physiology (including the immune system), and the study of comorbidities that accompany marital distress. A research agenda for the 21$^{st}$ century is then described.*

*Fam Proc 41:159–197, 2002*

T<small>HE</small> first published research study on marriage was a book by Terman, Butterweiser, Ferguson, Johnson, and Wilson's (1938). They had one major research question, namely, "What is fundamentally different about happily and unhappily married couples?" That question was to become a persistent one in the field of marital research throughout the 20$^{th}$ century. Terman et al. were operating within the long shadow cast by individual personality theory, and they therefore phrased the question as, "Are some personality traits more ideally suited to successful marriage?" In those early days of marital research, investigators firmly believed that self-report methods for measuring personality traits were adequate, and they had no worries about common method variance problems. Common method variance means that using the same method of measurement to measure two different ideas or constructs is problematic; it is related to many phenomena such as the phenomenon that measuring

---

† James Mifflin Professor; send correspondence to the University of Washington, Box 351525, Department of Psychology, Seattle WA 98195; e-mail: jgottman@gottman.com

‡ In private practice; office address: 5028 Wisconsin Ave. NW, Suite 303, Washington DC 20016; e-mail: cnmail@soon.com

two different constructs with the same method tends to yield higher correlations than measuring the same construct with two different methods. We have now learned that common method variance is a fatal flaw in a great deal of marital research. Unfortunately, this methodological problem (trying to "explain" one questionnaire solely with another questionnaire) also has pervaded most of 20th century research on marriage, at least until multiple measurement operations began to be employed in the same study.

Terman et al. found no evidence to support an optimal personality profile for happy marriage; people unhappy in their marriages tended to complain about a wide variety of things, a phenomenon that later was called both negative affectivity and neuroticism. In general, the first 30 years of research on marriage was based almost entirely on pencil-and-paper self-report measures of marital functioning and in dealing with variants of Terman's original question, eventually including stability as well as satisfaction (see Hicks & Platt, 1970). Little headway was made in the study of personality correlates of marital satisfaction until researchers thought of asking *each spouse* to describe the personality of the *partner*. Then, almost all partner-reported personality variables were related to marital satisfaction. However, it was unclear that personality was actually what was being measured.

By the mid-1950s it became evident to most researchers who studied marriage (by now almost entirely sociologists) that pencil-and-paper measures of marital functioning were significantly (usually moderately to highly) correlated if there were a wide enough range of marriages (from miserable to very happy) in a study (see Burgess, Locke, & Thomes, 1971). They began developing standardized short-form measures of marital satisfaction, obtaining norms, and studying de-

velopmental patterns over the life course. As with all factor analytic techniques applied to complex constructs (e.g., work on intelligence) this unidimensional nature of marital satisfaction does not imply that it isn't also multidimensional, since both solutions receive support; furthermore, it may be useful clinically to have an overall measure of marital quality as well as a self-report profile of various aspects of the marriage for diagnosis and clinical intervention.

The moderate to high relationship between most measures of marital functioning as well as moderate correlations of marital satisfaction with spouses' descriptions of their partners' personality traits led to the discovery of the first two replicated phenomena in the area of marital research. These phenomena were the positive and negative halo effects. Here are the two halo phenomena: in unhappy marriages, people tend to endorse almost any negative item about their partner; in happy marriages, people tend to endorse almost any positive item about their partner. Later, in the 1980s this same phenomenon was recast in attribution theory terms as follows: in unhappy marriages, people tend to attribute the negative things their partners do to lasting, unflattering personality traits (the most common being selfishness), and attribute positive things their partners do to fleeting, ephemeral, situational factors. In happy marriages people attribute the positive things their partners do to lasting flattering personality traits and attribute negative things their partners do to fleeting, ephemeral, situational factors. Hence, the early research on personality found that it wasn't so much each person's personality, but the partner's *perception* of the other's personality that was related to marital satisfaction. Note that these findings were, by themselves, of questionable use for clinical intervention.

With the study of norms and developmental patterns of marital satisfaction, some grim findings began emerging from research on marriage. Burgess' longitudinal study (Burgess & Wallin, 1953) found that, for most couples, marital satisfaction was high right after the wedding and then began a slow, steady, and nontrivial decline thereafter. The steady march toward disappointment, misery, and disillusionment appeared to be characteristic of almost all marriages. Although cross-sectional studies differed in their findings, most reported that marital satisfaction did, reliably, deteriorate steadily after marriage, reaching its minimum in mid-life, and began increasing again only when children left home. While there was initially much debate on this point, most studies—especially 13 of the 15 longitudinal studies—found that the arrival of children seemed to spell not conjugal bliss but stress and a precipitous and dangerous decrease in marital satisfaction (e.g., Belsky & Kelly, 1994). Hicks and Platt's (1970) decade-review article on marital happiness and stability concluded that "perhaps the single most surprising finding to emerge from research is that children tend to detract from, rather than contribute to marital happiness" (p. 569).

Then, in the mid-1950s, there was a sea change in marital research. While its historical roots can be traced back to the 1930s (especially to Ackerman, 1958), it was in the 1950s that the first dramatic conceptual break was made with the Terman personality-based tradition for studying marriage. The break was the advent of an *interactional perspective* on marriage rather than a personality perspective. This change was inaugurated by the classic double-bind article by Bateson, Jackson, Haley, and Weakland (1956). For marital research, it had powerful consequences. It suggested that characteristic and rigidly entrenched dysfunctional interaction patterns could be observed by watching clinical families, and dismantling the basic verbal and nonverbal components of messages sent and received. Furthermore, the authors suggested that these repetitive patterns of interactive behavior had profound implications for dysfunctional schemas of thought or even thought disorder. Thus, the interactional perspective focused simultaneously on cognition and interactive behavior. However, the interactional perspective *required* observational methods and *demanded* a focus on process. Indeed, in the 1960s the progenitors of the interactional view founded a new journal called *Family Process*. The new journal was to speak to both researchers and practitioners. Broderick's (1970) theoretical review piece—which initiated the decade-review articles in the *Journal of Marriage and the Family*—was entitled "Beyond the five conceptual frameworks," and attempted to introduce general systems concepts to sociological researchers.

Surprisingly, simultaneously in social psychology a similar sea change occurred, and it was also a breakthrough that emphasized interaction patterns. Thibaut and Kelly's (1959) book, *"The social psychology of groups,"* proposed a description of social interaction in terms of "payoff matrices" of costs and benefits for particular two-person interactions. They proposed that the repertoire of behavioral exchanges between two people could be listed and associated with particular costs and benefits, and that, in effect, the *payoff matrix* defined the relationship; this approach could be made mathematical by the notation that if person-1 displayed behavior $b_1$ to person-2 it was done with a particular payoff represented by a number. Using the idea of the payoff matrix, various relationship configurations could be described, such as win-lose and win-win configurations. One way of construing the payoff matrix is in terms of actual rewards or costs (and this was the way social psychologists preferred), while another way of construing behavior exchange is in terms of the *perceived* rewards and costs of particular exchanges; the latter is one way of operationalizing cognitive schema of interaction. This was not the mainstream approach taken by social psychologists, but it was the approach of some marital researchers.

We briefly depart from this historical review by noting that confluence in measuring both cognitions and interactive behavior was to come later in several forms. In the early 1970s, the Gottman laboratory built what they called a "talk table" whereby couples were videotaped in a conversation while they rated the perceived costs and benefits of each exchange. The behavior of the couple was then separately coded from the videotapes. In this way the positivity and negativity of exchanges could be separately assessed in the domains of behavior as well as cognition (Gottman, Markman, & Notarius, 1977). Later, in a brilliant study, Notarius, Benson, Sloane, et al. (1989) used a video recall method to create a time-synchronized stream of both behavior and Thibaut-Kelly-style of payoff matrix cognitions. This methodological breakthrough was important; the Gottman and Levenson laboratories, also using a video recall rating dial, were able to add physiological measures within the same time-synchronized stream to test hypotheses that previously had defied operationalization (Gottman & Levenson, 1985).

This time-synchronized blending of multiple measurements with observational measures in one investigation makes it possible to ask more sophisticated questions at the interfaces of the domains of behavior and perception. Notarius et al. (1989) pioneered a methodology for mapping the interface between perception and behavior in their experimental investigation of Weiss's (1980)

concepts of positive or negative sentiment override, and Gottman, Notarius, Gonso, and Markman's (1976) concept of editing. The concept of sentiment override implies a discrepancy between a spouse's subjective evaluation of partner's behavior and an outsider observer's evaluation of the same precise behavior. The valence of any discrepancy between spouse and unbiased observer in evaluating the partner's behavior would define positive or negative sentiment override. "Editing," however, implies a precise sequence of interaction in which a spouse responds positively (or even neutrally) immediately after accurately perceiving his or her partner's behavior to be negative (i.e., the perception matches an unbiased observer's assessment of the immediate antecedent). The important point is that these salient interactional processes can be studied only through an examination of the interface between behavior and perception. Applying log-linear modeling to the observational and subjective data, Notarius et al. (1989) found a surprising similarity among nondistressed wives and distressed and nondistressed husbands. The perception of distressed wives was heavily under the influence of negative sentiment override and these wives were least likely to edit out a negative reply to the their husband's negative interactions. In contrast, nondistressed wives and distressed and nondistressed husbands were subjectively more likely to evaluate their partner's negative messages as neutral or positive; even when they made a negative evaluation, they were less likely to respond negatively.

In the late 1960s and in the 1970s, a large set of suggestions emerged (without empirical support) about what was "dysfunctional" in both interactive behavior and social cognition in relationships. In the marital area, the dysfunctional cognitive schema identified by Paul Watzlawick was mindreading (Watzlawick, Beavin, &

Jackson, 1967), which is attributing things to a partner without adequate evidence or expecting a listener to know what the speaker needed without any explicit information provided by the speaker. Lederer and Jackson (1968), in their highly influential book *"The mirages of marriage,"* proposed several seminal hypotheses including: (1) the *quid pro quo,* or that a failure of a (usually covert) positive reciprocity contract characterized unhappy and unstable marriages; (2) unrealistic romantic illusions and unrealistic high standards about love characterized unhappy and unstable marriages.

Hence, by the mid-1970s there were two new approaches that suggested examining a relationship using interactive behavior and social cognitions about the interaction itself. In 1974, in a breakthrough research study, Raush, Barry, Hertl, and Swain were motivated to apply the thinking in these two approaches to the longitudinal study of couples going through the transition to parenthood. Using improvised conflict situations, they observed marital interaction and they then used an early form of sequential analysis (multivariate information theory) of these patterns of interaction to suggest cognitive schema associated with these patterns. The meta-theory they proposed was called "adaptive probabilism," which they intended to be a shift from a deterministic view of interactive behavior to a probabilistic one. Unfortunately, they did not use a separate method to measure cognitions or to operationalize Thibaut and Kelly's payoff matrices. Instead, they turned to a study of interactive games.

*Games or naturalistic interaction?* Initially, in the early years of observing couples, structured interactions with specified payoff matrices (also called games) were used in some studies (e.g., Ravich, Deutch, and Brown, 1966 used a trucking game; Straus and Tallman, 1971, used a game called SIMFAM, a shuffle-board

kind of game with uncertain rules; and Gergen, 1969, noted that the Prisoner's Dilemma game was used extensively). However, it turned out that behavior was so constrained in these games that they tended not to detect the actual level of distress. Thus, one can conclude that these situations had limited validity. The lack of correlation implies that there are many couples who are quite competent in communication and cooperation in constrained situations, but not during their own marital conflicts (and possibly conversely). This means it is possible to find contexts of communicative competence in even the most distressed marriages. Perhaps the therapist could build upon these inherent talents and generalize skills to marital situations.

One of the major conclusions of the Raush et al. (1974) study was that when interaction was *observed,* Talcott Parson and colleagues' (Parsons, Bales, Olds, et al., 1955) distinction of women as expressive and men as instrumental was not tenable. Women were highly instrumental in conflict interactions as well as expressive, and the same was true of men; gender differences were not quite so clearcut. In fact, Raush et al. concluded that, during pregnancy, women tended to be coercive and men conciliatory, but that these patterns changed after the baby's arrival (see also Broderick, 1970). Indeed, we are confident that anyone who actually observes women and men in families would conclude that both men and women are emotionally expressive and instrumental. In fact, the Tannen (1990) and Aries (1976) work on gender differences in language in the workplace has never held in families: women's language is not tentative during marital conflict, nor is it designed to facilitate conciliation and pair bonding; instead, it is strong, assertive, persuasive, thoughtful, and definite. It is well known that women start 80% of all marital conflict discussions; generally, women are not reticent in their presentation of the issues nor are they without analyses of the problem and suggestions for its solution (Ball, Cowan, & Cowan, 1995). None of these conclusions could have been drawn by collecting only self-report data.

Returning to the emergence of the interactional perspective: in the late 1960s, von Bertalanffy (1968) proposed a global approach called *General System Theory*. It stimulated a flurry of theoretical clinical writing suggesting that social interaction was very rich but could be dismantled and understood by examining its components. This led to a perspective on research as well as clinical work that was breathtaking in its scope. The idea was that psychopathology was caused by dysfunctional family interaction (and resultant dysfunctional thought patterns), and that the therapist should be viewed as a cybernetic engineer who would change these patterns by clarifying messages, build in self-sustaining feedback mechanisms, thus ending dysfunctional social cognitions (such as mindreading), and replacing dysfunctional patterns (double-bind messages) with functional ones (e.g., metacommunication).

But what exactly were the dysfunctional patterns? Theoreticians answered that they were patterns that prevented healthy development, which to some writers (Bateson, Jackson, Haley, & Weakland, 1962), meant double-binding messages; to some (Wynne, Ryckoff, Day, & Hirsch, 1958) meant pseudo-mutuality; to some (Bowen, 1961) meant blocks to differentiation (by which he meant being able to control emotion with reason); to others (Lidz, Cornelison, Fleck, & Terry, 1957) meant schism, skew, and symbiosis. These concepts were never clearly defined, and in his decade-review article on marital therapy Olson (1970) noted that most of these concepts had been derived from work with families of schizophren-

ics, and that they have no empirical validity. In the marital area, it is not necessary that one be right, just that one be interesting. That is to say, a great service was provided by suggesting hypotheses about what is functional and dysfunctional, especially if these ideas were measurable and potentially disconfirmable (which many were not).

The ideas about dysfunction and function were very good ideas, and they led to a new kind of research in the marital area. One of the things that these ideas accomplished is that they led to the use of observational methods in addition to the older self-report methods. They also led to the study of the *context* of the interaction (e.g., is the interaction conflictual or not), an idea that was never suggested by the study of personality, which presumably measures traits independent of situational context.

In the 1970s, a few behavioral and child psychologists entered the field of marriage research armed with observational systems that made it possible to measure marital interaction patterns with complex codes that could *describe* interaction. This is a subtle point, but observational measures (unlike personality scales) have the potential for providing just a description of interaction that is atheoretical and basically "dust-bowl" empirical. The process of quantitative description was skipped when studying marriages with other methods. However, observational methods could describe interaction. These methods therefore held a new potential for surprise and discovery. This spirit of discovery was also vitalized by the 1974 publication of an important volume edited by Lewis & Rosenblum entitled *"The effect of the infant on its caregiver."* The book called for new descriptive and analytic research on actual face-to-face interaction between babies and caregivers. It stimulated new methods of observational data collection and data analysis that led to the development and use of sequential analytic and time-series methods to describe the patterning of interaction between people over time.

This work, applying observational methods to the study of marriages, was begun with great energy and optimism. Unfortunately, the empirical research on troubled families was never able to support the interactive perspective's beautiful and complex hypotheses of dysfunction that had been proposed based largely on clinical observation. In general, research showed that troubled families were not characterized by more frequent use of double-binding messages, by more nonverbal-verbal channel inconsistency, by fewer metacommunicative messages, and so on. Instead, by and large, the data tended to support the conclusion that troubled families (or unhappy couples) were simply more negative (and to a smaller degree, less positive), and more likely to reciprocate negativity than was the case in well-functioning families (or happy couples). Hence, the observational data on the interactional perspective directed researchers to the importance of *affect* in understanding functional and dysfunctional marriages (e.g., Gottman, 1979).

This research work on emotion in the 1970s and 1980s was facilitated by two major methodological breakthroughs in the study of affect: the work of Ekman and Friesen (1978) and Izard (1972) on facial expressions of emotion, as well as the work of Scherer and Ekman (1982) on vocal expressions of emotion. Before Ekman and Friesen's work, a review by Bruner and Taguiri (1954) had suggested that the face was "a researcher's nightmare," and that no sense could be made of the thousands of potential facial actions. However, Ekman, Friesen, and Ellsworth's brilliant book (1972) decimated Taguiri and Bruner's position, and subsequent anatomical and physiological work by Ek-

man and Friesen's lab and Levenson's lab showed that there are indeed a set of cross-culturally universal facial expressions of emotion with distinct physiological profiles for at least seven primary affects (happiness, surprise, disgust, contempt, sadness, anger, and fear). Furthermore, although there is still some debate on this point, it now appears that these primary affects have particular autonomic profiles or "signatures"—much as had been suggested by Darwin's (1998/1882) classic work on emotion—that probably have adaptive value (Levenson, Ekman, & Friesen, 1990). For example, Darwin suggested that the facial expression of disgust closes the nostrils and protects against potentially harmful fumes.

The empirical *data* from the interactional perspective thus required a major shift from the original general systems ideas of the complex dismantling of the components of messages and feedback mechanisms and their accompanying cognitions to the importance of affect. It also required a major shift away from the model of the therapist as a cybernetic engineer of communication processes. Instead, it suggested that the marital therapist needs to be an expert in emotion. Unfortunately, few marital researchers (or therapists) were very interested in the study of emotion, nor were they knowledgeable about emotion research. The major exception in the marital therapy area was the seminal work of Greenberg and Johnson (1988) in their development of an emotionally focused marital therapy. Still, to date, few marital researchers have learned about emotion research in a scholarly manner; for example, they have not learned how to use the powerful, anatomically based Ekman and Friesen Facial Action Coding System (Ekman & Friesen, 1978), nor have many employed it in their own work with couples.

New work on the physiology of affect and relationships expanded the focus on marital satisfaction and stability to the functioning of the autonomic nervous system, to the functioning of the endocrine and immune systems (e.g., Kiecolt-Glaser, Fisher, Orgrocki, et al., 1987), and it expanded the focus of study from marital satisfaction and stability to other measures, such as health and longevity. To summarize briefly: a great deal of research, work on health, illness, and longevity, suggested that the most important predictors were the quality of people's closest relationships, particularly marriages and friendships; furthermore, it was the affective qualities of these relationships that did the work in prediction and understanding of correlations (Berkman & Breslow, 1983; Berkman & Syme, 1979; Friedman, Tucker, Schwartz, & Tomilson, 1995).

Despite these new findings on affect, relationships and health, unfortunately for the study of marriages, the mainstream focus in the social and behavioral sciences was to become *cognition* and not affect. We are living through the cognitive neuroscience revolution. Hence, while the research findings on relationships were leading researchers logically to a greater detailed study of affect, the field was becoming increasingly cognitive. However, the importance of affect could not be avoided. Even in the purely cognitive study of attributional processes, the research findings pointed to a systematic global distortion of cognitive processing that accompanied marital misery. This was a rediscovery of the twin halo effects that accompanied happy or unhappy marriages.

*Power* is a concept that sociologists early proposed as relevant in the understanding of marriages. It was logical to attempt an extension of the ideas of status and class from the societal level to the family or marital level. However, power turned out to be a complex and difficult notion in the study of marriages. The various ways of operationalizing power (such as who wins contested decisions) all made sense, but, unlike marital satisfaction, they tended to be uncorrelated with one another. In Broderick's (1993) brilliant monograph entitled *"Understanding family process,"* he wrote: "Literally hundreds of studies have been done on family power, who wields it and at whose expense. The matter has turned out to be complicated and elusive. As a result, the scholarly literature on family power is voluminous, complex, and often contradictory" (p. 164). This is true, despite the fact that most measures of power have been based on self-report. But the lack of convergence of different operations designed to measure power is a problem even when observational measures are used. Broderick's critique of the power concepts was that they all required conflict (the amount of which varies dramatically across families and across the life cycle), and that basic observational research (e.g., by Vuchinich, 1985) shows that most dinnertime family conflicts end in a standoff in which neither party yields but the topic is dropped. The remaining minority of such conflicts end most frequently by withdrawal; by far the least common response was submission. Hence, how is one to assess a family power structure in naturally occurring conflicts?

Other definitions of family or marital power that are not based so heavily on conflict resolution have emerged (e.g., the distribution of family resources, the allocation of household tasks, who speaks most, who interrupts most, the allocation of prestige, family coalitions, and alliances), and it remains to be seen whether these measures will add any light to the understanding of marriages. A promising mathematical approach was suggested initially by Rapoport (1960, 1972), using differential equations to represent parameters of mutual influence (for an explanation of the Rapoport model, see Broderick, 1993, pp 71–75). Rapoport had no data for his model, no idea of what to measure, and his equations were linear, which are well-known to be unstable. However, in recent years, *nonlinear* equations have been successfully applied (empirically) following the Rapoport example (Cook, Tyson, White, et al., 1995; Gottman, Murray, Swanson, et al., in press; Gottman, Swanson, & Murray, 1999). Nonlinear equations may be stable or unstable, and the models can specify a set of parameters of power that vary as a function of affect, that is, they specify mathematical power functions. The basic idea in this new approach is to define power in terms of affect, as the ability of one person's affect to change another person's affect. This development is a fulfillment of von Bertalanffy's (1968) general systems ideas, which proposed mathematical functions linking parts of an interacting system.

In the decade of the 1980s, there was a veritable explosion of theoretically based research on marriage. Spanier and Lewis's (1980) decade-review article on marital quality noted that there were more husbands in samples, more attention to couples and joint assessment of both spouses, the rapid expansion in the use of observational techniques, and greater attention to methodological and measurement issues. There was also an increasing awareness of the importance of male and female roles. Gelles' (1980) review noted that research on family violence emerged in the decade of the 1970s: research in the 1960s tended to view domestic abuse as "rare and confined to mentally disturbed and/or poor people, research in the 1970s revealed family violence as an extensive phenomenon which could not be explained solely as a consequence of psychological factors or income" (p. 873; see also Straus, 1979). Racial and cultural variations in American families became objects of study, with the first re-

ports of positive aspects of minority families emerging (Staples and Mirandé, 1980), as well as cross-societal family research (Osmond, 1980). Nontraditional and single-parent families began to be recognized and studied in the decade of the 1970s (Macklin, 1980), and attention began to be paid to older families (Streib & Beck, 1980). The phenomena of desertion, divorce, and remarriage also received attention (Price-Bonham & Balswick, 1980). In the 1980s marital quality continued as a topic of study with an increase in longitudinal investigations and the use of larger and more representative samples (Glenn, 1990); many studies began noting the decline in marital quality after the assumption of the parental role; there was more detailed study of marital communication (Noller & Fitzpatrick, 1990), the rise of feminist perspectives (Ferree, 1990), and the study of marital dissolution and the consequences of divorce (Kitson & Morgan, 1990; White, 1990), particularly for children. There was increasing attention to remarriage and stepfamilies (Coleman & Ganong, 1990), families with adolescents (Gecas & Seff, 1990), and families in later life (Berardo, 1990; Brubaker, 1990). The study of domestic violence had grown to include the sexual abuse of children (Gelles & Conte, 1990). There was a growing awareness of the impact of the family on health and longevity (Ross, Mirowsky, & Goldsteen, 1990), and of the impact of economic distress (Menaghan & Parcel, 1990; Voydanoff, 1990).

*Observational measurement and its contribution to marital process:* In the 1970 decade-review articles published by the *Journal of Marriage and the Family,* other than Broderick's theory monograph (1970), there is no separate recognition that observational measures can contribute anything unique to the study of process. Yet in the decade of the 1970s this was precisely the contribution of the few clinical and developmental psychologists who began studying and modifying marriages primarily from a behavioral perspective. In 1974 a major book was published edited by Lewis and Rosenblum, entitled *"The effects of the infant on its caregivers."* The book was a call for the study of bi-directional effects in parent-infant interaction, and also a call for the development of new methodological techniques for the study of temporal patterning in social interaction.

*The need for a tenacious focus on process:* Observational research plays a major role in research on marriage, both for purposes of description and for building theories of the mechanisms underlying central phenomena occurring within families. It is the main highway available for the precise study of family process. It has always been obvious to many scientists that observational research can enhance the study of marriages by adding a depth and richness to other, less expensive methods, such as surveys and questionnaires. Recently, however, it has also become clear that observational methods can also add predictive power and theoretical clarity. These important accomplishments stem, in part, from the power of observational data to reveal a replicable portrait of complex social interaction that lies beyond the usual awareness of even the most keenly sensitive spouse or partner, and thus lies beyond assessment with self-report instruments.

Many of these advances have also been enabled by significant technological breakthroughs in observational research that occurred in this past decade. With the arrival of inexpensive computer-assisted coding, live, real-time observational coding, or the rapid coding of videotapes, synchronized to computer-readable, video time-codes became feasible. Now, in the 21st century, an observer can code complex interaction between husbands and wives in real time and the com-

puter can later compute onsets, offsets, and durations of speaker/listener events, computer inter-observer reliability, and also perform sequential and time-series analyses that require knowledge of exactly when the events occurred. The merging of video and computer technology also has made it possible to time-synchronize the real-time acquisition of physiological and observational data from an interacting couple, and the use of video playback methods made it possible to time-synchronize spouses' perceptions and cognitions of the interaction. Thus, technology has made it possible to study, with time-synchronized data, the dynamic interplay between behavior, cognition, and physiology. Researchers discovered that the isolated study of behavior, cognition, or physiology without careful study of their interdependencies would severely limit being able to map findings onto the real interactional world of the couples we were studying. The relatively recent technical breakthroughs have narrowed the gap between couples' natural experience of their relationship and researchers' precise understanding of study participants.

Advances in understanding marriage stem not only from breakthroughs in technology but also from innovations in the methodologies used to extract information from the ongoing flow of interaction. Floyd (1989) reviewed research on the choice of coding units of different sizes and complexities. More and more interest was paid to developing global coding systems to capture targeted interactional processes. Basco, Birchler, Kalal, et al. (1991) developed and validated a rapid rating scale called the Clinician Rating of Adult Communication (CRAC). Bèlanger, Sabourin, Laughrea, et al. (1993) compared macroscopic global coding systems (MICS-Global and the Global Couple Interaction Coding System) and decided that the convergence was moderate and that it was premature to conclude that these macroscopic coding systems are interchangeable. Julien, Markman, and Lindahl (1989) presented a new global coding system and correlated it to the positive and negative codes of a more microanalytic Couples Interaction Scoring System (CISS). While negative codes between the two systems showed some convergence, the positive codes did not. Couples high in marital satisfaction reported higher Mutuality, while couples lower in marital satisfaction reported higher levels of Destructive Process, Coercion, and Post-Conflict Distress. Wampler and Halverson (1990) developed a Q-sort observational measure of marital interaction and they related it to their measures derived from the Couples Interaction Scoring System (CISS; Notarius, Markman, & Gottman, 1983).

A more powerful method of creating global categories from more microanalytic categories was a factor analysis reported by Heyman, Eddy, Weiss, and Vivian (1995), using 995 couples' videotaped conflict interactions with the MICS. The factors formed were: Hostility, Constructive Problem Discussion, Humor, and Responsibility Discussion. It is interesting that these super-categories are quite different from earlier suggestions for a global MICS system made by Weiss and Tolman (1990). An alternative approach to global coding was the work represented by the Gottman and Levenson laboratories, in which detailed microanalytic coding with multiple coding systems was undertaken (e.g., Gottman, 1994). This included the coding of facial expressions (the Emotion Facial Action Coding System, EMFACS; Ekman & Friesen, 1978), MICS coding, the development of a more rapid version of the CISS (RCISS; Krokoff, Gottman, & Hass, 1989), and a Specific Affect Coding System (SPAFF; Gottman, McCoy, Coan, & Collier, 1996) that codes macro-levels of emotional expression (e.g., anger, sad-

ness, fear). This work has led to reliable micro-analytic, real-time observational coding of marital interaction in both conflict and nonconflict contexts. One advantage of coding specific affects is greater precision in studying positive affect. Gottman, Coan, Carrère, and Swanson (1998) found that positive affect was the only predictor of both stability and happiness in a sample of newlyweds. Finally, a more macro look across time at marital interaction was offered in a review by Christensen and Pasch (1993). They broke down marital conflict into seven stages, beginning with the precipitating event and evolving through the fight and then a return to normal.

Recently, there has been a more widespread application of sequential analytic methods for the quantitative study of patterns of interaction between two people over time, the use of time-series analyses, and the mathematical modeling of marital interaction. In two landmark articles published in 1993, Griffin (1993a,b) demonstrated an innovative approach for how event-history analysis could be applied to the study of insider evaluations of marital interaction. The first article described the methodology, and the second article applied it in a study of marital interaction. Couples had two conversations, a pleasant memories and a problem conversation, and then they engaged in a video recall of affect procedure. The self-rating of affect during the video recall were the data for the analyses. The dependent measure was the time until there was a transition out of negative affect. In a logistic regression, Griffin found substantial gender differences. Griffin reported that, consistent with the Gottman and Levenson (1986, 1988) hypothesis, wives maintained a negative affect state longer than husbands, particularly on the problem task. The wife's transition time out of negative affect was determined by the wife's education, her marital satisfaction, and previous durations of negative affect. For husbands, the time already spent in a negative state determined the transition times out of that state; their exit behavior is less determined by their overall evaluation of the marriage than is the case for wives.

Griffin and Greene (1994) reported the results of analyzing one case of orofacial bradykinesia exacerbated during marital conflict. They used an interrupted time-series analysis to demonstrate that an increase of the symptoms followed a series of specific negative comments by the spouse in the conversation. Gottman et al. (1998) applied interrupted time-series analyses to their newlywed heart rate data to assess the extent to which a number of marital affective behaviors were either self-soothing or spouse-soothing; in a second step, they then used these data to predict marital outcomes 6 years later. As predicted by Gottman and Levenson (1988), only soothing of the male (primarily self-soothing) predicted positive marital outcomes.

We will focus the remainder of our review on what we see as the two primary advances recently made in the study of marital interaction. First, we examine how researchers have taken the fruits of cross-sectional, hypothesis-generating descriptive research and tested models for predicting the longitudinal course of relationships over time. These prospective studies were a major advance and their results demonstrate the maturation of the discipline. Second, we examine the empirical developments in several core content areas: 1) the study of power, 2) the exploration of marital interaction as a proximal determinant of individual well-being and distress, and 3) the study of interrelationships among interactional behavior, perception, and physiology.

## THE STUDY OF COUPLES OVER TIME

### Developmental Transitions

The family life cycle has been used to describe the natural history of couples over time. It is intuitively appealing to suppose that the interactional patterns characterizing the engaged couple, the newlyweds, the new parents, midlife couples, the empty nesters, the grandparents, for example, are stamped with unique qualities that determine if the couple is adaptively passing through these important and challenging transitions or not. Colloquially, couples expect the marriage to be different "once the honeymoon is over" and, empirically, we know that couples on the average experience a significant decline in satisfaction after the birth of the first child. Thus, it is encouraging to see that interactional researchers in the 1990s have begun to map the critical processes that define these developmental transitions.

*Divorce prediction:* Basic descriptive research during the 1980s paved the way in the 1990s for interactional research that can track the longitudinal course of marriages and can predict divorce. For a review of methodological issues, see Bradbury and Karney (1993). Gottman and Krokoff (1989) reported that a different pattern of interaction was related to concurrent marital satisfaction than to the change in marital satisfaction over time; for example, disagreement and anger were related to lower concurrent marital satisfaction, but also to improvement in marital satisfaction over time. Buehlman, Gottman, and Katz (1992) reported that, in a sample of families with preschool-aged children, their coding of an Oral History Interview was able to predict divorce or stability over a 3-year period with 94% accuracy, using a discriminant function analysis. The Oral History variables were also correlated in clear ways with Time-1 marital interaction in both problem solving and affect, the couple's physiological reactivity during marital interaction as well as Time-1 and Time-2 marital satisfaction. Gottman and Levenson (1992) reported the first prospective longitudinal study of divorce prediction that used observational data. They found that a couple's interaction and spouse's physiological responses observed at Time-1 were associated with a set of variables forming a cascade toward divorce. Couples starting on this cascade toward divorce at Time-1 had interactions that were marked by more negativity than positivity, and they rated their interactions more negatively upon video recall. Wives in these couples also had significantly higher heart rates and smaller finger pulse amplitudes (which could be part of a general alarm response in which blood is drawn into the trunk from the periphery). Subsequent work on the divorce prediction question with another sample of couples (Gottman, 1993, 1994) identified the ratio of positivity to negativity during the conflict discussion, and four specific negative interaction patterns (criticism, defensiveness, contempt, and stonewalling) as highly predictive of divorce. These findings were replicated with a third sample of newlywed couples (Gottman et al., 1998). In an independent replication and extension of the Gottman (1994) divorce prediction work, Matthews, Wickrama, and Conger (1996) reported that spousal hostility and lack of warmth predicted with 80% accuracy which couples would divorce within a year and with 88% accuracy which couples would be in the two most extreme marital groups. Furthermore, the observers' reports were related to marital instability both directly and indirectly through partners' perception of each other's behaviors.

*Transition to marriage:* Smith, Vivian, and O'Leary (1990) studied premarital problem-solving discussions and predicted marital satisfaction at 18 months and 30 months after marriage. The negativity of the premarital interaction correlated with concurrent marital unhappiness but was not predictive of post-marital satisfaction. Controlling for premarital relationship satisfaction, affective disengagement during a premarital problem-solving discussion was negatively associated with marital satisfaction at 18 months and 30 months after marriage. Cohan and Bradbury (1997) examined the longitudinal course of marital satisfaction and depressive symptoms in newlywed marriages over an 18-month period. Problem-solving behavior mediated but did not moderate the relationship between life events and adjustment. In particular, angry wives had better adjustment to major and interpersonal events so that their depressive symptoms were reduced and their marital satisfaction increased.

Gottman et al. (1998) reported the results of a multimethod, longitudinal study predicting the eventual 6-year marital happiness and stability from newlywed interactions observed in the first months after the wedding. Seven types of process models were explored: (a) anger as a dangerous emotion; (b) active listening; (c) negative affect reciprocity; (d) negative startup by the wife; (e) de-escalation; (f) positive affect models; and (g) physiological soothing of the male. Support was not found for the models of anger as a dangerous emotion, active listening, or negative affect reciprocity in kind, either low or high intensity. Support was found for models of the husband's rejecting his wife's influence, negative startup by the wife, a lack of de-escalation of low intensity negative wife affect by the husband, or a lack of de-escalation of high intensity husband negative affect by the wife, and a lack of physiological soothing of the male, all predicting divorce. Support was also found for a contingent positive affect model and for balance models (i.e., ratio models) of positive-to-negative affect predicting satisfaction among stable couples.

*Transition to parenthood:* In 1957, LeMasters claimed that 83% of new parents went through moderate to severe crisis in the transition from being a couple to becoming parents. His claims were initially refuted and subsequently strongly debated by scholars. They were based entirely on the results of retrospective studies. Beginning in the 1980s, prospective longitudinal studies began to appear and they primarily confirmed LeMasters' claims (for reviews, see Belsky & Pensky, 1988; Cowan & Cowan, 1988). After 15 longitudinal studies, it is now generally accepted that the transition to parenthood is a stressful period for marriages, and because of decreased marital quality and parent-child interaction, a potentially stressful period for the development of the baby (Cowan & Cowan, 1995; Cowan, Cowan, & Kerig, 1993; Cowan, Cowan, Coie, & Coie, 1978). Recently, four landmark books were published that summarized key longitudinal research projects on the transition to parenthood (Cowan & Cowan, 1992 and Belsky & Kelly, 1994; Belsky & Rovine, 1990; Belsky, Spanier, & Rovine, 1983; see also Lewis, 1989; Michaels & Goldberg, 1988). There have been approximately 15 longitudinal studies on the transition to parenthood; many of the others were not prospective longitudinal studies. The longitudinal findings are remarkably consistent. Most have concluded that, for the overwhelming majority of couples this transition can be both extremely stressful and pleasurable. For approximately 40 to 70% of couples there is a drop in marital quality. In general, marital conflict increases by a factor of 9: people are at risk for depression; there is a precipitous drop in marital quality within one year after the birth of the first child; people revert to stereotypic

gender roles; they are overwhelmed by the amount of housework and childcare; fathers withdraw into work; and marital conversation and sex sharply decrease. There is also an increase in joy and pleasure with the baby. The longitudinal studies have all discovered the strong linkages between the pre-birth marital system (particularly highlighting the couple's conflict resolution skills, and a sense of we-ness), the parent-child system, and the baby's subsequent emotional/social and cognitive development. Belsky's study is a rich source of information for understanding the transition. The Cowans' study is the only controlled, preventive marital intervention study in the field. They demonstrated the powerful intervention effect of 24 hours of group supportive therapy during pregnancy in reducing the drop in marital satisfaction, preventing divorce, and improving parenting quality. However, by the time the child is 5, there were no differences between the experimental and control groups; it is still a mystery as to what happened to create relapse in the experimental group between years 3 ½ and 5. Lewis' (1989) landmark work defines very specific pre-birth marital "competencies" that provide links to child developmental outcomes through parenting.

*Couples at mid-life and beyond:* Overwhelmingly, the existing observational research on marriage has studied relatively young couples. The data that exist about older marriages have been limited to self-report data, derived primarily from questionnaires and interviews (Erikson, Erikson, & Kivnick, 1989; Guilford & Bengtson, 1979; Stinnett, Carter, & Montgomery, 1972). Although self-report data can be useful, they are well-known to have severe limits, especially when people are reporting very personal material. Amazingly, the only other studies that employed observational data are an unpublished dissertation by Illig (1977) and a study by Zietlow and Sillars (1988) of couples from only one Lutheran church in Milwaukee.

In the 1990s, this state of affairs began to be remedied. Using an observational system for coding emotional behavior, Carstensen, Gottman, and Levenson (1995) studied the interactions of a representative sample of couples in their 40s or 60s as they attempted to resolve marital conflicts. With respect to negative emotions, the interactions of older couples were clearly less emotional than those of middle-aged couples. Older couples showed less anger, disgust, belligerence, and whining than middle-aged couples. With respect to the more positive emotions, however, the evidence was mixed. Middle-aged couples expressed more interest and more humor, but older couples expressed more affection. Importantly, these findings of lesser negative emotion and greater affection in older couples when discussing marital problems still held when the authors controlled for differences in the severity of the problems being discussed. The reports of the couples themselves were quite consistent with their behavioral coding. When they showed spouses the videotapes of their interactions and had them rate how they were feeling from moment to moment during the interaction, older couples indicated feeling more emotionally positive than middle-aged couples (Levenson, Carstensen, & Gottman, 1993, 1994).

## THE CORE CONTENT AREAS

### The Study of Power

In 1993, the late Calfred Broderick published an important book entitled "Understanding family process." Broderick organized family process literature, which he called "relational space," into three major areas, the *regulation* of interpersonal distance, the *regulation* of transactions, and the *regulation* of "vertical space," by which he meant power. The idea of "reg-

ulation" implied a homeostatic set point theory. In a therapy context, these three areas were respectively discussed as positivity/caring, responsiveness, and status/influence (Gottman, Notarius, Gonso, & Markman, 1976). We will briefly discuss these three areas. Historically, the regulation of interpersonal distance was first explored by examining the clarity of communication. Hypotheses were advanced to explore the role of unclear communication in dysfunctional families and family distress. More specific hypotheses were advanced that unclear communication was responsible for psychopathology (e.g., Bateson, Jackson, Haley, & Weakland, 1956; Watzlawick et al., 1967), and the cybernetic model or the systems approach to family process was born. However, subsequent research over three decades has shown that the regulation of interpersonal distance is all about *affect,* not about communication clarity (e.g., Gottman, 1993). So the field of family and marital process had been led very gradually toward the greater specification of emotional expression and experience, as we noted above. The regulation of transactions (e.g., signals of switches in speaking turns) has been studied with strangers (e.g., Duncan & Fiske, 1977; Jaffe & Feldstein, 1970) and has yet to be applied to the study of marital interaction.

The regulation of "vertical space," that is, the study of power, has been much more elusive. It remains an area of important activity, particularly as the study of physically abusive marriages became a major focus of research attention (e.g., Jacobson & Gottman, 1999). The empirical fabric of power always appears to disintegrate upon closer examination. Broderick (1993) wrote: Literally hundreds of studies have been done on family power, who wields it and at whose expense. The matter has turned out to be complicated and elusive. As a result, the scholarly literature on power is voluminous, complex, and often contradictory (see Szinovacz, 1987). The great majority of these studies are based on questionnaires that ask the respondent to report on who wins the most contested decisions in his or her family. Critics have noted several problems with this approach (p. 164). Questionnaires filled out by independent observers do not correlate very well, nor are different measures well correlated (see Gray-Little & Burks, 1983); nor have patterns of domination proven stable over time (see Babcock, Waltz, Jacobson, & Gottman, 1993). An older article by Gray-Little (1982) is noteworthy because it combined the observational assessment of talk time during a 6-minute marital conflict discussion, and power during a marital game (the SIMFAM game, Straus & Tallman, 1971). Results were complex, but included the result that balance in husband-wife power was related to marital quality; however, self-report and observational measures did not show a high level of agreement in classifying couples. The issues of blending the study of affect and power are central to the integration of psychological and sociological approaches to marriage. As we will note, the issue of how to conceptualize and study power may become clarified either through the use of more precise observational measures or the use of more precise analytic techniques using data from two people that unfolds over time.

*Power studied with more precise observations:* An example of this approach to clarifying power is a recent study by Gray-Little, Baucom, and Hamby (1996). They assessed power more precisely, using a coding of the couple's influence patterns during a discussion of the Inventory of Marital Conflicts (IMC; Olson & Ryder, 1970). They found that egalitarian couples had the highest Time-1 marital satisfaction, fewer negative Marital Interaction Coding System (MICS) behaviors (Weiss, Hops, & Patterson, 1973); also,

wife-dominant couples improved the most in a 12-week marital therapy study.

*Power explored in the context of gender and relational hierarchy:* Feminist writers have pointed to the central role that power must play in understanding marriages. Quantitative observational research has also explored these ideas. Women typically start most of the marital conflict discussions in laboratories that use observational methods (Ball et al., 1995; Oggins, Veroff, & Leber, 1993). The degree of negative affect and the amount of criticism with which a conflict discussion starts is also critical in determining its outcome. In one study, for example, the way a marital conflict interaction *began* determined its subsequent course 96% of the time (Gottman, 1994; Gottman et al., 1998, p. 7). White (1989), in a sequential analysis using the Raush et al., (1974) coding system, found evidence for the contention that men display a more coercive style in resolving marital conflict, while women display a more affiliative style. Ball et al., (1995) reported that couples perceived women to be more important than the husband in the mobilization phase of problem talk, which involved raising the issues, planning on how to solve them, being active and taking control by silence and nonresponse. Husbands and wives both viewed this phase as the most stressful aspect of marital problem solving. Men were perceived as more influential in determining the content and emotional depth of later phases of the discussion. Women viewed their power in the early phases as illusory—"their behavior was shaped primarily by the effort to choose strategies that would avoid upsetting their husbands" (p. 303).

Coan, Gottman, Babcock, and Jacobson (1997) used sequential analysis to investigate the propensity of two types of physically violent men to reject influence from their wives during a marital conflict discussion. The sequence of escalation of the negativity (from complaining to hostility, for example) was used to operationalize the sequence of rejecting influence. As hypothesized, abusive husbands whose heart rates decreased from baseline to the marital conflict discussion (labeled as Type-I abusers in the study), rejected any influence from their wives. These men were also generally violent outside the marriage and were more likely to have used a knife or gun to threaten their wives than abusive husbands whose heart rates accelerated from baseline to the conflict discussion (label as Type-II abusers in the study). These analyses were repeated for a representative sample of nonviolent newlywed couples in the first few months of marriage, and the escalation sequence of men rejecting influence from their wives predicted subsequent divorce (Gottman et al., 1998). The sequence of women rejecting influence from their husbands did not predict divorce. This report was the first time that negative affect reciprocity was broken down into responding negatively *in kind* (e.g., anger is met with anger) or *escalation* (e.g., anger is met with contempt). Negative reciprocity in kind was characteristic of all marriages; only the escalation sequence was characteristic of marriages that were later to end in divorce. These findings reconceptualize negative affect reciprocity as the rejection of influence. More research is necessary to validate this suggested interpretation of the escalation sequence.

*Power studied with the mathematical modeling of marital interaction:* Power, according to Broderick (1993) "may be most simply defined as the ability to win contested decisions" (p. 164). However, an alternative definition has recently emerged using mathematical modeling of marital interaction. This alternative definition defines power quantitatively as the ability of one partner's affect to influence the other's affect. In this modeling (Cook et al., 1995; Gottman et al., in press) two

influence functions are computed across the affective range of a conversation, one for the husband's influence on the wife, and one for the wife's influence on the husband. This approach to modeling is based on writing down two interlocking nonlinear difference equations for husband and wife, with *influence functions* computed after controlling for autocorrelation. The method has a venerable history in the marital field. Long ago, Anatol Rapoport (1960, 1972) suggested that two linear differential equations for husband and wife interaction could describe a marital system as escalating out of control, or being self-regulated. He never operationalized these variables or applied them to real data, and, unfortunately, his equations were linear, and linear equations are usually unstable. However, Cook et al. (1995), applying the new mathematics of nonlinear dynamic modeling (e.g., Murray, 1989), showed that, depending on the shape of the influence functions, couples can have several stable steady states or "attractors," which are self-regulating, homeostatic set points for the marital system. A homeostatic attractor is a point in husband-wife phase space toward which the interaction is repeatedly drawn, and if the system is perturbed, it will move back to the attractor. These influence functions describe the impact of one person's affect on the partner's subsequent affect. This determination is made across the range of affects in the husband-wife dialogue. The influence functions make the study of power more detailed and specific. Power may be specific to particular affects. Asymmetries in influence reflect a power imbalance, and they reported that these asymmetries were predictive of divorce.

*Power and marital typologies:* An important research monograph was published by Fitzpatrick (1988). In it she presented the results of a series of studies that combined observational data on marital interaction with questionnaire data.

She presented a typology of marriage from her analyses of ideology, communication, interdependence, and power dynamics in the marriage. Three main types emerged from her analysis: *Traditional* couples, who were high on conflict and highly interdependent, but who have a conventional ideology; *Separate* couples, who were low on conflict and low in interdependence; and *Independent* couples, who were high on conflict and high on interdependence, but who have an unconventional ideology. She also presented results on mixed types. Her work was another example of the integration of the study of power with marital interaction. In a monograph on what marital processes predict divorce, Gottman (1994) also presented a marital typology with three types, looking at interaction and influence, and his types appear to be similar to Fitzpatrick's types. On a conflict task Gottman's types were: *Validating* couples, who are high on conflict but wait a while in the discussion and ask questions before engaging in persuasion attempts; *Volatile* couples, who are high in conflict and engage in persuasion attempts immediately; and *Conflict Avoiding* couples, who are low in conflict and do not engage in persuasion attempts at all. All three types were equally likely to have stable marriages, but Cook et al. (1995) discovered that *mismatches in influence* functions between Gottman's types predicted divorce. The question remains as to what fundamental mismatches in typology are dysfunctional.

Vanlear & Zietlow (1990) correlated Fitzpatrick's couple typology, marital satisfaction, and relational control. "Relational control" attempts to capture the sequential communication of power or status between spouses (e.g., from assertion to dominance, from collaborative deference to submission). Across couple types, marital satisfaction was associated with interactions confirming equality between

partners (i.e., there was an absence of "putting" self or partner, up or down). More importantly, the study revealed an interaction effect between couple type and relational control on marital satisfaction. This finding, along with Fitzpatrick's and Gottman's, further encourages researchers to challenge a uniformity assumption holding that all distressed and nondistressed couples are alike in their reactions to specific interactional behaviors.

*Demand-withdraw pattern and power:* Although the pursuer-distancer pattern was first identified and noted as a focus of clinical work by Virginia Satir (see "foreword" in McCann & Shannon, 1985), the pioneering research work quantifying this pattern was done by Christensen and his associates; he called it the demand-withdraw pattern (e.g., Christensen & Heavey, 1990; Sagrestano, Christensen, & Heavey, 1998). The Christensen wife-demand/husband-withdraw pattern does not imply that the wife is dominant in this interaction pattern. The husband's withdrawal could be driving the wife's demandingness, for example. In an innovative analysis, Klinetob and Smith (1996) continuously coded demand and withdraw behaviors for both husband and wife. Using bivariate time-series analysis, and controlling for autocorrelation, they assessed the direction of influence between demand-withdraw behaviors (and between withdraw-demand) in both husbands and wives. They found that in the wife-demand/husband-withdraw pattern, the overwhelming percentage of couples showed a bi-directional influence pattern (especially when it was her issue), with wife dominance as the next most frequent pattern. For the husband-demand/wife-withdraw pattern, once again a bi-directional influence pattern was most common, with husband dominance the next most frequent pattern (particularly when it was his issue). This was an elegant approach to the study of marital power.

## Marital Interactions as Determinants of Family Well-Being

Historically, an important revolution took place in the study of family processes when interactional hypotheses were advanced to explain how specific family interactions were related to and perhaps responsible for an individual family member's psychopathology (e.g., Bateson et al., 1956; Watzlawick et al., 1967). This marked the beginning of a major conceptual shift away from individual personality as the primary determinant of personal well-being and distress and toward social interaction with significant others as among the most significant determinant of physical and psychological well-being. We will examine the evidence to emerge in the 1990s that represents the next evolution in this 30-year-old revolution.

*Health and longevity:* An outstanding review by Burman and Margolin (1992) crystallized ongoing work that the psychosocial quality of marriages is linked to mortality and morbidity. In searching for a mechanism for these linkages, they decided that the effect is indirect and nonspecific. Previous research has identified strong links between marital quality and health (c.f. Burman & Margolin, 1992), and between being married and better health and longevity (e.g., Berkman & Syme, 1979; Berkman & Breslow, 1983). Research now indicates that marital distress is associated with suppressed immune function (e.g., Kiecolt-Glaser et al., 1987; Malarkey, Kiecolt-Glaser, Pearl, & Glaser, 1994), cardiovascular arousal (e.g., Brown & Smith, 1992; Ewart, Burnett, & Taylor, 1983; Ewart, Taylor, Kraemer, & Agras, 1991; Gottman, 1994; Gottman & Levenson, 1992; Levenson & Gottman, 1983, 1985), and increases in stress-related hormones such as catecholamines and corticosteroids (e.g., Kiecolt-Glaser et al., 1993). There is extensive literature

that indicates, that for men, marriage offers health-buffering effects (e.g., Berkman & Syme, 1979; Berkman & Breslow, 1983; Bernard, 1982; Burman & Margolin, 1992; Shumaker & Hill, 1991) and that women are more likely to experience health-related problems if the marriage is distressed (Ewart et al., 1991; Gaelick, Bodenhausen, & Wyer, 1985; Huston & Ashmore, 1986; Kiecolt-Glaser et al., 1993). Recently, researchers also broadened the search for associations between marital interaction and specific disorders. Many of these studies are somewhat weak in methodology but nevertheless point the way toward the benefits of more refined study.

*Child outcomes:* Recently, research has been rich in discovering linkages across interacting subsystems within the family, and to the child's peer relations as well. The mediating variable in many of these investigations is the concept of *emotional regulation* of arousal in children, variously defined. Marital conflict, distress, and dissolution are linked to problematic childhood outcomes including: depression, withdrawal, poor social competence, deleterious health outcomes, lower academic achievement, and conduct-related incidents (Cowan & Cowan, 1987, 1992; Emery & O'Leary, 1982; Forehand, Brody, Long, et al., 1986; Goldberg & Easterbrooks, 1984; Gottman & Katz, 1989; Hetherington, Cox, & Cox, 1978; Katz & Gottman, 1991, 1993, 1995; Peterson & Zill, 1986; Porter & O'Leary, 1980; Rutter, 1971; Whitehead, 1979). For example, Cummings and colleagues found that children exposed to angry inter-adult conflict tend to use negative behavior such as physical aggression to cope (Cummings, Zahn-Waxler, & Radke-Yarrow, 1984). El-Sheikh (1994) found that pre-school children from highly conflictual marriages displayed behavioral distress and heart rate reactivity when shown tapes of angry adult interactions. Brody, Arias, & Fincham (1996) reported a link between conflict-promoting marital attributions (e.g., seeing one's partner as selfish) and ineffective parent-child communication, and to the child's attributions for negative parental behavior. Davies, Myers, and Cummings (1996) showed videotaped segments of adults engaged in brief verbal conflicts, with various endings, to two groups of children, 7–9 year olds and 13–15 year olds. They reported that emotionally harmonious endings were crucial in creating a sense of emotional security in both groups of children, regardless of whether the adults' conflicts were about adult or child issues. Explicit verbal resolution was unnecessary. Across both age groups, female children reported more fear while male children offered more task-oriented interventions. See also Davies and Cummings (1994) for an attachment-based theory of emotional regulation.

Margolin, Christensen, and John (1996), in a sequential analysis, reported that distressed couples showed greater continuance of tensions and more spillover, particularly from marital to parent-child interaction. However, there may at times be an inverse relationship between marital conflict and parent-child interaction. Mahoney, Boggio, and Jouriles (1996) found that mothers were more empathic toward their 4- to 10-year-old clinic-referred sons after an episode of marital conflict.

Gottman, Katz, and Hooven (1996) reported the results of a longitudinal study in which there were clear linkages between observed marital, parent-child, and child-peer interaction when the child was 4 years old. Furthermore, these linkages were mediated by the child's ability to regulate physiological arousal during parent-child interaction. These linkages predicted a range of longitudinal child outcomes, including child peer relations at age 8. The central concept of this research was "meta-emotion," which refers to the feelings and cognitions that parents had about their own and their children's anger and sadness. Katz and Gottman (1993) found that two distinct and uncorrelated patterns of marital interaction were related to distinct child outcomes. A mutually hostile pattern (which predicted marital dissolution) correlated with child externalizing behavior, whereas a husband angry and withdrawn pattern correlated with child internalizing disorders. Katz and Gottman (1997) reported that variables that index a "coaching" meta-emotion philosophy buffer children from almost all the deleterious consequences associated with marital conflict and dissolution. Coaching parents are aware of their child's emotion, they listen empathically to the child's feelings, they help the child find words to express the emotion, and then they explore and implement strategies to deal with the emotion. There was a physiological substrate to this buffering effect. Katz and Gottman (1995) found that a central child physiological dimension, called "vagal tone," protected children from marital conflict. Broadly, vagal tone is related to the ability of the parasympathetic branch of the autonomic nervous system to calm the child down. The concept has become central theoretically for many researchers in organizing the bases for the infant's emotional and social development (e.g., Fox, 1994; Garber & Dodge, 1991; Thompson, 1994).

Rogers and Holmbeck (1997) reported that more frequent and intense interparental aggression was associated with greater adjustment problems for children. They identified cognitive appraisal strategies that were maladaptive for the children and also noted that peer social support could buffer the negative effects of marital conflict.

Once again, after a hiatus of many years, links are again being made between the marital relationship and child sibling relationships. For example, among children aged approximately 4 to 9 years,

Erel, Margolin, and John (1998) reported linkages between the wives' negative reports of the marital relationship, the mother-child relationship, and the older siblings' observed negative interaction. The younger siblings' negative interaction was linked with the mother-child and the differential mother-child interaction (across siblings). No such relationship was found for siblings' positive interactions.

Adolescent adjustment was also studied in the context of couples undergoing the transition to remarriage (Hetherington & Clingempeel, 1992). There were three groups of families: stepfamilies with a divorced custodial mother who was in the first months of a remarriage, families with a divorced custodial mother who had not remarried, and nondivorced families. Authoritative parenting was associated with positive adjustment of children in all family groups, but children in nondivorced families were more competent and had fewer behavior problems than children in divorced or remarried families. Nondivorced and remarried couples looked very similar on the observational measures. There was remarkable stability in marital interaction over time. However, in their chapter, Deal, Hagan, and Anderson (1992) noted that the new stepfather is in a tenuous position in his new family: "It may thus be that the primary difference between first marriages and remarriages lies not in the quality of the marital relationship but in the relative importance of the marital relationship within the whole family system" (p. 93).

*Common co-morbidities:* Research in this past decade firmly established that marital interaction is also strongly associated with a broad range of outcomes for family members. Although the direction of cause and effect between marital interaction and spousal or child well-being is often unclear, the strength and importance of these relations will surely be pursued in the 21st century.

**1.** Depression: Schmaling, Whisman, Fruzzetti, and Truax (1991) assessed the marital interaction behaviors associated with wives' depression. They found that active summarization by the wife was associated with fewer depressive symptoms and the absence of a diagnosis of major depression. Johnson and Jacob (1997) examined the marital interactions of control couples and couples in which either the wife or the husband was clinically depressed. Depressed couples were more negative than nondepressed, and couples with a depressed wife were more negative than couples with a depressed husband. McCabe and Gotlib (1993), in a study of depressed and nondepressed couples, reported that depressed wives became increasingly more negative in their verbal behavior over the course of the interaction, and they perceived the interactions as more hostile. After breaking the interaction into thirds, they found that only depressed couples were fairly immediately reactive to their spouse's behavior in the interaction.

Biglan, Hops, Sherman, et al. (1985) discovered an interesting set of interactions using sequential analysis, which led to an exciting flurry of theoretically based research. They examined the potential "function" of depressed and aggressive behavior in depression, using sequential analyses. They compared distressed and nondistressed couples, both of which included a depressed wife, with community controls. First, they found that the couples with a depressed spouse exhibited higher rates of depressive behavior than the community control couples. Second, using sequential analysis they also noted two additional patterns: (1) husbands of depressed wives in distressed marriages were less likely to behave aggressively following a wife's depressive behavior than were husbands of depressed wives in nondistressed marriages; (2) depressed wives in distressed marriages were less likely than depressed wives in a nondistressed marriage to show depressive behavior after their husbands exhibited an aggressive behavior. These were exciting findings, suggesting that the marital system might be covertly maintaining depressive symptoms, and thereby suggesting the direction of the causal relationship between interaction and individual outcomes.

Biglan et al.'s (1985) study was criticized because the investigators had difficulty obtaining nondepressed distressed couples. Schmaling and Jacobson (1990) conducted the full design, crossing high or low marital distress with high or low depression. They did not find interactional patterns that were unique to depression, but did find that these marital patterns were due to marital distress rather than depression. Similarly, Nelson and Beach (1990) found that the suppression of aggressive behavior was an artifact of the number of months the couples had been discordant. Interestingly, these means were quite long: 65.0 months for the nondepressed discordant and 94.5 months for the depressed discordant couples. Greater suppression of aggressive behavior was associated with shorter durations of discord within both groups of couples.

**2.** Violence: There has been an impressive increase in observational research applied to the study of violent marriages. Burman and Margolin (1993) used sequential analysis to compare the re-enactments of physically aggressive, verbally aggressive, withdrawing, and nondistressed low-conflict couples. Physically aggressive couples were characterized by reciprocity of hostile affect and by rigid, highly contingent behavior patterns that were stronger and longer lasting than those of other couples. Nondistressed couples also reciprocated hostility, but were able to exit these negative interaction cycles quickly. These sequential results were also obtained by Cordova, Jacobson, Gottman, et al. (1993)

for actual marital conflicts in the laboratory rather than re-enactments of conflicts at home. These investigators designed elaborate procedures to guarantee the safety of the abused women following actual marital conflicts in the laboratory. The data suggest that violent couples are missing an exit or withdrawal ritual from either reciprocated or escalating hostility.

Gottman, Jacobson, Rushe, and Shortt (1995) reported a typology of batterers based upon heart rate reactivity. Two types of batterers were identified: Type-1 men, who lowered their heart rates from baseline to a marital conflict interaction, and Type-2 men, who raised it. Compared to Type-2 men, Type-1 men were more violent outside the marriage (to strangers, co-workers, friends, and bosses), were higher on antisocial and sadistic aggression personality scores, lower on dependency, and were more verbally aggressive toward their wives during marital conflict; wives responded to these men with anger, sadness, and defensiveness. Type-1 men were more likely to threaten their wives using a knife or gun, but both types had inflicted as much actual physical damage (for more detail see Jacobson & Gottman, 1999). In a subsequent article on divorce prediction, Jacobson, Gottman, Gortner, et al. (1996) reported that among their batterers, there was a high divorce/separation rate of 38%, and that two variables predicted the divorce with 85.7% accuracy: 1) husband dominance and 2) the wife's reports of his emotional abuse. During the Time-1 marital interaction, more husband's contempt, less husband humor, less husband neutral affect, more wife defensiveness, and less wife humor predicted divorce. Physiological reactivity variables in both husbands and wives at Time-1 also predicted divorce. As noted above, the research on violence in marriages has focused attention on the power aspects of marriage. In an unpublished dissertation, Rushe (1995) analyzed marital transactions in terms of power and control strategies and concluded that the violent marriage is basically engaged in a power struggle, which is reminiscent of the analyses carried out by Coan et al. (1997) on violent men rejecting influence from women. This notion of violence as a form of power struggle is distinctly different from the emphasis on anger management for batterers in the therapy literature. The power dimension of violence suggests a systematic use of violence to intimidate and control the abused wife, instead of periodic uncontrolled outbursts (see Jacobson & Gottman, 1999). Babcock et al. (1993) reported that violent couples were more likely than nonviolent distressed and happily married couples to engage in the husband demand/wife withdraw pattern. Also, within the domestically violent group, husbands who had less power were more physically abusive toward their wives. Power was measured by communication skill using a structured interview about previous arguments, marital power outcomes with the Who Does What scale (Cowan et al., 1978). Positive affect and social support in violent couples have been studied by Holtzworth-Munroe, Stuart, Sandin, et al. (1997). They found that, compared to nonviolent men, violent husbands in the Bradbury social support task (Pasch & Bradbury, 1998; Pasch, Bradbury, & Davila, 1997) offered less social support than nonviolent husbands. Instead, they were more belligerent/domineering, more contemptuous/disgusted, showed more anger and tension, and were more upset by the wife's problem.

**3.** Chronic Physical Pain: Romano, Turner, Friedman, et al. (1991) developed a methodology for the behavioral observations of chronic pain patients and their spouses. Pain and control groups could be discriminated with ratings of overt verbal and nonverbal pain-related behaviors. Spouses of pain patients showed more so-

licitous behavior than control spouses. Turk, Kerns, and Rosenberg (1992), however, reviewed evidence that suggested the complexity of the problem: positive attention from spouses to displays of pain were associated with reports of more intense pain, higher observed pain frequency, and greater disability; but, negative spouse responding to pain was associated with increased affective distress.

**4.** Hostility and Type-A Personality: Sanders, Smith, and Alexander (1991) reported a relationship between marital hostile/dominant behavior and Type A or Type B personality pattern in both husbands and wives. Brown and Smith (1992) found a strong relationship between hostility during marital interaction and heart rate reactivity.

**5.** Alcohol Abuse: Jacob and Krahn (1987) used three different analytic methods to cluster the marital interactions of 96 couples (with the MICS) in which the husband was either alcoholic, clinically depressed, or a normal control. Cluster analysis revealed that there were three salient dimensions of the behaviors: Negative Evaluation, Problem Solving, and Positive Evaluation. Jacob and Leonard (1992) performed a highly detailed sequential analysis of these marital interactions. They found that couples with a depressed husband were different from the normal controls and couples with an alcoholic husband; couples with an alcoholic husband and normal controls were characterized by *similar* interaction patterns. Negative reciprocity was lower among the couples with depressed husbands, and husbands were less likely to follow their wives' problem solving with problem solving of their own.

**6.** Drug Abuse: Fals-Stewart and Birchler (1998) used their macro-CRAC coding system to study the marital conflict interactions of couples with drug-abusing husbands, and a well-selected control group of nonsubstance abusing, but distressed couples. They thus controlled for distress and varied only the active ingredient of drug abuse. No differences were found between couple types on the self-report inventories, but the couples with the substance-abusing husband interacted significantly differently than the distressed nondrug-abusing couples: they showed higher Abusiveness, lower Problem-Solving Skills, and more Attribution of Blame than the distressed non-drug-abusing couples. In addition, they found that the CRAC total score was negatively related to the husband's percentage of days abstinent during the year before entering substance abuse treatment.

## INTERRELATIONSHIPS AMONG KEY DOMAINS

More recently, research has witnessed the *blending of multiple measurements with observational measures in one investigation,* which makes it possible to ask more sophisticated questions at the interfaces of these three domains. We reviewed the Notarius et al. (1989) methodology in their experimental investigation of Weiss's (1980) concepts of positive or negative sentiment override and Gottman et al.'s (1976) concept of editing. We suggested that these salient interactional processes can be studied only through a time-synchronized examination of the interface between behavior and perception.

Bradbury and Fincham (1992) reported the results of two studies. In study 1, maladaptive attributions were related to less effective problem-solving behaviors (coded globally with rating scales), particularly for wives. In study 2, a more detailed coding system was used, combined with lag sequential analysis (Bakeman & Gottman, 1997; Bakeman & Quera, 1995). In this study maladaptive attributions (controlling for marital satisfaction) were related to the reciprocation of negative partner behavior (hostility or rejection of partner's views). Attributions and behavior

were most strongly related for distressed wives. Miller and Bradbury (1995) found that maladaptive attributions were related to hindering problem resolution on two tasks, one a problem-solving and one a social support discussion. Attributions and behavior were more strongly related for wives than husbands, and for distressed than for nondistressed spouses; again showing that cognitive factors function to impair interaction. Vanzetti, Notarius, and NeeSmith (1992) studied specific and generalized expectancies that couples had for the outcomes of marital conflict interactions. Distressed couples expected fewer positive and more negative behaviors. Couples high on relational efficacy chose relationship-enhancing attributions more often than low-efficacy couples. Halford and Sanders (1990) used a video recall procedure to assess cognition of each partner during a problem discussion and a relaxed discussion. Both domains discriminated distressed from nondistressed couples; and negative behavior in the interaction could be predicted better by accounting for both past cognition and behavior than by relying on past behavior alone. Thomas, Fletcher, and Lange (1997), using a thought-stream video recall method pioneered by Ickes (e.g., Ickes, Stinson, Bissonnette, & Garcia, 1990), in a study of empathic accuracy, had couples review their own videotapes and describe their own and their partners' "on-line" thoughts and feelings. Partners' assumed similarity was related to marital satisfaction and the positivity of the verbal interaction. Mendola, Beach, and Tesser (1996) found that the responsiveness to one's partner's self-evaluations was associated with favorable marital interaction during a conflict discussion, whereas responsiveness to one's own self-evaluation was associated with unfavorable marital interaction. These findings may suggest a possible mechanism underlying defensiveness. Fincham, Garnier, Gano-Phillips, and Osborne (1995) developed a new methodology for studying a couple's pre-interaction expectations and the "accessibility" of marital satisfaction. To operationalize accessibility, they used two computer tasks and measured response latencies to specific questions about the spouse or the marriage. Response latencies moderated the relationship between satisfaction and expected partner behavior for husbands. Since there is considerable complexity in studying each separate domain, it is not surprising that work exploring the interrelations that exist between behavior and cognition is not well advanced.

### Physiology and Interaction

The use of physiological measures in studies of marital interaction has increased in the decade. Ewart et al. (1991), in a study of essential hypertension, investigated high blood pressure and marital conflict. They reported that "not being nasty matters more than being nice." This was based on the finding that, among women, supportive or neutral messages were unrelated to blood pressure, but hostile interaction and marital dissatisfaction were related. Among men, blood pressure was related only to speech rate. Levenson and Ruef (1992) reported a physiological substrate for empathy. They asked subjects to view a videotaped 15-minute marital interaction of a couple and to indicate how a particular spouse reported feeling. When the rater's physiological responses matched those of the target spouse being observed, the rater was more accurate predicting the targeted spouse's feelings. Gottman and Levenson (1992) combined physiological assessment with observational coding of interaction, specific affect, and the subjective evaluation of affect. Using an index based on the aggregate valence of all statements spoken during a speaker turn, two groups of couples were formed. The

speaking turns of regulated couples were characterized by a positive slope (i.e., speaker turns were generally characterized by positive affect) over the course of a conversation while the speaking turns of nonregulated couples were characterized by a negative slope (i.e., speaker turns were generally characterized by negative affect) for one or both spouses. Wives in nonregulated interactions showed higher levels of arousal than all other spouses and Gottman and Levenson speculated that this heightened arousal may play a role in the poorer health of wives in distressed marriages. Gottman et al. (1998), using interrupted time-series analysis, found that only husband's physiological soothing (via self-soothing or through wives' humor) predicted marital stability among newlyweds.

Smith and Brown (1991) related husbands' and wives' MMPI cynical hostility scale scores to two marital interaction conditions, one in which they simply discussed a problem area, and one in which they received rewards for trying to persuade their wives in a win-lose contest. In husbands, their cynical hostility scores in the win-lose condition was related to their own increased systolic blood pressure (SBP) and heart rate (HR) reactivity. Husbands' cynical hostility scores also were related to increased systolic blood pressure reactivity in their wives. Wives' cynical hostility scores were unrelated to their own or to their husbands' physiological responses. Brown & Smith (1992) reported that in this win-lose condition husbands' SBP increases were accompanied by increases in anger and a hostile, coldly assertive style. In wives this same interactive style occurred but it was not associated with their own elevated SBP.

### MARITAL RESEARCH AGENDA FOR THE 21ST CENTURY

There is a need to extend this work to representative and international samples as well as a need to integrate sociological and psychological methodologies. Psychological studies have relied on samples of convenience that have limited generalizability. A recent exception is Escudero, Rogers, and Gutierrez (1997), who, in a detailed microanalytic investigation also employing sequential analysis, studied marital interaction in Spain, comparing clinic distressed couples with nonclinic nondistressed couples. They used the Rogers relational coding system (Rogers, 1972), which directly codes power transactions, and the Couples Interaction Scoring System (Gottman et al., 1977) for coding affect. They found that clinic couples displayed more domineering, more negative affect, and a stronger association between one-up control and negative affect than was the case for nonclinic couples. Krokoff, Gottman, and Roy (1989) conducted the only random sample study of blue- and white-collar marital interaction known to us. They used Markov model sequential analysis of interaction. Among their findings, there was more negative affect and negative affect reciprocity for unhappy couples, regardless of occupational status. Blue-collar husbands displayed more negative affect than white-collar husbands. Job distress was able to account for this difference between blue- and white-collar husbands; white-collar wives, when unhappy, were more negative than blue-collar wives when they were unhappy. Zamsky (1997) compared the interactions of distressed and nondistressed, white and African American couples. Replicating interactional findings on more homogeneous groups, Zamsky found large differences between distressed and nondistressed couples, particularly for the negative, emotionally invalidating behaviors. Surprisingly, communication differences between couples were not attributable to factors of race, socioeconomic status, or any interaction between these variables and marital satisfaction.

Observational study of distressed and nondistressed couples continued in the 1990s to be used in international settings. In studies in Germany, Kaiser, Hahlweg, Fehm-Wolfsdorf, and Groth (1998) showed that a short-term psychoeducational program increased the frequency of self-disclosure, problem solving, acceptance, and nonverbal positive behavior, and decreased the frequency of criticism relative to a control group. Hahlweg, Markman, Thurmaier, et al. (1998) showed that many of the changes in communication behaviors following the short-term intervention were maintained through a 3-year followup. Gender differences have frequently been observed in studies with US couples (see Baucom, Notarius, Burnett, & Haefner, 1990), particularly concerning wives negativity, and similar differences were observed in the German samples. At the 3-year followup, wives in the treatment and control group were observed to display more nonverbal negative behavior and more self-disclosure compared to their husbands, and wives in the control group displayed more criticism than their husbands.

In a study of distressed and nondistressed Dutch couples, Van Widenfelt (1995) confirmed a pattern of interactional differences that have been replicated in several studies carried out in the United States. She defined interactional behaviors and found that nondistressed couples display significantly more statements to facilitate problem solving, to emotionally validate the partner, and to self-disclose thoughts and feelings, while distressed couples display significantly more statements to inhibit problem solving and to emotionally invalidate the partner. Van Widenfelt also observed wives in her Dutch sample to display significantly more statements that were emotionally invalidating of their husbands (e.g., criticisms, guilt inductions, character assassinations). Sequential analyses revealed the interaction of nondistressed couples to be characterized by statements that facilitated problem solving that were followed by self-disclosure or emotional validation. In contrast, the interaction of distressed couples was characterized by a high frequency of emotional invalidation that was followed by statements that either facilitated or interfered with problem solving, but without any consequent emotional validation.

**There is a need for more observation in naturalistic settings:** Melby, Ge, Conger, and Warner (1995), in an elegant analysis, compared a marital discussion and a problem-solving task and reported on the importance of task in detecting positive marital interaction. However, there have been very few studies of marital interaction outside laboratory settings, and this is a direction that needs continuing exploration. An exception is Vuchinich (1985), who studied naturally occurring dinner-time disputes. He found that in 200 examples of conflict, 67% ended in standoffs in which no one yielded and the topic was dropped. In 33% of the conflicts the most frequent reaction was withdrawal, in which one person refused to continue the discussion. The reaction of submission, in which one person gave in or compromised was very rare. However, even if not naturalistic, laboratory observations may have validity, particularly if they can be shown to predict important marital outcomes. Older evidence shows that interaction in the lab underestimates differences between distressed and nondistressed couples, compared to tape recordings made in couples' homes (Gottman, 1979). More recently, Hayden, Schiller, Dickstein, et al. (1998) related the mealtime interactions of families to multiple levels of family assessment; the measures were strongly related to both mother and father involvement. The use of a marital interaction diary was pioneered in a study by Halford, Gravestock,

Lowe, and Scheldt (1992) in an attempt to discover the behavioral ecology of stressful marital interaction. For example, they found that most stressful interaction occurred in the kitchen during the weekdays and were associated with everyday life stresses; the most stressful interactions resulted from one partner leaving the scene.

**There is a need for continued focus on sequences or patterns of interaction:** Either using various tools of sequence analysis, or through the direct observation of sequences, the observational study of marital interaction expanded to the analysis of patterned communication. Probably the most important of these patterns was the investigation of the demand-withdraw pattern. Most commonly this is observed as wives demanding change (through emotional requests, criticism, and complaints) and husbands withdrawing (through defensiveness and passive inaction). Christensen and his students pioneered the study of this sequence (Christensen & Heavey, 1990; Sagrestano et al., 1998) and showed that this pattern was most likely when discussing a wife issue, and could be reversed for a husband issue (Heavey, Layne, & Christensen, 1993). However, since a consistent finding is that women typically raise most of the issues in most marriages, this finding may be of only theoretical interest. Heavey, Christensen, and Malamuth (1995) demonstrated that the withdrawal by men and the female-demand/male-withdraw pattern predicted decline in wives' marital satisfaction 2.5 years later.

**There is a need to recognize the importance of positive affect:** Part of the accomplishments in the study of marital interaction over the last 20 years can be traced to the use of common methodologies and data analytic strategies in independent laboratories throughout the United States, in the Netherlands, Germany, and Australia. One feature of the typical paradigm was a focus on conflict discussions and the negative behaviors that marked the interaction of distressed couples in this context. As we enter the next decade, interactional researchers are beginning to look beyond conflict to understand better the contribution that intimacy and other affectional processes make to relationship satisfaction and stability.

The importance of looking at positive affective reactions is suggested by several studies of marital interaction. Gottman et al. (1998) found that only positive affect during conflict discussions in the early months of marriage predicted both later divorce and the marital happiness of stable couples. Pasch and Bradbury (1998) and Pasch et al. (1997) studied social support in marital interaction using a task of only moderate conflict in which spouses discussed personal, nonmarital issues. Longitudinal data showed that wives' "support solicitation and provision behaviors" predicted marital outcomes 2 years later, independent of the negative behaviors exhibited during marital conflict. Beach, Martin, Blum, and Roman (1993) reported that co-workers and marital quality played a significant role in reducing negative affective symptoms (depression and interpersonal stress).

De Koning and Weiss (1997) studied the use of instrumental humor and found that it appears to function differently during the problem-solving conversations of younger couples married an average of 14 years than during the conversations of older couples married an average of 39 years. Among younger couples, instrumental humor was negatively associated with marital satisfaction, but among older couples, instrumental humor was strongly associated with marital happiness. The authors speculated that humor may function as an avoidance maneuver in the younger couples and more genuinely represent positive affect in the older

couples. Cordova (1998) is developing a promising behavioral model of intimacy. Intimacy is operationalized as a dyadic event sequence in which one partner's expresses a personal vulnerability and the spouse responds in an accepting, nonpunitive manner. Clearly the field is just beginning to explore the interactional basis of marital intimacy.

**There is a need to revisit personality:** Karney and Bradbury (1997), in a longitudinal study, examined the relationship between neuroticism, marital interaction, initial levels of marital satisfaction, and rates of change in marital satisfaction. They found that neuroticism was associated with initial levels of marital satisfaction but not with rates of change in marital satisfaction. However, behavior during marital interaction (total positive minus negative codes using Sillars' 1982 coding system) was associated with rates of change in marital satisfaction, but not with initial levels. Kobak and Hazan (1991), using an attachment theory framework with Q-sort methodology, reported that the accuracy of spouse's internal working models as relying on one's partner, and the partner being psychologically available, were both related to observers' positive ratings of communication in problem-solving and confiding tasks. Sayers and Baucom (1991) studied the relationship between femininity and masculinity and marital interaction using the MICS. Femininity was positively related to greater rates of negative behavior among both husbands and wives. A sequential analysis supported the idea that wives' femininity was associated with greater negative reciprocity of the wives. Men's femininity was associated with husbands' tendency to terminate fewer negative sequences of behavior in comparison to their wives. High masculinity of the wives was related to shorter sequences of negative behavior.

**There is a need to study the management of stress spill-over into the marriage:** In 1987, Jacobson, Schmaling, and Holtzworth-Munroe conducted a 2-year telephone followup study of the couples from their marital therapy study. They studied two groups of couples, those who maintained change, and those who relapsed. The only significant difference between the two groups was in the management of stress from nonmarital situations to the marital relationship. Couples who relapsed had more spillover of stress into the marriage than those who maintained change. A Swiss psychologist, Bodenman (1997a) reported that "dyadic coping" with stress predicted longitudinal outcomes (stability and happiness) in a 2-year study of 70 Swiss couples. Bodenman has developed an intervention program focusing of dyadic coping with stress (Bodenman, 1997b). This is an area that needs greater development.

To close our review, we suggest that in the past century we learned to use a multimethod approach that honors the study of multiple channels of information (affective behavior, perception, physiology) as they unfold over time. This attention to detail about marital process has led to empirical breakthroughs in both the prediction and the theoretical understanding of marriages, and it has set a research agenda that will carry the field forward into the 21st century on a sound scientific course.

## REFERENCES

Ackerman, N.W. (1958). *The psychodynamics of family life.* New York: Basic Books.

Aries, E. (1976). Interaction patterns and themes in male, female, and mixed groups. *Small Group Behavior 7:* 7–18.

Babcock, J.C., Waltz, J., Jacobson, N.S., & Gottman, J.M. (1993). Power and violence: The relation between communication patterns, power discrepancies, and domestic violence. *Journal of Consulting and Clinical Psychology 61:* 40–50.

Ball, F.L.J., Cowan, P., & Cowan, C.P. (1995). Who's got the power? Gender differences in partners' perceptions of influence during marital problem-solving discussions. *Family Process 34:* 303–321.

Bakeman, R., & Gottman, J.M. (1997). *Observing interaction: An introduction to sequential analysis* (2nd ed.). New York: Cambridge University Press.

Bakeman, R., & Quera, V. (1995). *Analyzing interaction: Sequential analysis with SDIS and GSEQ.* New York: Cambridge University Press.

Basco, M.R., Birchler, G.R., Kalal, B., Talbott, R., & Slater, M.A. (1991). The clinician rating of adult communication (CRAC): A clinician's guide to the assessment of interpersonal communication skill. *Journal of Clinical Psychology 47:* 368–380.

Bateson, G., Jackson, D.D., Haley, J., & Weakland, J.H. (1956). Toward a theory of schizophrenia. *Behavioral Science 1:* 251–264.

Bateson, G., Jackson, D.D., Haley, J., & Weakland, J.H. (1962). A note on the double bind—1962. *Family Process 2:* 154–161.

Baucom, D., Notarius, C., Burnett, C., & Haefner, P. (1990). Gender differences and sex-role identity in marriage (pp. 150–171). In F. Fincham & T. Bradbury (eds.), *The psychology of marriage: Basic issues and applications.* New York: Guilford Press.

Beach, R.H., Martin, J.K., Blum, T.C., & Roman, P.M. (1993). Effects of marital and coworker relationships on negative affect: Testing the central role of marriage. *The American Journal of Family Therapy 21:* 313–323.

Bèlanger, C., Sauborin, S., Laughrea, K., Dulude, D., & Wright, J. (1993). Macroscopic marital interaction coding systems: Are they interchangeable? *Behavior Research and Therapy 8:* 789–795.

Belsky, J., & Kelly, J. (1994). *The transition to parenthood: How a first child changes a marriage. Why some couples grow closer and others apart.* New York: Dell Publishing.

Belsky, J., & Pensky, E. (1988). Marital change across the transition to parenthood. *Marriage and Family Review 12*(3–4): 133–156.

Belsky, J., & Rovine, M. (1990). Patterns of marital change across the transition to parenthood: Pregnancy to three years postpartum. *Journal of Marriage and the Family* 52(2): 5–19.

Belsky, J., Spanier, G., & Rovine, M. (1983). Stability and change in a marriage across the transition to parenthood. *Journal of Marriage and the Family* 45(3): 567–577.

Berardo, F. (1990). Trends and directions in family research in the 1980s. *Journal of Marriage and the Family* 52: 809–817.

Berkman, L.F., & Breslow, L. (1983). *Health and the ways of living: The Alameda County Study.* New York: Oxford University Press.

Berkman, L.F., & Syme, S.L. (1979). Social networks, host resistance, and mortality: A nine-year follow-up study of Alameda County residents. *American Journal of Epidemiology* 109: 186–204.

Bernard, J. (1982). *The future of marriage.* New Haven: Yale University Press.

Biglan, A., Hops, H., Sherman, L., Friedman, L.S., Arthur, J., & Osteen, V. (1985). Problem solving interactions of depressed women and their spouses. *Behavior Therapy* 16: 431–451.

Bodenman, G. (1997a). The influence of stress and coping on close relationships: A two-year longitudinal study. *Swiss Journal of Psychology* 56: 156–164.

Bodenman, G. (1997b). Can divorce be prevented by enhancing the coping skills of couples? *Journal of Divorce and Remarriage* 27: 177–194.

Bowen, M. (1961). The family as the unit of study and treatment. *American Journal of Orthopsychiatry* 31: 40–60.

Bradbury, T.N., & Fincham, F.D. (1992). Attributions and behavior in marital interaction. *Journal of Personality and Social Psychology* 63: 613–628.

Bradbury, T.N., & Karney, B.R. (1993). Longitudinal study of marital interaction and dysfunction: Review and analysis. *Clinical Psychology Review* 13: 15–27.

Broderick, C.B. (1970). Beyond the five conceptual frameworks: A decade of development in family theory. *Journal of Marriage and the Family* 33: 139–159.

Broderick, C.B. (1993). *Understanding family process: Basics of family systems theory.* Newbury Park CA: Sage Publications.

Brody, G.H., Arias, I., & Fincham, F.D. (1996). Linking marital and child attributions to family processes and parent-child relationships. *Journal of Family Psychology* 10: 408–421.

Brown, P.C., & Smith, T.W. (1992). Social influence, marriage, and the heart: Cardiovascular consequences of interpersonal control in husbands and wives. *Health Psychology* 11: 88–96.

Brubaker, T.H. (1990). Families in later life: A burgeoning research area. *Journal of Marriage and the Family* 52: 959–981.

Bruner, J.S., & Taguiri, R. (1954). The perception of people (pp. 634–654). In G. Lindzey (ed.), *Handbook of social psychology, Vol. 2.* Reading MA: Addison-Wesley.

Buehlman, K.T., Gottman, J.M., & Katz, L.F. (1992). How a couple views their past predicts their future: Predicting divorce from an Oral History Interview. *Journal of Family Psychology* 5: 295–318.

Burgess, E.W., Locke, H.J., & Thomes, M.M. (1971). *The family.* New York: Van Nostrand Reinhold.

Burgess, E.W., & Wallin, P. (1953). *Engagement and marriage.* Philadelphia: J.B. Lippincott.

Burman, B., & Margolin, G. (1992). Analysis of the association between marital relationships and health problems: An interactional perspective. *Psychological Bulletin* 112: 39–63.

Burman, B., & Margolin, G. (1993). America's angriest home videos: Behavioral contingencies observed in home reenactments of marital conflict. *Journal of Consulting and Clinical Psychology* 61: 28–39.

Carstensen, L.L., Gottman, J.M., & Levenson, R.W. (1995). Emotional behavior in long-term marriage. *Psychology and Aging* 10: 140–149.

Christensen, A., & Heavey, C.L. (1990). Gender and social structure in the demand/withdraw pattern of marital conflict. *Journal of Personality and Social Psychology* 59: 73–81.

Christensen, A., & Pasch, L. (1993). The sequence of marital conflict: An analysis of seven phases of marital conflict in distressed and nondistressed couples. *Clinical Psychology Review 13:* 3–14.

Coan, J., Gottman, J.M., Babcock, J., & Jacobson, N.S. (1997). Battering and the male rejection of influence from women. *Aggressive Behavior 23:* 375–388.

Cohan, C.L., & Bradbury, T.N. (1997). Negative life events, marital interaction, and the longitudinal course of newlywed marriages. *Journal of Personality and Social Psychology 73:* 114–128.

Coleman, M., & Ganong, L.H. (1990). Remarriage and stepfamily research in the 1980s: Increased interest in an old family form. *Journal of Marriage and the Family 52:* 925–940.

Cook, J., Tyson, R., White, J., Rushe, R., Gottman, J., & Murray, J. (1995). Mathematics of marital conflict: Qualitative dynamic modeling of marital interaction. *Journal of Family Psychology 9:* 110–130.

Cordova, J. (1998). A behavioral theory for the study of intimacy: Intimate events, suppressive events and the construction of intimate partnerships. Paper presented at the meeting of the Association for the Advancement of Behavior Therapy, Washington DC.

Cordova, J.V., Jacobson, N.S., Gottman, J.M., Rushe, R., & Cox, G. (1993). Negative reciprocity and communication in couples with a violent husband. *Journal of Abnormal Psychology 102:* 559–564.

Cowan, C.P., & Cowan, P.A. (1988). Who does what when partners become parents: Implications for men, women, and marriage. *Marriage & Family Review 12*(3–4): 105–131.

Cowan, C.P., & Cowan, P.A. (1992). *When partners become parents.* New York: Basic Books.

Cowan, C.P., & Cowan, P.A. (1995). Interventions to ease the transition to parenthood: Why they are needed and what they can do. *Family Relations 44:* 412–423.

Cowan, C.P., Cowan, P.A., Coie, L., & Coie, J.D. (1978). Becoming a family: The impact of the first child's birth on the couple's relationship (pp. 296–324). In W.B. Miller & L.F. Newman (eds.), *The first child and family formation.* Chapel Hill NC: Carolina Population Center.

Cowan, P.A., & Cowan, C.P. (1987, April). Couple's relationships, parenting styles, and the child's development at three. Paper presented at the Society for Research in Child Development, Baltimore MD.

Cowan, P.A., Cowan, C.P., & Kerig, P.K. (1993). Mothers, fathers, sons and daughters: Gender differences in family formation and parenting style (pp. 165–195). In P. A. Cowan & D. Field (eds.), *Family, self and society: Toward a new agenda for family research.* Hillsdale NJ: Lawrence Erlbaum Associates.

Cummings, E.M., Zahn-Waxler, C., & Radke-Yarrow, M. (1984). Developmental changes in children's reactions to anger in the home. *Journal of Child Psychology 25:* 63–75.

Darwin, C. (1996/1882). *The expressions of emotions in man and animals* (3rd ed.; commentary by Paul Ekman). New York: Oxford University Press.

Davies, P.T., & Cummings, M.E. (1994). Marital conflict and child adjustment: An emotional security hypothesis. *Psychological Bulletin 116:* 387–411.

Davies, P.T., Myers, R.L., & Cummings, M.E. (1996). Responses of children and adolescents to marital conflict scenarios as a function of the emotionality of conflict endings. *Merrill-Palmer Quarterly 42:* 1–21.

De Konig, E., & Weiss, R.L. (1997). A funny thing happened during my marriage. Paper presented at the meeting of the Association for the Advancement of Behavior Therapy, Miami FL.

Deal, J.E., Hagan, M.S., & Anderson, E.R. (1992). The marital relationship in remarried families (pp. 73–93). In E.M. Hetherington & W.G. Clingempeel (eds.), Coping with marital transitions: A family systems perspective. *Monographs of the Society for Research in Child Development 57* (Serial No. 227).

Duncan, S.D., Jr., & Fiske, D.W. (1977). *Face-to-face interaction: Research methods and theory.* Hillsdale NJ: Lawrence Erlbaum Associates.

El-Sheikh, M. (1994). Children's emotional and physiological responses to interadult angry behavior: The role of interparental history. *Journal of Abnormal Child Psychology 22:* 661–678.

Ekman, P., & Friesen, W.V. (1978). *Facial ac-*

*tion coding system.* Palo Alto CA: Consulting Psychologists Press.

Ekman, P., Friesen, W.V., & Ellsworth, P. (1972). *Emotion in the human face: Guidelines for research and an integration of findings.* New York: Pergamon Press.

Emery, R.E., & O'Leary, K.D. (1982). Children's perception of marital discord and behavior problems of boys and girls. *Journal of Abnormal Child Psychology 10:* 11–24.

Erel, O., Margolin, G., & John, R.S. (1998). Observed sibling interaction: Links with the marital and mother-child relationship. *Developmental Psychology 34:* 288–298.

Erikson, E.H., Erikson, J.M., Kivnick, H.P. (1989). *Vital development in old age.* New York: W.W. Norton.

Escudero, V., Rogers, L., & Gutierrez, E. (1997). Patterns of relational control and nonverbal affect in clinic and nonclinic samples. *Journal of Social and Personal Relationships 14:* 5–29.

Ewart, C.K., Burnett, K.F., & Taylor, C.B. (1983). Communication behaviors that affect blood pressure: An A-B–A-B analysis of marital interaction. *Behavior Modification 7:* 331–344.

Ewart, C.K., Taylor, C.B., Kraemer, H.C., & Agras, S.W. (1991). High blood pressure and marital discord: Not being nasty matters more than being nice. *Health Psychology 10:* 155–163.

Fals-Stweart, W., & Birchler, G.R. (1998). Marital interactions of drug-abusing patients and their partners: Comparisons with distressed couples and relationship to drug-using behavior. *Psychology of Addictive Behaviors 12:* 28–38.

Ferree, M.M. (1990). Beyond separate spheres: Feminism and family research. *Journal of Marriage and the Family 52:* 866–884.

Fincham, F.D., Garnier, P.C., Gano-Phillips, S., & Osborne, L.N. (1995). Preinteraction expectations, marital satisfaction, and accessibility: A new look at sentiment override. *Journal of Family Psychology 9:* 3–14.

Fitzpatrick, M.A. (1988). *Between husbands and wives: Communication in marriage.* Newbury Park CA: Sage Publications.

Floyd, F.J. (1989). Segmenting interactions: Coding units for assessing marital and family behaviors. *Behavioral Assessment 11:* 13–29.

Forehand, R., Brody, G., Long, N., Slotkin, J., & Fauber, R. (1986). Divorce/divorce potential and interparental conflict: The relationship to early adolescent social and cognitive functioning. *Journal of Adolescent Research 1:* 389–397.

Fox, N.A. (ed.), (1994). The development of emotion regulation: Biological and behavioral considerations. *Monographs of the Society for Research in Child Development 59*(2–3, Serial No. 240). Chicago IL: The University of Chicago Press.

Friedman, H.S., Tucker, J.S., Schwartz, J.E., & Tomilson, (1995). Psychosocial and behavioral predictors of longevity: The aging and death of the "Termites". *American Psychologist 50:* 69–78.

Gaelick, L., Bodenhausen, G.V., & Wyer, J. (1985). Emotional communication in close relationships. *Journal of Personality and Social Psychology 49:* 1246–1265.

Garber, J., & Dodge, K.A. (eds.), (1991). *The development of emotion regulation and dysregulation.* New York: Cambridge University Press.

Gecas, V., & Seff, M.A. (1990). Families and adolescents: A review of the 1980s. *Journal of Marriage and the Family 52:* 941–958.

Gelles, R. (1980). Violence in the family: A review of research in the seventies. *Journal of Marriage and the Family 42:* 873–885.

Gelles, R.J., & Conte, J.R. (1990). Domestic violence and sexual abuse of children: A review of research in the 1980s. *Journal of Marriage and the Family 52:* 1045–1058.

Gergen, K. (1969). *The psychology of behavior exchange.* Reading MA: Addison-Wesley.

Glenn, N.D. (1990). Quantitative research on marital quality in the 1980s: A critical review. *Journal of Marriage and the Family 52:* 818–831.

Goldberg, W.A., & Easterbrooks, M.A. (1984). Role of marital quality in toddler development. *Developmental Psychology 20:* 504.

Gottman, J.M. (1979). *Marital interaction: Experimental investigations.* New York: Academic Press.

Gottman, J.M. (1993). The roles of conflict engagement, escalation or avoidance in marital interaction: A longitudinal view of five types of couples. *Journal of Consulting and Clinical Psychology 61:* 6–15.

Gottman, J.M. (1994). *What predicts divorce: The relationship between marital processes and marital outcomes.* Hillsdale NJ: Lawrence Erlbaum Associates.

Gottman, J.M., Coan, J., Carrère, S., & Swanson, C. (1998). Predicting marital happiness and stability from newlywed interactions. *Journal of Marriage and the Family 60:* 5–22.

Gottman, J.M., Jacobson, N.S., Rushe, R.H., Shortt, J.W. (1995). The relationship between heart rate reactivity, emotionally aggressive behavior, and general violence in batterers. *Journal of Family Psychology 9:* 227–248.

Gottman, J.M., & Katz, L.F. (1989). Effects of marital discord on young children's peer interaction and health. *Developmental Psychology 25:* 373–381.

Gottman, J.M., Katz, L.F., & Hooven, C. (1996). Parental meta-emotion philosophy and the emotional life of families: Theoretical models and preliminary data. *Journal of Family Psychology 10:* 243–268.

Gottman, J.M., & Krokoff, L.J. (1989). Marital interaction and satisfaction: A longitudinal view. *Journal of Consulting and Clinical Psychology 57:* 47–52.

Gottman, J.M., & Levenson, R.W. (1985). A valid procedure for obtaining self-report of affect in marital interaction. *Journal of Consulting and Clinical Psychology 53:* 151–160.

Gottman, J.M., & Levenson, R.W. (1986). Assessing the role of emotion in marriage. *Behavioral Assessment 8:* 31–48.

Gottman, J.M., & Levenson, R.W. (1988). The social psychophysiology of marriage (pp. 183–200). In P. Noller & M.A. Fitzpatrick (eds.), *Perspectives on marital interaction.* San Diego: College Hill Press.

Gottman, J.M., & Levenson, R.W. (1992). Marital processes predictive of later dissolution: Behavior, physiology, and health. *Journal of Personality and Social Psychology 63:* 221–233.

Gottman, J.M., Markman, H.J., & Notarius, C. (1977). The topography of marital conflict: A study of verbal and nonverbal behavior.

*Journal of Marriage and the Family 39:* 461–477.

Gottman, J.M., McCoy, K., Coan, J., & Collier, H. (1996). The Specific Affect Coding System (SPAFF) for observing emotional communication in marital and family interaction (pp. 112–195). In J.M. Gottman (ed.), *What predicts divorce? The measures.* Mahwah NJ: Lawrence Erlbaum Associates.

Gottman, J.M., Murray, J., Swanson, C., Swanson, K., & Tyson, R. (in press). *The mathematics of marital conflict.* Cambridge MA: M.I.T. Press.

Gottman, J.M., Notarius, C., Gonso, J., & Markman, H. (1976). *A couple's guide to communication.* Champaign IL: Research Press.

Gottman, J.M., Notarius, C., Markman, H., & Mettetal, G. (1977). *Codebook for the CISS.* Unpublished laboratory manual.

Gottman, J., Swanson, C., & Murray, J. (1999). The mathematics of marital conflict: Dynamic mathematical nonlinear modeling of newlywed interaction. *Journal of Family Psychology 13:* 3–19.

Gray-Little, B. (1982). Marital quality and power processes among Black couples. *Journal of Marriage and the Family 44:* 633–646.

Gray-Little, B., Baucom, D.H., & Hamby, S.L. (1996). Marital power, marital adjustment, and therapy outcome. *Journal of Family Psychology 10:* 292–303.

Gray-Little, B., & Burks, N. (1983). Power and satisfaction in marriage: A review and critique. *Psychological Bulletin 93:* 513–538.

Greenberg, L.S., & Johnson, S.M. (1988). *Emotionally focused marital therapy.* New York: Guilford Press.

Griffin, W.A. (1993a). Event history analysis of marital and family interaction: A practical introduction. *Journal of Family Psychology 6:* 211–229.

Griffin, W.A. (1993b). Transitions from negative affect during marital interaction: Husband and wife differences. *Journal of Family Psychology 6:* 230–244.

Griffin, W.A., & Greene, S.M. (1994). Social interaction and symptom sequences: A case study of orofacial bradykinesia in Parkinson's disease during negative marital interaction. *Psychiatry: Interpersonal and Biological Processes 57:* 269–274.

Guilford, R., & Bengston, V. (1979). Measuring marital satisfaction in three generations: Positive and negative dimensions. *Journal of Marriage and Family 41*(2): 387–398.

Hahlweg, K., Markman, H., Thurmaier, F., Engl, J., & Eckert, V. (1998). Prevention of marital distress: Results of a German prospective longitudinal study. *Journal of Family Psychology 12:* 543–556.

Halford, W.K., Gravestock, F.M., Lowe, R., & Scheldt, S. (1992). Toward a behavioral ecology of stressful marital interactions. *Behavioral Assessment 14:* 199–217.

Halford, W.K., & Sanders, M.R. (1990). The relationship between cognition and behavior during marital interaction. *Journal of Social and Clinical Psychology 9:* 489–510.

Hayden, L.C., Schiller, M., Dickstein, S., Seifer, R., Sameroff, A.J., Miller, I., Keitner, G., & Rasmussen, S. (1998). Levels of family assessment I: Family, marital, and parent-child interaction. *Journal of Family Psychology 12:* 7–22.

Heavey, C.L., Christensen, A., & Malamuth, N.M. (1995). The longitudinal impact of demand and withdrawal during marital conflict. *Journal of Consulting and Clinical Psychology 63:* 797–801.

Heavey, C.L., Layne, C., & Christensen, A. (1993). Gender and conflict structure in marital interaction: A replication and extension. *Journal of Consulting and Clinical Psychology 61:* 16–27.

Hetherington, E.M., & Clingempeel, W.G. (1992). Coping with marital transitions: A family systems perspective (pp. 1–242). *Monographs of the Society for Research in Child Development 57* (Serial No. 227).

Hetherington, E.M., Cox, M., & Cox, R. (1978). The aftermath of divorce (pp. 110–155). In J.H. Stevens, Jr., & M. Matthews (eds.), *Mother-child, father-child relations.* Washington DC: National Association for the Education of Young Children.

Heyman, R.E., Eddy, J.M., Weiss, R.L., & Vivian, D. (1995). Factor analysis of the Marital Interaction Coding System (MICS). *Journal of Family Psychology 9:* 209–215.

Hicks, M.W., & Platt, M. (1970). Marital happiness and stability: A review of the research in the sixties. *Journal of Marriage and the Family 32:* 553–573.

Holtzworth-Munroe, A., Stuart, G.L., Sandin, E., Smutzler, N., & McLaughlin, W. (1997). Comparing the social support behaviors of violent and nonviolent husbands during discussions of wife personal problems. *Personal Relationships 4:* 395–412.

Huston, T.L., & Ashmore, R.D. (1986). Women and men in personal relationships (pp. 167–21). In D. Ashmore & F.D. Boco (eds.), *The social psychology of female-male relationships.* New York: Academic Press.

Ickes, W., Stinson, L., Bissonnette, V., & Garcia, S. (1990). Naturalistic social cognition: Empathic accuracy in mixed-sex dyads. *Journal of Personality and Social Psychology 59:* 730–742.

Illig, D.P. (1977). Distributional structure, sequential structure, multivariate information analysis, and models of communicative patterns of elderly and young married and friendship dyads in problem-solving situations. Unpublished doctoral dissertation, Pennsylvania State University.

Izard, C. (1972). *The face of emotion.* New York: Addison-Wesley.

Jacob, T., & Krahn, G. (1987). The classification of behavioral observation codes in studies of family interaction. *Journal of Marriage and the Family 49:* 677–687.

Jacob, T., & Leonard, K. (1992). Sequential analysis of marital interactions involving alcoholic, depressed, and nondepressed men. *Journal of Abnormal Psychology 101:* 647–656.

Jacobson, N.S., & Gottman, J.M. (1999). *When men batter women.* New York: Simon & Schuster.

Jacobson, N.S., Gottman, J.M., Gortner, E., Berns, S., & Shortt, J.W. (1996). The longitudinal course of battering: When do couples split up? When does the abuse decrease? *Violence and Victims 11:* 371–392.

Jacobson, N.S., Schmaling, K., & Holtzworth-Munroe, A. (1987). Component analysis of behavioral marital therapy: 2-year followup and prediction of relapse. *Journal of Marital and Family Therapy 13:* 187–195.

Jaffe, J., & Feldsein, S. (1970). *Rhythms of dialogue.* New York: Academic Press.

Johnson, S.L., & Jacob, T. (1997). Marital interactions of depressed men and women. *Journal of Consulting and Clinical Psychology 65:* 15–23.

Julien, D., Markman, H.J., & Lindahl, K.M. (1989). A comparison of a global and a macroanalytic coding system: Implications for future trends in studying interactions. *Behavioral Assessment 11:* 81–100.

Kaiser, A., Hahlweg, K., Fehm-Wolfsdorf, G., & Groth, T. (1998). The efficacy of a compact psychoeducational group training program for married couples. *Journal of Consulting and Clinical Psychology 66:* 753–760.

Karney, B.R., & Bradbury, T.N. (1997). Assessing longitudinal change in marriage: An introduction to the analysis of growth curves. *Journal of Personality & Social Psychology 72(5):* 1075–1092.

Katz, L.F., & Gottman, J.M. (1991). Marital discord and child outcomes: A social psychophysiological approach (pp. 129–155). In J. Garber & K.A. Dodge (eds.), *The development of emotion regulation and dysregulation.* New York: Cambridge University Press.

Katz, L.F., & Gottman, J.M. (1993). Patterns of marital conflict predict children's internalizing and externalizing behaviors. *Developmental Psychology 29:* 940–950.

Katz, L.F., & Gottman, J.M. (1995). Vagal tone protects children from marital conflict. *Developmental Psychopathology 7:* 83–92.

Katz, L.F., & Gottman, J.M. (1997). Buffering children from marital conflict and dissolution. *Journal of Clinical Child Psychology 26:* 157–171.

Kiecolt-Glaser, J.K., Fisher, L., Ogrocki, L.D., Stout, J.C., Speicher, C.E., & Glaser, R. (1987). Marital quality, marital disruption, and immune function. *Psychosomatic Medicine 49:* 13–34.

Kiecolt-Glaser, J.K., Malarkey, W.B., Chee, M., Newton, T., Caciopppo, J.T., Mao, H.Y., & Glaser, R. (1993). Negative behavior during marital conflict is associated with immunological down-regulation. *Psychosomatic Medicine 55:* 395–409.

Kitson, G.C., & Morgan, L.A. (1990). The multiple consequences of divorce: A decade review. *Journal of Marriage and the Family 52:* 913–924.

Klinetob, N.A., & Smith, D.A. (1996). Demand-withdraw communication in marital interaction: Tests of interpersonal contingency and gender role hypotheses. *Journal of Marriage and the Family 58:* 945–957.

Kobak, R.R., & Hazan, C. (1991). Attachment in marriage: Effects of security and accuracy of working models. *Journal of Personality and Social Psychology 60:* 861–869.

Krokoff, L.J., Gottman, J.M., & Hass, S.D. (1989). Validation of a global rapid Couples Interaction Scoring System. *Behavioral Assessment 11:* 65–80.

Krokoff, L.J., Gottman, J.M., & Roy, A.K. (1989). Blue-collar and white-collar interaction and communication orientation. *Journal of Personal and Social Relationships 5:* 201–221.

Lederer, W.J., & Jackson, D.D. (1968). *The mirages of marriage.* New York: W.W. Norton.

LeMasters, E.E. (1957). Parenthood as a crises. *Marriage and Family Living 19:* 352–355.

Levenson, R.W., Carstensen, L.L., & Gottman, J.M. (1993). Long-term marriage: age, gender and satisfaction. *Psychology and Aging 8:* 301–313.

Levenson, R.W., Carstensen, L.L., & Gottman, J.M. (1994). The influence of age and gender on affect, physiology, and their interrelations: A study of long-term marriages. *Journal of Personality and Social Psychology 67:* 56–68.

Levenson, R.W., Ekman, P., & Friesen, W.V. (1990). Voluntary facial action generates emotion-specific autonomic nervous system activity. *Psychophysiology 27:* 363–384.

Levenson, R.W., & Gottman, J.M. (1983). Marital interaction: Physiological linkage and affective exchange. *Journal of Personality and Social Psychology 45:* 587–597.

Levenson, R.W., & Gottman, J.M. (1985). Physiological and affective predictors of change in relationship satisfaction. *Journal of Personality and Social Psychology 49:* 85–94.

Levenson, R.W., & Ruef, A.M. (1992). Empathy: A physiological substrate. *Journal of Personality and Social Psychology 63:* 234–246.

Lewis, J. (1989). *The birth of the family: An*

*empirical inquiry.* New York: Brunner/Ma-zel.

Lewis, M., & Rosenblum, L. (eds.). (1974). *The effect of the infant on its caregiver.* New York: John Wiley & Sons.

Lidz, T., Cornelison, A.R., Fleck, S., & Terry, D. (1957). The intrafamilial environment of schizophrenic patients: Marital schism and marital skew. *American Journal of Psychiatry 114:* 241–248.

Macklin, E.D. (1980). Nontraditional family forms: A decade of research. *Journal of Marriage and the Family 42:* 905–921.

Mahoney, A., Boggio, R.M., & Jouriles, E.N. (1996). Effects of verbal marital conflict on subsequent mother-son interactions in a child clinical sample. *Journal of Child Clinical Psychology 25:* 262–271.

Malarkey, W.B., Kiecolt-Glaser, J.K., Pearl, D., & Glaser, R. (1994). Hostile behavior during marital conflict alters pituitary and adrenal hormones. *Psychosomatic Medicine 56:* 41–51.

Margolin, G., Christensen, A., & John, R.S. (1996). The continuance of spillover of everyday tensions in distressed and nondistressed families. *Journal of Family Psychology 10:* 304–321.

Matthews, L.S., Wickrama, K.A.S., & Conger, R.D. (1996). Predicting marital instability from spouse and observer reports of marital interaction. *Journal of Marriage and the Family 58:* 641–655.

McCabe, S.B., & Gotlib, I.H. (1993). Interactions of couples with and without a depressed spouse: Self-report and observations of problem-solving situations. *Journal of Personal and Social Relationships 10:* 589–599.

McCann, E., & Shannon, D. (1985). *The two-step: The dance toward intimacy* [foreword by Virginia Satir]. New York: Grove Press.

Melby, J.N., Ge, X., Conger, R.D., & Warner, T.D. (1995). The importance of task in evaluating positive marital interactions. *Journal of Marriage and the Family 57:* 981–994.

Menaghan, E.G., & Parcel, T.L. (1990). Parental employment and family life: Research in the 1980s. *Journal of Marriage and the Family 52:* 1079–1098.

Mendola, M., Beach, S.R.H., & Tesser, A. (1996). The relationship between marital in-teraction behaviors and affective reactions to one's own and one's spouse's self-evaluation needs. *Personal Relationships 3:* 279–292.

Michaels, G.Y., & Goldberg, W.A. (eds.). (1988). *The transition to parenthood: Current theory and research.* New York: Cambridge University Press.

Miller, G.E., & Bradbury, T.N. (1995). Refining the association between attributions and behavior in marital interaction. *Journal of Family Psychology 9:* 196–208.

Murray, J.D. (1989). *Mathematical biology.* Berlin: Springer-Verlag.

Nelson, G.M., & Beach, S.R.H. (1990). Sequential interaction in depression: Effects of depressive behavior on spousal aggression. *Behavior Therapy 21:* 167–182.

Noller, P., & Fitzpatrick, M.A. (1990). Marital communication in the 1980s. *Journal of Marriage and the Family 52:* 832–843.

Notarius, C.I., Benson, P.R., Sloane, D., Vanzetti, N.A., & Hornyak, L.M. (1989). Exploring the interface between perception and behavior: An analysis of marital interaction in distressed and nondistressed couples. *Behavioral Assessment 11:* 39–64.

Notarius, C.I., Markman, H.J., & Gottman, J.M. (1983). Couples interaction scoring system: Clinical implications (pp. 117–136). In E.E. Filsinger (ed.), *Marriage and family assessment.* Beverly Hills: Sage Publications.

Oggins, J., Veroff, J., & Leber, D. (1993). Perceptions of marital interactions among Black and White newlyweds. *Journal of Personality and Social Psychology 65:* 494–511.

Olson, D.H. (1970). Marital and family therapy: Integrative review and critique. *Journal of Marriage and the Family 32:* 501–537.

Olson, D.H., & Ryder, R.G. (1970). Inventory of marital conflicts (IMC): And experimental interaction procedure. *Journal of Marriage and the Family 32:* 443–448.

Osmond, M.W. (1980). Cross-societal family research: A macrosociological overview of the seventies. *Journal of Marriage and the Family 42:* 995–1016.

Parsons, T., Bales, R.F., Olds, J., Zelditch, M., & Slater, P.E. (1955). *Family socialization and interaction process.* Glencoe IL: Free Press.

Pasch, L.A., & Bradbury, T.N. (1998). Social support, conflict, and the development of marital dysfunction. *Journal of Consulting and Clinical Psychology 66:* 219–230.

Pasch, L.A., Bradbury, T.N., & Davila, J. (1997). Gender, negative affectivity, and observed social support in marital interaction. *Personal Relationships 4:* 361–378.

Peterson, J.L., & Zill, N. (1986). Marital disruption, parent-child relationships, and behavior problems in children. *Journal of Marriage and the Family 48:* 295–307.

Porter, B., & O'Leary, K.D. (1980). Marital discord and childhood behavior problems. *Journal of Abnormal Psychology 8:* 287–295.

Price-Bonham, S., & Balswick, J.O. (1980). The noninstitutions: Divorce, desertion, and remarriage. *Journal of Marriage and the Family 42:* 959–972.

Rapoport, A. (1960). *Fights, games, and debates.* Ann Arbor: University of Michigan Press.

Rapoport, A. (1972). The uses of mathematical isomorphism in general systems theory (pp. 42–77). In G.J. Klir (ed.), *Trends in general systems theory.* New York: Wiley Interscience.

Raush, H.L., Barry, W.A., Hertl, R.K., & Swain, M.A. (1974). *Communication, conflict, and marriage.* San Francisco: Jossey-Bass.

Ravich, R., Deutch, H., & Brown, B. (1966). An experimental study of marital discord and decision making (pp. 105–135). In I.M. Cohen (ed.), *Family structure, dynamics and theory.* Washington DC: American Psychiatric Association.

Rogers, L.E. (1972). *Relational Communication Control Coding Manual.* Unpublished lab manual, Michigan State University.

Rogers, M.J., & Holmbeck, G.N. (1997). Effects of interparental aggression on children's adjustment: The moderating role of cognitive appraisal and coping. *Journal of Family Psychology 11:* 125–130.

Romano, J., Turner, J.A., Friedman, L.S., Bulcroft, R.A., Jensen, M.P., & Hops, H. (1991). Observational assessment of chronic pain patient-spouse behavioral interactions. *Behavior Therapy 22:* 549–567.

Ross, C.E., Morowsky, J., & Goldsteen, K. (1990). The impact of the family on health: The decade in review. *Journal of Marriage and the Family 52:* 1059–1078.

Rushe, R.H. (1995). Tactics of power and influence in violent marriages. Unpublished Doctoral Dissertation, Department of Psychology, University of Washington, Seattle.

Rutter, M. (1971). Parent-child separation: Psychological effects on the children. *Journal of Child Psychology and Psychiatry 12:* 233–260.

Sagrestano, L.M., Christensen, A., & Heavey, C.L. (1998). Social influence techniques during marital conflict. *Personal Relationships 5:* 75–89.

Sanders, J.D., Smith, T.W., & Alexander, J.F. (1991). Type A behavior and marital interaction: Hostile-Dominant responses during conflict. *Journal of Behavioral Medicine 14:* 567–580.

Sayers, S.L., & Baucom, D.H. (1991). Role of femininity and masculinity in distressed couples' communication. *Journal of Personality and Social Psychology 61:* 641–647.

Scherer, K., & Ekman, P. (eds.). (1982). *Handbook of research on nonverbal behavior.* New York: Cambridge University Press.

Schmaling, K.B., & Jacobson, N.S. (1990). Marital interaction and depression. *Journal of Abnormal Psychology 99:* 229–236.

Schmaling, K.B., Whisman, M.A., Fruzzetti, A.E., & Truax, P. (1991). Identifying areas of marital conflict: Interactional behaviors associated with depression. *Journal of Family Psychology 5:* 145–157.

Shumaker, S.A., & Hill, D.R. (1991). Gender differences in social support and physical health. *Health Psychology 10:* 102–111.

Sillars, A.L. (1982). Verbal Tactics Coding Scheme: Coding Manual. Unpublished manuscript, Ohio State University, Columbus.

Smith, D.A., Vivian, D., & O'Leary (1990). Longitudinal prediction of marital discord from premarital expressions of affect. *Journal of Consulting and Clinical Psychology 58:* 790–798.

Smith, T.W., & Brown, P.C. (1991). Cynical hostility, attempts to exert social control and cardiovascular reactivity in married couples. *Journal of Behavioral Medicine 14:* 581–592.

Spanier, G.B., & Lewis, R.A. (1980). Marital quality: A review of the seventies. *Journal of Marriage and the Family 42:* 825–839.

Staples, R., & Mirandé, A. (1980). Racial and

cultural variations among American families: A decade review of the literature on minority families. *Journal of Marriage and the Family 42:* 887–903.

Stinnett, N., Carter, L., & Montgomery, J. (1972). Older persons' perceptions of their marriages. *Journal of Marriage and the Family 34:* 665–676.

Straus, M. (1979). Measuring interfamily conflict and violence: The Conflict Tactics (CT) Scales. *Journal of Marriage and the Family 41:* 75–88.

Straus, M., & Tallman, I. (1971). SIMFAM: a technique for observational measurement and experimental study of families (pp. 379–438). In J. Aldous, T. Condon, R. Hill, M. Straus, & I. Tallman (eds.), *Family problem solving.* Hinesdale IL: Dryden.

Streib, G.F., & Beck, R.W. (1980). Older families: A decade review. *Journal of Marriage and the Family 42:* 937–956.

Szinovacz, M.E. (1987). Family power (pp. 651–694). In M.B. Sussman & S.K. Steinmetz (eds.), *Handbook of marriage and the family.* New York: Plenum Press.

Tannen, D. (1990). *You just don't understand.* New York: William Morrow & Co.

Terman, L.M., Butterweiser, P., Ferguson, L.W., Johnson, W.B., & Wilson, D.P. (1938). *Psychological factors in marital happiness.* Stanford CA: Stanford University Press.

Thibaut, J.W., & Kelley, H.H. (1959). *The social psychology of groups.* New York: John Wiley & Sons.

Thomas, G., Fletcher, G.J.O., & Lange, C. (1997). On-line empathic accuracy in marital interaction. *Journal of Personality and Social Psychology 72:* 839–850.

Thompson, R.A. (1994). Emotion regulation: A theme in search of definition (pp. 25–52). In N.A. Fox (ed.), The development of emotion regulation: Biological and behavioral considerations. *Monographs of the Society for Research in Child Development 59*(2–3, Serial No. 240). Chicago IL: The University of Chicago Press.

Turk, D.C., Kerns, R.D., & Rosenberg, R. (1992). Effects of marital interaction on chronic pain and disability: Examining the down side of social support. *Rehabilitation Psychology 37:* 259–273.

Vanlear, C.A., & Zietlow, P.H. (1990). Toward a contingency approach to marital interaction: An empirical integration of three approaches. *Communication Monographs 57:* 202–218.

Van Widenfelt, B.M. (1995). *The prediction and prevention of relationship distress and divorce.* The Haag: Cip-Gegevens Koninklijke.

Vanzetti, N.A., Notarius, C.I., & NeeSmith, D. (1992). Specific and generalized expectancies in marital interaction. *Journal of Family Psychology 6:* 171–183.

von Bertalanffy, L. (1968). *General system theory.* New York: George Braziller.

Voydanoff, P. (1990). Economic distress and family relations: A review of the 1980s. *Journal of Marriage and the Family 52:* 1099–1115.

Vuchinich, S. (1985). Arguments, family style. *Psychology Today 19:* 40–46.

Wampler, K.S., & Halverson, C.F., Jr. (1990). The Georgia Marriage Q-Sort: An observational measure of marital functioning. *The American Journal of Family Therapy 18:* 169–178.

Watzlawick, P., Beavin, J.H., & Jackson, D.D. (1967). *Pragmatics of human communication.* New York: W.W. Norton.

Weiss, R.L. (1980). Strategic behavioral marital therapy: Toward a model for assessment and intervention (pp. 229–271). In J.P. Vincent (ed.), *Advances in family intervention, assessment and theory, Vol 1.* Greenwich CT: JAI Press.

Weiss, R.L., Hops, H., & Patterson, G.R. (1973). A framework for conceptualizing marital conflict (pp. 309–342). In L.A. Hamerlynck, L.C. Handy, & E.J. Marsh (eds.), *Behavior change: Methodology, concepts, and practice.* Champaign IL: Research Press.

Weiss, R.L., & Tolman, A.O. (1990). The marital interaction coding system—Global (MICS-G): A global comparison to the MICS. *Behavioral Assessment 12:* 271–294.

White, B.B. (1989). Gender differences in marital communication patterns. *Family Process 28:* 89–106.

White, L.K. (1990). Determinants of divorce: A review of research in the eighties. *Journal of Marriage and the Family 52:* 904–912.

Whitehead, L. (1979). Sex differences in children's responses to family stress. *Journal of Child Psychology and Psychiatry 20:* 247–254.

Wynne, L.C., Ryckoff, I.M., Day, J., & Hirsch, S.I. (1958). Pseudo-mutuality in the family relations of schizophrenics. *Psychiatry 21:* 205–220.

Zamsky, E. (1997). Racial and socioeconomic status differences in marital interaction. Unpublished Doctoral Dissertation, Catholic University of America, Washington DC.

Zietlow, P.H., & Sillars, A.L. (1988). Life-stage differences in communication during marital conflicts. *Journal of Social and Personal Relationships 5:* 223–245.

Manuscript received September 4, 2001; final revision submitted and accepted March 19, 2002.

# The History of Couple Therapy: A Millennial Review

ALAN S. GURMAN, Ph.D.†
PETER FRAENKEL, Ph.D.‡

*In this article, we review the major conceptual and clinical influences and trends in the history of couple therapy to date, and also chronicle the history of research on couple therapy. The evolving patterns in theory and practice are reviewed as having progressed through four distinctive phases: Phase I—Atheoretical Marriage Counseling Formation (1930–1963); Phase II—Psychoanalytic Experimentation (1931–1966); Phase III—Family Therapy Incorporation (1963–1985); and Phase IV—Refinement, Extension, Diversification, and Integration (1986–present). The history of research in the field is described as having passed through three phases: Phase I—A Technique in Search of Some Data (1930–1974), Phase II—Irrational(?) Exuberance (1975–1992), and Phase III—Caution and Extension (1993–present). The article concludes with the identification of Four Great Historical Ironies in the History of Couple Therapy.*

*Fam Proc 41:199–260, 2002*

C OUPLE therapy is an area of psychotherapy practice that is long on history, but short on tradition. One tradition that has been established solidly, however, is that historians of the field periodically assess its status from a metaphorically developmental perspective. Olson (1970), the field's first chronicler, referred to marital therapy as a "youngster" which had "not yet developed a solid theoretical base nor tested [its] major assumptions and principles" (p. 501). Six years later, Olson and Sprenkle (1976), continuing the individually oriented metaphor, asserted that the field was "no longer in its infancy" and was "showing signs of maturing," although it "appeared like an adolescent, full of undirected energy . . ." (p. 326), and a mere four years later, asserted that it had "reached young adulthood" (Olson, Russell, & Sprenkle, 1980, p. 974). Unfortunately, such loose metaphorical assessments appear quite unreliable. For example, in 1995, Gurman and Jacobson (p. 6) declared that "couple therapy has come of age," by virtue of its

greater awareness of the significance of personal and cultural values; a more balanced appreciation of the interdependence of interpersonal and intrapsychic factors in couple relationships . . . an increasing emphasis on . . . operationalizing interventions . . . a more honest assessment of . . . the efficacy of couple therapies . . . and . . . more solid links

† Professor and Director of Family Therapy Training, Department of Psychiatry, University of Wisconsin Medical School, 6001 Research Park Boulevard, Madison, Wisconsin 53719; e-mail: asgurman@facstaff.wisc.edu.

‡ Associate Professor, Dept. of Psychology, City College of New York; e-mail: pfraenkel@aol.com.

with ... relevant professions and disciplines. [p. 6]

But commentators Johnson and Lebow (2000) soon questioned this position as being "premature" (p. 34), while ironically documenting the striking developments in the field during the previous decade that, in fact, corresponded almost exactly to those identified by Gurman and Jacobson!

To strain an admittedly tired metaphor once more, just after the first year of the new millennium, we suggest that a more interpersonal, systems-oriented appraisal of the current evolutionary status of couple therapy is appropriate. Such an appraisal should include consideration not only of the field's ability to stand on its own two feet, but also of its capacity to remain appropriately and respectfully connected to its origins, while at the same time, establishing viable, peer-like relationships with representatives of the contemporary world outside. In this article, we present just such an appraisal. But first, we must consider just why this millennial assessment is necessary.

## Myth of Recent Ascendancy

It is certainly significant that the first (and, to our knowledge, only) invited millennial reviews of couple therapy appear in *Family Process*. While *Family Process* has never had explicit, formal affiliations with any professional mental health associations, highly influential and visible members of the journal's governing board and its editorial advisors played pivotal roles in the founding of the American Family Therapy Academy (AFTA) (née "Association") in the late 1970s. As Framo (1989), a leading historian of that period of AFTA's saga, noted:

The founding of AFTA had ... aroused considerable alarm in the AAMFC [now AAMFT, American Association for Marriage

and Family Therapy] ... From AFTA's point of view the fields of marriage counseling and family therapy were two separate areas, each with their own histories, concepts, and practices. [p. 12]

The AAMFT, of course, was the professional organization that had originated in the marriage counseling movement. The irony that such a special series on couple therapy appears here, rather than in any of several other more organizationally affiliated, similar journals, should not be minimized, and its meaning is, indeed, profound. Most of the early pioneers of family therapy either explicitly disavowed couple therapy as not central to their work, or effectively cast it into conceptual oblivion merely by not referring to its role. Rare, indeed, for example, were early family therapy textbooks that gave more than a passing nod to the theory or practice of couple therapy. Even widely acclaimed, recent state-of-the-art texts such as M.P. Nichols and Schwartz' (1998) volume, devote only a small fraction of their pages to couple therapy (for Nicholas and Schwartz, about 2%). Indeed, even in our own family therapy textbooks (Gurman & Kniskern, 1981b, 1991), couple therapy accounted for about one quarter of the chapters.

Such representations of the less-than-secondary importance of couple therapy in the broader family field persist even today, despite family therapy's unofficial founder, Nathan Ackerman, having identified "the therapy of marital disorders as the core approach to family change" (1970, p. 124). Although Fraenkel (1997) has suggested that, at least historically, "the two modalities [of family and couple therapy] draw from the same body of concepts and techniques" (p. 380), this is becoming increasingly less true, as we will show.

But such representations of couple therapy's secondary status have flown in the face of what Gurman & Kniskern (1992, p. 66) called "the long-denied fact that most 'family therapists' predominantly work with couples rather than two-generational families." Thus, Rait's (1988) survey of family therapists showed that about one-fifth of their typical caseload was couple work, and just over one-third was whole family work, notwithstanding the related finding that the most frequently identified (63%) patient complaints among the three most common problems identified by survey respondents were "marital difficulties." Similarly, Simmons and Doherty's (1995) first study of family therapists' practice patterns found that "couple problems" (59%) exceeded "whole family problems" (42%), and their followup national survey (Doherty & Simmons, 1996) of family therapists showed that these clinicians treated about twice as many couples as families. Whisman, Dixon, and Johnson's (1997) survey of practicing family psychologists and family therapists likewise showed that couple problems dominated the landscape of their clinical work. And recent multiauthor volumes, such as those by Donovan (1999) and Dattilio and Bevilacqua (2000) make it clear that therapists of every major (and some minor) "family" theoretical orientation regularly devote large portions of their work to couples. In sum, the "family" therapy literature of the last thirty years presents a grossly distorted view of what family therapists actually do.

Why has the professional myth that "family" therapists do little couple or marital work been both so pervasive and so persistent? This is one of the implicit themes found throughout the history of marital and couple therapy, which will be examined in our description of the conceptual history of the field. It is important to note that the undeniably increased visibility of books, articles, workshops, and conference presentations on couple ther-

apy in the past decade indirectly support the myth that this area of clinical practice has become commonplace only very recently. Certainly, some models of couple therapy and the scientific study of couple therapy have ascended only recently. But despite appearances in the broader family therapy field to the contrary, the practice of couple therapy never actually vanished. Still, it is undoubtedly the case that the credibility attributed to such clinical practice is much more recent. The increased visibility of this work via books, conferences, and the like, reflects increased recognition of the centrality of couple therapy. Indeed, as our analysis will show, there are understandable, though unfortunate, reasons why couple therapy remained hidden in the shadows of the world of family therapy and individual psychotherapy for many years, despite the fact that couple therapy has probably been the modal clinical activity of family therapists for decades.

### The Public Health Importance of Couple Therapy

In addition to countering the myth of couple therapy's "disappearance," there is one other especially salient and far-reaching justification for this millennial review: the breakdown of marriage and other long-term, committed, intimate relationships, whether through divorce or chronic conflict and distress, exacts an enormous cost to public health, and so commands our attention at a societal level.

Couples seek therapy mostly because of relational concerns, such as emotional disengagement, power struggles, problem-solving and communication difficulties, jealousy and extrarelational involvements, value and role conflicts, sexual dissatisfaction, and violence, and this kind of help-seeking is not a recent phenomenon. Even more strikingly, a large percentage of persons seeking help from therapists practicing individually based therapy do so for marital difficulties. For instance, as early as 1960, Gurin, Veroff, and Feld found that over forty percent of all people seeking psychological help viewed the nature of their problem as marital. Such concerns alone are sufficient to warrant the development of effective couple interventions. But recurring marital conflict and dissolution are associated with a wide array of negative noninteractional sequelae in both adults and children. The partners in troubled relationships themselves are more likely to suffer from anxiety, depression and suicidality, and substance abuse, and from both acute and chronic medical problems and disabilities such as impaired immunological functioning and high blood pressure, and health-risk behaviors such as susceptibility to sexually transmitted diseases and accident-proneness (Bloom, Asher, & White, 1978; Burman & Margolin, 1992; Kiecolt-Glaser, Fisher, & Ogrocki et al., 1993). Moreover, the children of distressed marriages are more likely to suffer from anxiety, depression, conduct problems, and impaired physical health (Gottman, 1994).

### Defining Couple Therapy

In order to appreciate adequately the current status of couple therapy, and the significance of the pathways traveled to its current position, a historical perspective must be taken. In this article, we offer just such a history, but one that differs from earlier similar undertakings. By far, the most comprehensive and compelling history of couple therapy to date is that of Broderick and Schrader (1981, 1991), who trace the histories of marriage counseling and marital therapy with a primary emphasis on the development of the professionalization of these therapeutic movements. Our purpose here is quite different. Except when it is essential to do so, we will not address the emergence of

professional organizations and associations in the field, the decades-long (in the United States) struggles of relationship clinicians to achieve parity with other mental health service providers via licensing and graduate program accreditation, or the training and education of couple clinicians.

Rather, our focus will be on the conceptual history of the field of couple intervention, highlighting and commenting on emerging trends in theory and practice, and research pertaining to such practice. To do so, we must first define what we mean by "couple therapy." While we recognize that "couple therapy" can involve whole-family meetings, individual sessions, contact with other community members, etc., the emphasis here is on the prototypic case that focuses primarily on dyadic relational elements.

Thus, our focus is on conjoint therapy, a term coined by Jackson (1959) in regard to both family and couple work, and popularized by Satir (1964) in her classic, *Conjoint Family Therapy*. Of course, there are models of systems-oriented therapy (e.g., the Brief Therapy of the Mental Research Institute, Narrative Therapy) that regularly deal with couple issues with individual patients, just as there are many "individual" psychotherapists who do not subscribe to any particular systems orientation, yet who regularly work with individuals in troubled relationships. We believe that, for practical purposes, it is reasonable to consider couple therapy as involving the presence of both relationship partners. Although there exists a debate (e.g., Gurman & Kniskern, 1986; Gurman, Kniskern, & Pinsof, 1986; Wells & Gianetti, 1986a,b) as to whether individual treatment of couple problems is as helpful as conjoint treatment, we consider the formats of therapy just mentioned to be individual therapy, albeit, at times with a systemic twist. As one of us has commented, "therapeutic intents are not the same as therapeutic events" (Gurman & Kniskern, 1979, p. 5).

*On "couples" and "marriages":* The term "couple therapy" has recently come to replace the historically more familiar and limiting term "marital therapy" because of its emphasis on the link and bond between two people, without the associated judgmental tone of social value implied by the more traditional term. We ourselves have followed this contemporary convention (Fraenkel, 1997; Gurman & Jacobson, 1995), along with others (e.g., Halford & Markman, 1997; Johnson & Lebow, 2000). In the therapy literature, the two terms are overwhelmingly used interchangeably. The word "couple" has been intended to mean, in effect, "committed, but not 'married' in the legal sense." With some important exceptions (e.g., Laird & Green, 1996), the relevant literature and clinical practices considered here, whether dealing with therapy or prevention, rarely address committed, nontraditional intimate relationships. The terms are the same, but different. Whether therapeutic methods operate similarly or differently with "couples" vs. "marriages" is presently unknown. For our present purposes, we assume that they do operate similarly. In this article, we generally use the more inclusive term "couple therapy," which, of course, subsumes "marital therapy."

*The temporal aspect of couple intervention:* In addition to the distinctions made above, it is useful to differentiate couple interventions in terms of the phase of the relationship at which they occur. The focus of most couple therapy is remedial, and therapy typically occurs during the long phase of the relationship that follows some sort of symbolic ritual affirming a long-term commitment. When nonremedial intervention occurs in this phase, it usually falls under the heading of "pri-

mary prevention" or "enrichment." Both of these areas are considered here.

When intervention occurs before a legal commitment ritual, it is usually considered "premarital counseling" if it has a remedial intent, and "prevention," if not. Preventive intervention has developed tremendously in recent years, but premarital counseling seems never to have developed either a substantial body of theory or research, and is not addressed here. Likewise, separation/divorce therapy with couples, though a common activity of couple therapists, contains no critical mass of clinical theory apart from generic couple therapy, or widely accepted practices, nor is its research base extensive (Sprenkle & Storm, 1983), and thus, it is also not addressed here as a distinct entity.

## FOUR-PHASE CONCEPTUAL HISTORY OF COUPLE THERAPY

Our review suggests that there have been four main phases in the theoretical and clinical history of couple therapy. These phases, visually represented in the timeline in the Figure (see below), refer to conceptually distinguishable time periods in the development of the field. These phases, of course, are not discrete, i.e., they do not literally begin or end in particular years. This phasic representation serves as an organizational heuristic to examine the evolving conceptual and clinical trends of the couple therapy field. Moreover, this phasic analysis reflects the dominant, but not exclusive, thrusts and influences at work during each time period.

In this analysis, we will examine the major conceptual influences in couple therapy in each period, with particular attention paid to theories and methods that have shown clearly enduring and pervasive influences. We will also show the ways in which these four phases in-

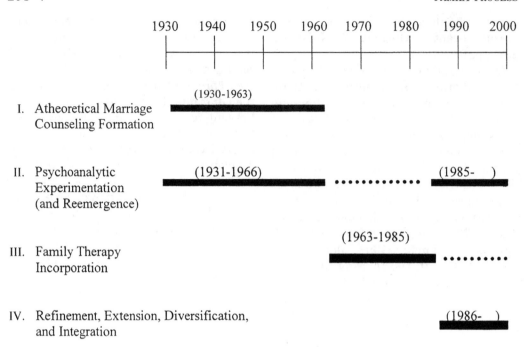

FIG. The four-phase history of couple therapy.

volved complex, mutual influence processes among the dominant forces in the field.

We will draw attention to certain basic elements that would seem to convey something of the essential character of the dominant couple therapies practiced in that period: the models' views of relational health vs. dysfunction; typical treatment goals associated with the models (e.g., degree of emphasis on the attachment vs. power dimension of couple interaction); the theory of change associated with the models (e.g., the balance between interpersonal vs. intrapsychic factors); the nature of the therapeutic relationship in the models (e.g., the degree of therapist directiveness); typical and preferred techniques (e.g., preferred time-frame perspective); and the types of problems and patients treated (e.g., remedial vs. preventive emphasis). Elsewhere, we have separately (Fraenkel, 1997; Gur-

man, 1978, 1979) presented comprehensive, comparative analyses of how such interventive dimensions and foci characterize significant distinctions among the different major schools of couple therapy, but without respect to the unfolding history of those schools.

**PHASE I: ATHEORETICAL MARRIAGE COUNSELING FORMATION (1930–1963)**

Broderick and Schrader's (1981, 1991) classic tracing of the history of marital counseling identified four distinct phases; Phase I (1929–1932), the "Pioneer" stage, dominated by a small handful of forward-lookng practitioners; Phase II (1934–1945), the "Establishment" stage, signaled by the formation of the American Association of Marriage Counselors (AAMC); Phase III (1946–1963), the "Consolidation" stage, leading to the the first legal recognition of the marriage counseling profession (in California, in 1963); and Phase IV (1964–1978), the "Formative" stage, marked by the building of a professional literature, an occasional effort at scientific study, and what L'Abate and McHenry (1983, p. 3) called "intense growth and clarification of standards and competencies" for training and practice. In our view, what clearly links these stages is the understandable and overwhelming emphasis on the formation of a professional identity for marital practitioners, especially those coming out of the "marriage counseling" tradition. For Broderick and Schrader (1981, 1991), there were four phases to the "marriage counseling" movement. For us, by contrast, these four phases conceptually constitute four subphases in one long phase in the atheoretical formation of the marriage counseling profession.[1]

## What Was "Marriage Counseling"?

As already noted, "marriage counseling" died a political-administrative death in 1978. If we arbitrarily date modern marriage counseling as having been born, organizationally at least, about 1930 (in that three major marriage counseling clinical institutes were formed from 1929 to 1932 in the United States; Broderick & Schrader, 1981, 1991), then we may justifiably wonder just what was going on in

the field for almost forty years, and why "counseling" came to such a sudden halt.

Broderick and Schrader (1981) described the early marriage counselors as "a more or less naively service-oriented group" (p. 11) for whom their counseling was "the auxiliary activity of a professional whose primary commitment was elsewhere" (p. 4), in their work, e.g., as obstetrician-gynecologists, clergyman, social workers, family life educators, etc. Their clients were pre-marrieds, newlyweds and married couples seeking guidance about the everyday facets of marriage and family life, in some ways presaging the contemporary psychoeducational-preventive movement, as we shall see. They most decidedly were not severely maladjusted or suffering from diagnosed psychiatric disorders, and marriage counseling, even later in its history, was not viewed by the world-at-large as a "mental health" discipline (Haley, 1984; Shields, Wynne, McDaniel, & Gawinski, 1994). Early marriage counseling, however, clearly took a health/strength perspective and, in this way, foreshadowed the later emergence of more comprehensively delineated preventive couple interventions, as we discuss later.

Barker (1984) vividly described the modal clinical activity of clergy and social worker marriage counselors in the 1920s: "They told their clients how to make their marriages work better. They educated couples as to their legal and social obligations and they extolled the values inherent in family life" (p. 11). Marriage counselors stayed close to couples' presenting problems, provided advice and information, e.g., about the biological aspects of marriages, and helped couples solve relatively uncomplicated practical problems of everyday life. A marriage counselor's approach was typically very focused, very short-term, and quite didactic.

---

[1] Parenthetically, but significantly, we think Broderick and Schrader (1981, p. 30) erred in identifying the early contributions of behavioral marriage therapists in the 1970s (e.g., Jacobson & Martin, 1976; Stuart, 1969) as having any connection to the "marriage counseling area." At that time, Stuart was a university-based Professor of Social Work, and Jacobson was affiliated with an academic program in clinical psychology. They both came from, and were leaders in, the field of behavior therapy. With this in mind, we have amended Broderick and Schrader's Phase IV to end, not in 1981 when their chapter was published, but in 1978, when the term "marriage counseling" was officially terminated as the AAMFC became the AAMFT.

## Treatment Format

If all of this seems to bear little resemblance to modern couple therapy (though it has more in common with modern psychoeducational programs), there is even less resemblance than may meet the eye. Ironically, though interested in the emotional welfare of couples, early marriage counselors rarely met in what we now consider the routinely preferred format of the conjoint interview. In 1963, thirty years into the history of the profession, Michaelson estimated from the case records of the three major marriage and family clinics in the United States that, in the 1940s, only 5% of marriage counselors' cases met conjointly, rising to 9% during the 1950s and to a whopping 15% in 1960. By the mid-1960s, clinicians who primarily identified themselves as marital therapists overwhelmingly used the conjoint format in couple cases, while mental health professionals from other disciplines who also practiced marital therapy were more divided between conjoint and individual approaches (Alexander, 1968). It was not until the end of that decade, now forty years after the founding of marriage counseling, that Olson (1970), in the field's first comprehensive analytical review, identified the "predominant use of the technique of conjoint therapy" (p. 503). As we shall soon see, the conjoint approach did not originate within marriage counseling, but within psychoanalytically dominated psychiatric circles (Sager, 1966), thus portending the virtual downfall of the marriage counseling profession.

## Dominant Treatment Models

While Olson (1970) correctly identified the routine emergence of the conjoint approach, he also noted that the field was "seriously lacking in empirically tested principles, and it is without a theoretically derived foundation on which to op-

erate clinically" (p. 503). Likewise, Broderick and Schrader (1981) noted that during this period, there was a "lack of clear commitment to any particular clinical philosophy" (p. 12). And Manus' (1966) classic and often-cited article provocatively declared that marriage counseling was a mere "technique in search of a theory" (p. 449).

And when marriage counselors of the day went searching for a theory, where did they find it? In the "peer group" of psychoanalysis. Apparently, few heeded the warning of psychiatrist/marriage counselor Laidlaw (1957): "If, as therapy progresses, unconscious factors are discovered . . . the case ceases to be in the field of marriage counseling" (p. 56). By the mid-1960s, marriage counselors had latched onto the independently emerging psychoanlaytic and psychodynamic approaches to marital therapy. As Manus (1966) noted, "The most generally influential hypothesis . . . is that marital conflict is based on the neurotic interaction of the partners . . . a product of psychopathology in one or both . . . partners" (p. 449). And, in a classic and very influential marriage counseling article of the mid-1960s, Leslie (1964) identified the central technical issues in working with couples: the "identification of distortions" (p. 68) in the partners' mutual perceptions; the "handling of transference and countertransference" (p. 69); the "drawing out of conflict" (p. 70), i.e., allowing the marital conflict to be fully manifest in-session; and the "direct alteration of interaction (p. 70)." Whereas marriage counseling in its first thirty-plus years had maintained an almost sole focus on the present and on patients' conscious experience, the past and the unconscious were now explicitly entering the conjoint counseling process, albeit with a focus still maintained on the current relationship. And yet, as Leslie (1964, p. 66) unabashedly acknowledged, and indeed emphasized, "There is no sharp line between marriage counseling and reconstructive therapy." Marriage counseling, as W.C. Nichols (1973) would say in another influential article, included "long-term, intensive psychotherapeutic work" (p. 5).

It was understandable that marriage counseling had begun to take on a psychoanalytic flavor. First, family therapy was in the wings, but had not yet gained credibility in the broader world of psychotherapy. While the marriage counseling movement had taken the bold and groundbreaking step of defining marriage as a suitable target for social science investigation and for clinical intervention, marriage counseling was becoming professionally and intellectually marginalized, and, as clinical psychology had done after emerging post-World War II, attempted to attach itself to the most prestigious peer group it could.

Unfortunately, marriage counseling had unwittingly chosen to consort with the devil, as the growing and soon-dominating field of family therapy would generally come to view psychoanalytic thought. Although many of family therapy's early leaders had been trained in psychoanalytic thinking, and some in psychoanalysis proper, family therapy largely emerged as a collective statement against the excess and limitations of highly individual-oriented theory and practice. The marriage counseling profession had not produced an influential clinical theorist in its first four decades, and now it had hitched its wagon not to a rising star, but to the falling star of psychoanalytic marriage therapy that would soon be in a different psychotherapy atmosphere, and would evaporate and largely disappear from visibility for about two decades.

## PHASE II: PSYCHOANLAYTIC EXPERIMENTATION (1931–1966)

While all the feverish ferment involved in establishing a professional identity was taking place in the field of marriage counseling over a period of four decades, an entirely separate type of marriage interventionist was straining to emerge as a viable therapeutic force. A small coterie of psychoanalytic clinicians (all psychiatrists, of course, since non-M.D.'s were not then allowed entrance to psychoanalytic training institutes), were growing impatient with the ineffectiveness of treating analysands with primary marital complaints, and even of the sluggish pace of success when it did occur. Despite their understandable cautiousness, a few rebels began an era of daring experimentation.

### Precursors to Conjoint Approach

Psychoanalytic writers for decades had been deeply interested in the complex processes of mate selection, the meaning of marriage in family life, and the effects of psychoanalysis on the spouse (Meissner, 1978). As early as 1931, Oberndorf made the first presentation at a major professional (psychiatric) conference on the psychoanalysis of married couples, focusing on the role of "interlocking neuroses" in symptom formation. This paper was followed by one (Oberndorf, 1934) on the phenomenon of "folie à deux" in couples. The original paper, appearing in print several years later (Oberndorf, 1938), described the "consecutive" psychotherapy of marital partners treated by the same analyst, in which the second analysis commenced only when the first ended.

A significant step forward, especially in terms of therapeutic efficiency and length, was taken by Mittelman (1948), who conducted "concurrent" treatment, in which "both spouses are treated individually but synchronously by the same therapist" (Greene, 1965, p. 3). This action was quite a divergence from the psychoanalytic tradition that warned of the dangers of the analyst's contact with the relatives of analysands, because of its assumed contamination and complication of transference and countertransference phenomena. But Mittelman's next step was even more daring for its time. He initiated two joint sessions with one couple, as Sager (1966) noted, "because their stories conflicted" (p. 460).

This action was certainly theoretically and politically very incorrect in this tradition, but more tellingly, it also captured the essence of the presumed mechanism of change in concurrent treatment. That is, it was the *therapist's* task to disentangle the partners' irrational, distorted mutual perceptions, as if he (few analysts were then female) "knew" what was rational, and what was not. Significantly, it was when Mittelman had trouble keeping his patients' stories straight, when he could not understand their different stories, that he arranged for conjoint meetings. His conceptual error (from our constructivist-informed, millennial perspective), and the possible error of all the early psychoanalytic marital therapists, was to search for "truth," rather than to entertain and incorporate multiple perspectives. In addition, concurrent therapy, which excluded joint sessions, certainly must have heightened certain technical problems, such as the maintenance of impartiality and the regulation of countertransference reactions. But even Mittelman was not wholly enamored of the conjoint method, and believed that it was the indicated approach for only about twenty percent of couples, with the rest requiring two analysts.

Other psychonanalytic experimentation cautiously occurred during the late 1950s and early 1960s. But, as Sager (1966) noted, "Most of these contributions . . . evidenced no new fundamental development of theory . . ." (p. 460). These contributions mostly involved alternative formats for therapy, e.g., "collaborative" therapy (Martin, 1965), in which partners simultaneously were "treated by different therapists, who communicate for the purpose of maintaining the marriage (Greene, 1965b, p. 3), and "combined" treatment, which involved combinations of family therapy, group therapy, individual, concurrent, and, later, conjoint sessions "in various purposeful combinations" (Greene, 1965b, p. 3). Greene's (1965a) classic, *The Psychotherapies of Marital Disharmony*, summarized the extant theories of marital therapy circa the mid-1960s.

In all the emerging nonconjoint psychoanalytic marital treatment methods, the centrality of the individual(s) prevailed. At the same time, there was increasing intuitive sense among practitioners (so it seems in retrospect) that "something" was still missing from the dominant conceptualizations of both marital conflict and of requisite therapist interventions. As long as the marital partners remained either exclusively or predominantly in individually formatted therapies, the therapist remained the central agent through which change must perforce occur. Psychoanalytic marriage therapists challenged rigid adherence to core analytic practices, such as the necessity of free association and dream analysis, and a focus on the patient-therapist transference, and increasingly recognized the salience of the "real," as well as the transferential, marital relationship. These therapists, however, continued to practice in ways that kept them in the position of being *the* pivotal agent of change. They did not yet recognize the healing potential within couples' own relationships (Dicks, 1967; Lewis & Gossett, 2000).

*The ambivalent transition to the conjoint approach:* To be sure, by the early 1960s, psychoanalytic couple therapy was moving inexorably toward an emphasis on the conjoint approach. But the transition had not yet been completed. Thus, for example, even A. S. Watson (1963), in one of the most influential articles of the decade on the "conjoint treatment of marriage partners," still regularly held two or three individual anamnestic, formulation sessions with each spouse before convening the threesome on a regular basis. The assumption was still that, in order to understand a couple's *"interlocking* adaptive and communication *systems"* (p. 914) and their "interlocking homeostatic balance" (p. 913), the therapist needed to have a clear appreciation of each partner's individual psychodynamics and developmental history, assessed not in the couple transactional setting, but in the traditional patient-therapist dyadic setting. There was still, to an important degree, a belief in content over context.

During the 1960s, therapeutic methodology remained largely unchanged, even as conjoint practice increased. Treatment emphasized the interpretation of defenses (which now also included joint as well as individual defenses); the use of the techniques of free association and dream analysis (which now also included each spouse's associations to the other's, as well as their own, productions); and the ventilation and examination of previously unexpressed feelings (which now included feelings toward both one's partner and the therapist).

Even as psychoanalytic therapists were moving inevitably toward modern conjoint methods, they seemed to still cling to a core individual mindset. Thus, Sager (1967b), certainly the most widely influential marriage therapist in the psychoanalytic tradition during the 1960s and 1970s (e.g., Sager, 1967a, 1976, 1981; Sager, Kaplan, Gundlach et al., 1971) wrote, "I am not primarily involved in treating marital disharmony, which is a symptom, but rather in treating the two individuals in the marriage" (Sager, 1967b, p. 185). Sager had not yet moved (cf. Sager, 1976, 1981) to a balanced intrapsychic/interpersonal approach, and still emphasized "triangular transference transctions" (p. 185), including attention to "oedipal elements."

The same year Sager penned the above, he also recognized a common therapeutic problem, and an associated therapist error involved in "the attempt of husband or wife to talk to the analyst rather than to one another. The alert therapist avoids an omnipotent role so that he allows patients to work toward finding their own creative solutions . . ." (Sager, 1967a, p. 144). In effect, the (traditional) transference should be paramount, but the therapist paradoxically should be more decentralized.

Such paradoxes expressed psychoanalytic marriage therapists' profound uncertainty in their work about the centrality of the defining characteristic of psychoanalysis, the analysis of transference. And yet, the marital therapist still had primary responsibility to serve what would later be thought of as the essential "holding" function (Catherall, 1992; Scharff, 1995) for both members of the couple, when partners experienced unacceptable feelings, thoughts, and impulses.

More than a decade after Sager's early influential writings, Skynner (1980), one of the most widely cited psychoanalytic marital/family therapists (e.g., Skynner, 1976, 1981), already strongly influenced by the object relations theories that had not yet influenced most psychoanalytic marital therapists of this era, discussed the conjoint therapeutic aim of "getting the projections back somehow into the individual selves" (p. 205). He emphasized, after Gurman (1978), that the psychodynamic approach seemed to have "lost [its] way" (p. 276) in identifying change-inducing techniques, beyond the basic psychoanalytic understanding of couple dynamics that it clearly offered. He attributed this technical vacuum to "the inappropriate focus on the concept of 'transference' . . . in relation to the *therapist* (usually cast in a parental role)—and interpretation to bring it to awareness . . ." (p. 276; original emphasis). Skynner emphasized that "the unconcious conflicts are already fully developed in the mutual projective system between the couple, and could be better dealt with directly rather than by the indirect methods of 'transference'" (pp. 276–277).

*The psychoanalytic conjoint approach in apparent limbo:* One of psychoanalytic marital therapy's most influential articles, Sager's (1966) "The Development of Marriage Therapy: An Historical Review," appeared "at the very zenith of its independent development" (Broderick & Schrader, 1981, p. 17), and yet psychoanalytic couple therapy would soon almost drop out of the race for leadership and influence for nearly two decades. It suffered from two interrelated, near-fatal challenges. The first challenge, the lack of effective interventions, came from within the field. As already noted, to the degree that it continued to include a significant emphasis on the traditional patient-therapist transference, it reciprocally failed to evolve interventions that significantly emphasized the partner-partner transference, thus placing a solid ceiling on its capacity to help induce change. But the second challenge was not self-imposed and could not be fended off. It was called the family therapy movement. Despite the fact that most of the pioneers of family therapy had been trained psychoanalytically, and the fact that some of the field's early influential clinical theorists (e.g., Ackerman, 1970; Framo, 1965) creatively integrated psychodynamic and systems concepts, in large measure, the early history of family therapy was marked by a strong, and at times, unyielding, disavowal of most accepted psychoanalytic/ psychodynamic therapy principles and the practices of traditional mental health disciplines (Gurman, 2001; Nichols & Schwartz, 1998). Psychoanalytic marriage therapy soon publicly plummeted from its mid-1960s "zenith" to a two-decade nadir. Psychoanalytic and psychodynamic thought seemed to disappear from

the marital therapy scene. In fact, it did not really vanish, but it did really recede in visibility, although important, though undervalued, contributions from theorists such as Framo (1976, 1981), N. Paul (1969; N. Paul & B. Paul, 1975), and Sander (1979) appeared during this period. Psychoanalytic thinking did not actually die out, but, as we shall see, it was certainly fragmented and marginalized by the dominant therapy schools of the era.

## PHASE III: FAMILY THERAPY INCORPORATION (1963–1985)

The changes in clinical practice that were reflected by increasing attention to conjoint couple therapy were experienced not merely as controversial, but as revolutionary, within psychoanalytic circles. But these changes paled in comparison to the magnitude of the changes among the influential conceptual forces in marital therapy that had just begun, near marital therapy's "zenith." Family therapy had arrived.

It is interesting to note the varied tones with which the impact of family therapy's arrival on couple therapy, and psychotherapy more generally, has been described. For example, a perfectly accurate and tempered representative description was offered by Fraenkel (1997): "Systems approaches developed in large part as a reaction against the perceived limitations of therapies that attributed psychological and social dysfunction to problems solely within the individual, whether these were viewed as biological, psychodynamic or behavior in nature" (p. 380).

In similar tones, widely cited historians of the field have described seemingly gentle processes of change in marital therapy. For example, Broderick and Schrader (1991, p. 15) speak of the "amalgamation" and "merger" of the fields; Nichols and Schwartz (1998, p. 37) refer to family therapy as "absorbing" marital therapy;

and Olson et al. (1980, p. 973) write somewhat wistfully that, by 1980, the "traditional distinctions between marriage counseling and family therapy [had] faded." Politically correct, understated descriptions of the changes taking place abounded, and were nowhere more strikingly expressed than in Olson et al.'s (1980, p. 973) euphemistic conclusion that the fields had become "unitary, but not fully unified and integrated."

Part of the reason for what Olson (1970, p. 501) referred to as the "parallel but unrelated development" of the marital and family therapy fields was that, as he put it, "None of the pioneers were recognized as innovators in both fields" (p. 506). And Haley (1984) more caustically argued that there was not "a single school of family therapy which had its origin in a marriage counseling group, nor is there one now" (p. 6). More generally, as Haley (1984) put it, "marriage counseling did not seem relevant to the developing family therapy field" (pp. 5–6).

The second related major reasons for the "parallel but unrelated development" of the two fields, beyond the mere matter of creative personnel, was also trenchantly touched upon by Haley (1984), who noted, "Marriage counselors adopted the ideas of other therapies. When individual therapy was psychodynamic, marriage counseling tended to propound those ideas" (p. 7). And, of course, as discussed earlier, "those ideas" that couple therapists adopted were those of the psychoanalytic/psychiatric establishment. Although L'Abate and McHenry (1983) have offered the perplexing view that "marriage counseling evolved rapidly in the 1970s" (p. 325), it is more accurate to say that, in what Nichols and Schwartz (1998, p. 9) referred to as "family therapy's golden age" (1975 to 1985), family therapy essentially killed marriage counseling (although it could be argued that the demise was the result of self-inflicted wounds),

and severely maimed psychoanalytic marital therapy.

**Four Influential Voices**

As a reasonably thorough reading of the history of the family therapy movement and its most influential theories inevitably reveals (Broderick & Schrader, 1981, 1991; Framo, 1989; Guerin, 1976; Kaslow, 1980; Nichols & Schwartz, 1998), almost every major family therapy theorist and clinical innovator has had something to say about the place of marriage in overall family functioning and individual symptom formation, the requirements of a healthy marriage and the sources of couple disharmony, and guiding principles for intervening with couples in conflict. Still, it is well beyond the scope of this article to review and comment on all these contributions to our understanding of long-term, committed relationships (see Fraenkel, 1997, for a review). Of the numerous approaches to family therapy that flowered during this Third Phase of couple therapy, we identify four clinical theorists as having made signal contributions to theory development and/or clinical practice: Don D. Jackson, Virginia Satir, Murray Bowen, and Jay Haley. These contributions either generated ground-breaking new ideas or stimulated a line of thinking that continues strongly to influence contemporary practices. What is more, we believe these pioneers' contributions are the most representative of the kinds of conceptual changes family therapy brought to bear on couple therapy during its "golden age."

*Don D. Jackson and the Marital Quid Pro Quo:* Jackson, founder of the Mental Research Institute (MRI), was one of that group's groundbreaking investigators of the family's role in schizophrenia (e.g., Bateson, Jackson, Haley, & Weakland, 1956). His work made household names in family therapy of such influential concepts as the "report" and "command" dimensions of communication (Jackson, 1965b), the "double bind" (Bateson et al., 1956), and relational "symmetry" and "complementarity" (Lederer & Jackson, 1968). His most pervasively influential concept of "family homeostasis" (Jackson, 1957) has been aptly referred to by Nichols and Schwartz (1998) as "the defining metaphor of family therapy's first three decades" (p. 39). Homeostatic mechanisms referred to systemic properties of families that resist change. And family "rules," inferred patterns of redundant interaction (Jackson, 1965a), were the homeostatic mechanisms that received the most attention in Jackson's study of marital relationships.

Nichols and Schwartz (1998) perceptively note that while Jackson sought to create a language descriptive of whole-family interactions, his "major success was in describing relationships between husbands and wives" (p. 41). Indeed, his best-known book, *The Mirages of Marriage* (Lederer & Jackson, 1968) focused entirely on couples. And the "defining metaphor" in Jackson's discussions of marital relationships was the "marital quid pro quo" (Jackson, 1965a).

The marital "quid pro quo" was also the cornerstone concept in Jackson's methods of couple therapy. As we will discuss, this concept would become absolutely central to the early development of behavior marital therapy (Azrin, Naster, & Jones, 1973; Jacobson & Margolin, 1979; Stuart, 1969), Indeed, Jackson's two major treatments of this concept (Jackson, 1965a; Lederer & Jackson, 1968) are universally considered classics.

But, as Mark Twain (1897) said, a classic is "A book which people praise and don't read."[2] Contrary to common percep-

tions, for Jackson, the quid pro quo was "not overt, conscious or the tangible result of *real bargaining*" (Jackson, 1965a, p. 592; emphasis added), and was not "time-bound" (Lederer & Jackson, 1968, p. 272). That is, quid pro quo exchanges are not point-for-point exchanges, e.g., of the kind commonly found in the "behavioral exchange" interventions of behavioral couple therapists (Jacobson & Margolin, 1979).

The essence of the quid pro quo was "an *unconscious* effort of both partners to assure themselves that they are equals, that they are peers. It is a technique enabling each to preserve his *dignity* and *self-esteem*" (Lederer & Jackson, 1968, p. 179; emphasis added). The "*quid pro quo* pattern becomes an unwritten (usually not consciously recognized) set of ground rules" (p. 179). Consistent with the non-time-boundedness and nonliteralness of the concept, is the notion that the "marital quid pro quo is a *metaphorical* statement of the marital relationship bargain; that is, how the couple has agreed to *define themselves within this relationship*" (Jackson, 1965b, p. 12).

Despite Jackson's efforts to throw off his psychoanalytic/Sullivanian roots, and to move from "mentalistic inference to behavioral observation of sequences" (Nichols & Schwartz, 1998, p. 39), he never fully succeeded in casting them aside. Indeed, his writings on the marital quid pro quo exude an emphasis on the importance of patients' phenomenology, and humanistic sensitivity to self-perception and self-valuing. It might be said that they could take Jackson out of Chestnut Lodge, but they could not take Chestnut Lodge out of Jackson.[3]

---

[2] Twain, M. (1897). *Following the Equator,* vol. I: *Pudd'nhead Wilson's New Calendar,* epigraph for Chapter 25.

[3] Chestnut Lodge, in Rockville MD, is a private psychiatric hospital where Jackson did his psychiatric residency. Its training philosophy was heavily Sullivanian, i.e., both interpersonally *and* intrapsychically oriented.

Although he originated the term "conjoint therapy," Jackson (1959, p. 122) did not publish a great deal on matters of therapeutic technique, and yet his writings were salient in two very different ways: first, for the ways in which they were misread and misapplied, and second, for the ways in which they presaged some of the practices in couple therapy that are most prevalent at the start of the new millennium.

Despite his efforts to minimize attention to the individual through his communicational analysis of dyads, Jackson wrote that "It is at the level of exchange of definitions of the relationship (and, therefore, of *self-definition within the relationship*) that we can *usefully analyze* in terms of quid pro quo" (Jackson, 1965a, p. 592; emphasis added). And one of the main ways to "usefully analyze" the quid pro quo was, Jackson said, "to bring it from the *unconscious* to the conscious level" (Lederer & Jackson, 1968, pp. 179–180; emphasis added). Later, in the *Mirages of Marriage,* Jackson added that "one of the *main functions* of the marriage counselor is to . . . *make them aware of those unconscious rules* which are causing friction . . . and *help them develop new rules* which *may be more workable*" (Lederer & Jackson, 1968, p. 442; latter emphasis in original).

To this end, Jackson added, "Insight alone is insufficient" (Lederer & Jackson, 1968, p. 442). But, note that, unlike most of the family therapy "systems purists" (Beels & Ferber, 1969) of the "golden era," including some of his prominent MRI colleagues, Jackson did not assert that insight was either harmful, irrelevant, or unnecessary. It was merely not enough.

And Jackson believed that what was necessary in addition to insight was "to have them consciously engage in behavior that demonstrates the presence or absence of this [particular covert] rule, and then to help them begin to formulate a new one" (Lederer & Jackson, 1968, p. 443). And, keep in mind that the "new one" was not a point-for-point exchange, but a new "bargain" about each partner's definition-of-self-in-the relationship.

To this end, Jackson described in great detail the "quid pro quo meetings" (Lederer and Jackson, 1968, p. 287) he used in order to help couples fashion new, more adaptive, conscious rules for their relationship. Interestingly, his procedures are rarely, if ever, specifically cited by contemporary writers on couple therapy. Yet, these procedures are more than mildly reminiscent of widespread (and empirically supported) treatment principles in behavioral couple (cf. Christensen, Jacobson, & Babcock, 1995) and preventive intervention programs (Floyd, Markman, Kelly, et al., 1995; Fraenkel, 1997; Fraenkel, Markman, & Stanley, 1997) aimed at improving couple communication. Examples of this overlap include: taking turns expressing one's views on a focused topic, followed by the listener's summarization of what he or she has heard; an emphasis on behavioral specificity in making relational requests; a prohibition against mind-reading; the use of "the floor" by the speaker; and the termination of negative quid pro quo meetings in order to prevent escalation, followed by calmer resumption of the conversation.

And Jackson was not at all insistent on what would soon become the fashionable push for ever-briefer therapy, noting that while some couples can be helped in "as few as three to ten sessions" (Lederer & Jackson, 1968, p. 447), couples with "serious marital problems" (p. 447) might wisely anticipate a treatment course of one to two years, with perhaps the majority requiring six months to a year!

In sum, Jackson struggled against the two-heavy individual emphasis of psychoanalytic psychotherapy, and used core ideas such as family homeostasis and marital quid pro quo to balance the extant explanatory models in the mental health fields. He used such concepts, in effect, as pragmatic interventions into the field, noting that "notions of family rules and marital quid pro quo are levers to *force us away* from the characteristics of individuals onto the nature of their interactions" (Jackson, 1965b, p. 29; emphasis added). And, he urged that we "avoid the pitfalls of reification and acknowledge the fictitious nature of all our constructs" (p. 29). Jackson never intended to obliterate an awareness of and sensitivity to the individual, as others would soon do. Indeed, Jackson might well have constructed the much needed bridge between both the moribund field of marriage counseling and the floundering psychoanalytic marital therapy of the day, on the one hand, and the rapidly proliferating field of family therapy on the other, but his life was tragically cut short in 1969, at the age of forty-eight.

*Virginia Satir, Self-Esteem, and Congruent Communication:* There can be no doubt that the charismatic Virginia Satir was the most visible and influential popularizer of family and marital therapy among both professional and lay audiences from the mid-1960s until about the mid-1970s. The author of such mega-sales books as *Peoplemaking* (Satir, 1972) and *Conjoint Family Therapy* (Satir, 1964), she held a unique place in the early history of systems-oriented therapy, in that she was the only nationally and internationally influential female clinician in the field. Although the titles of most of her published work referred to family rather than couple therapy, the lion's share of her systems-oriented therapeutic contributions, like Jackson's, were about dyads, and especially the marital dyad.

Satir, like Jackson, was one of the MRI pioneers, arriving there in 1959. Unlike many of the pioneers of family therapy, Satir was not uncomfortable about her links to the field of psychiatry, and in fact had established the first formal family therapy training program in a psychiatric residency program (at the Illinois State Psychiatric Institute, in 1955). Her clinical attitude of inclusiveness and acceptance was also manifest in the way she related to her colleagues and to the mental health professions in general.

Unlike the popular "systems purists" of the day, Satir was not disinterested in the historical family origins of presenting problems, nor was she mute on the matter of marital choice, a topic of great concern, of course, to psychoanalytic marriage therapists. She believed that people chose partners with similar difficulties and degrees of selfhood (Satir, 1964, 1967). And also unlike emerging systems theorists in the field, Satir had definite views on what constituted individual psychological health. These criteria included an ability to accept oneself and others, comfort in acknowledging such acceptance, awareness of one's own needs and feelings, the ability to communicate clearly, and the ability to accept disagreements and others' points of view. Symptoms in individuals, she argued, "develop when the rules for operating do not fit needs for survival, growth, getting close to others, and productivity . . ." (Satir, 1965, p. 122); and she believed that dysfunctional marriages follow dysfunctional rules that limited individual growth as well as dyadic intimacy. Little did Satir know that she was laying one of the cornerstones for later models of couple therapy grounded in attachment theory (e.g., Greenberg & Johnson, 1986, 1988; Johnson, 1996; Johnson & Greenberg, 1995).

In all of her thinking, primacy was given to the functioning and experiencing of the individual, as much as to the individual-in-relational context. For Satir, the narrow roles people assumed in close relationships (e.g., "victim," "placater," "defiant one," "rescuer"), and the dysfunctional communication styles they exhibited (e.g., "blamer," "placater," "being irrelevant," "being super reasonable"), while certainly reinforced by pathological patterns of interaction over time, were fundamentally expressions of low self-esteem and poor self-concept. Significantly, self-esteem and one's quality of communication were thought to exist in a circular relationship, so that poor self-esteem leads to poor communication (of various types), which in turn, leads to poor self-esteem, etc.

Although Satir was always aware of the systemic nature of problem formation and problem maintenance, she viewed the couple system rather differently than did most of the family therapy theorists of this era. Satir focused on one's perceptions of self and other, how one thinks and feels and shows ("manifests") these experiences, and how one reacts to others. For Satir (1965), "these three parts form the patterns of interaction that *compose the couple's system*" (p. 122; original emphasis). In keeping with Jackson's (1965b) warning about the dangers of reifying systemic constructs, Satir always kept in view what M. P. Nichols (1987) later called the "self in the system."

The overriding ultimate goal of couple therapy for Satir, then, was to foster greater self-esteem and self-actualization, to be achieved through such mediating goals as increasing the congruence and clarity of self-expression about relational needs, self-perceptions, and perceptions of one's partner; increasing self-awareness; removing protective "masks" that shield authentic self-revelation; and accepting and, indeed valuing, differences. These goals were toward growth, not stability. As Satir (1965) expressed it, the goal was "not to maintain the relationship nor to separate the pair but to help each other to *take charge of himself*" (p. 125; emphasis added).

To these ends, a wide variety of interventions and experiential techniques were used, ranging from verbal methods such as emphasis on the use of "I-statements," talking to rather than about one's mate, emphasizing people's positive motives more than their accumulated resentments, intensifying the immediacy of one's emotional self-awareness, clarifying communication, urging direct expression of feelings, encouraging validation of one's mate, and acceptance of differences: to nonverbal methods such as family sculpting and even, at times, dance movement, and massage. While the emphasis of Satir's work was on the present, her "Family Reconstruction" method (Nerin, 1986) made special efforts to unlock patients from dysfunctional historical patterns learned in their families of origin. The therapist's roles were multiple, and included prominently, pointing out unspoken family rules, eliciting conscious but unexpressed feelings, use of the therapist's self through expressions of warmth and caring, and serving as a "model of communication" and "a resource person" who shares her "special knowledge" (Satir, 1965, p. 132). Satir saw the effective couple therapist as a nurturing teacher, whose aim was to help orchestrate corrective emotional experiences.

Satir left the MRI in 1966, to become the first director of the famous Esalen Institute in California. Her increasing involvement in the "human potential movement" of Rogers, Maslow, Perls, and others took her more and more outside the mainstream of family and couple therapy, despite her abundant popularity among laypeople. Her direct leadership role in the field was also decelerated by a pivotal public debate in 1974 with a leader of the "systems purist" forces of the field, in which she was criticized for her humanitarian zeal, and felt unappreciated and marginalized by the newer waves of (male) family systems engineers (Pittman, 1989).

Among the most influential values Satir almost singularly represented, and the therapeutic stances she adhered to during her heyday, were: the importance of direct, authentic communication and self-disclosure; the importance of esteeming both oneself and one's intimates; the salience of relational closeness and security over and above mere problem resolution; the relevance of having an explicit model of individual and relational health and pathology; the belief in the restorative potential of committed couple relationships rather than the notion that they almost inevitably resist change; and the role of the therapist as an encouraging, nurturant healer, rather than as either an intellectualizing "analyst" or an uninvolved, yet provocative, problem-fixer.

Satir died in 1988, leaving no true "school" of couple (or family) therapy with her name. While she had been seen by many leaders in the field, including some of her very own MRI colleagues, as a "naïve and fuzzy thinker" (Nichols & Schwartz, 1998, p. 122), it could be argued that she left a more enduring and pervasive legacy for the treatment of couple problems than any of her pioneering contemporaries.

*Murray Bowen and the Differentiation of Self:* For Murray Bowen, never one to be described as a "naïve and fuzzy thinker," theory was first and foremost, standing far ahead of therapeutic technique, the therapeutic relationship, and the like. The father of multigenerational or transgenerational family systems theories, Bowen began a conceptual approach that has outlived his own passing in 1990, and been carried on by a number of influential thinkers, not only in the family therapy realm (e.g., Friedman, 1985; Kerr & Bowen, 1988), but in the couple therapy realm as well (e.g., Aylmer, 1986; Gerson, Hoffman, Sauls, & Ulrici, 1993; Guerin, Fay, Burden, & Kautto, 1987; Papero, 1995, 2000; Roberto-Forman, 2002). In-

deed, while Bowen's earliest clinical involvement in intergenerational thinking occurred in the 1950s in the context of working with families with a schizophrenic member (Broderick & Schrader, 1991), his clinical work, and that of his students, strongly emphasized the marital dyad as the central treatment unit.

And yet, as Papero (1995) notes, "Bowen family systems theory (BFST) is not primarily a theory about marriage" (p. 11). Nonetheless, as Bowen (1976) emphasized, "Practically, the two spouses are usually the only ones who are important enough to the rest of the family and who have the motivation and dedication for this kind of [therapeutic] effort" (p. 392). Thus, working with the marital couple was Bowen's preferred format for therapy, even when the presenting problem was not marital conflict but, rather, the symptom of one partner, or even of a child. Bowen believed in relational causes of all psychological and psychiatric problems. He began working regularly with couples in part as a way of attempting to block pathological multigenerational processes.

And it was multigenerational process that Bowen focused on, even as his systemic family therapy contemporaries were highlighting observable, present-day interactions. The central concept of BFST was the differentiation of self, essentially the ability to distinguish between thoughts and feelings. Differentiation was, importantly, two-fold: differentiation within self, and differentiation from others. The latter required the former. Such two-fold differentiation was equivalent to psychological health, and a precondition for systemic health, including marital or couple health. Differentiation allows internal direction, autonomy, and the possibility of intimacy. Poor differentiation is associated with defensiveness, externalization, and discrediting of one's partner.

Like Satir, Bowen had strong views on the matter of marital choice, and believed that people choose partners who are at similar levels of differentiation. The pathological expression of low differentiation, according to BFST, could take four forms: emotional distancing, marital conflict, one spouse's symptoms, or scapegoating (e.g., of a child). Marital conflict might ensue when the anxiety level of one or both partners rose, whether because of factors outside the relationship, or within the relationship, e.g., anxiety over intimacy. In such circumstances of emotional tension, the partners inevitably intuitively recruit in ("triangulate") a third factor to stabilize the dyad. The third point of such pathological triangles can be persons (e.g., affairs) or individual symptoms. But, for Bowen, marital conflict pointed not only to problems in the dyad, but more prominently to problems in the larger family systems of the partners, i.e., the families of origin. Thus, dysfunctional marriages bespoke undifferentiated individuals who, by definition, were insufficiently differentiated not only within themselves (affectively), but, just as important, from their families of origin.

The therapeutic focus in BFST with couples, then, is the "recursive, repetitive, chronic cycles of symptoms between marital partners and key extended family members" (Roberto-Forman, 2002). The shift was from a marital focus to a self-focus. Before experimenting in direct interactions with each partner's family of origin, each partner had to focus on anxiety reduction. To this end, the process of therapy, and the nature of the therapist's role were central. Little attention was paid to the immediate couple interaction, and interpersonal skills per se were not taught. While the "therapeutic relationship," as usually conceived, with a view of the therapist as a healer, was downplayed, the therapist's stance as an involved, yet dispassionate, objective "coach"

would allow him to remain in contact with each partner, and still stay affectively "detriangulated." So central was this concept to Bowen's theory of change, that he even asserted that "Conflict between two people will resolve *automatically* if both remain in emotional contact with a third person who can relate actively to both without taking sides with either" (Bowen, 1978, p. 177; emphasis added).

To keep BFST sessions calm, partners are typically encouraged to communicate through the therapist rather than to each other. The therapist is generally cerebral and intellectual, regulating his own emotional reactivity, taking clear "I-positions" without judging the partners, and teaching the (BFST) principles of emotional processes in individuals and in relationships. This ("detriangulated") therapist stance was seen as more important than any specific therapist techniques or interventions. Indeed, the therapist's capacity for objectivity, and his knowledge of family systems principles (à la BFST) provided the central mechanism of therapeutic change. BFST even asserts that marital partners cannot achieve higher levels of differentiation than their therapist has achieved.

BFST has attained a most interesting place in the history of couple (and, of course, family) therapy. On the one hand, there are relatively few true "Bowenian" therapists, since high-level training centers in this approach are small in number and tend to cluster in the Northeast. On the other hand, there has definitely not been any other historically oriented, transgenerational method of couple treatment emerging out of the world of mainstream family therapy with as much widespread influence as BFST. The constructs and language of BFST have pervaded the practice of multigenerational couple therapy more than any other model.

Rising to prominence during the heyday of the powerful family therapy movement, it was no small achievement that BFST bucked the dominant trends in the field toward present-centered, interaction-centered, and symptom-centered methods. In addition to the attractiveness of the theory itself, there are at least three interrelated contextual explanations for the status and influence earned by BFST. First, Bowen's well-known assertions that BFST had nothing in common with psychoanalytic/psychodynamic thinking notwithstanding, this approach certainly did seem to resonate with some central notions of object relations theory. In this way, BFST probably provided the field of family therapy not merely with "a bridge between individual and family therapy" (Lebow & Gurman, 1998, p. 486), but also a legitimized theory from outside the tradition of psychoanalytic marital therapy which retained the individual without ever losing sight of the larger family system. Psychoanalytic thinking was becoming déclassé, if not formally forbidden, within mainstream family therapy, and BFST provided a conceptual lifeline to the "inner man" for those who were not yet ready to abandon such interest.

Relatedly, BFST also seems to have provided if not an antidote to, then at least a reliable refuge from, the heavily technique-oriented, symptom-focused approaches that were rapidly overtaking the field of family therapy. Just as the "persons" of patients in couple (and family) therapy were being submerged, so, too, was the role of the therapist's own personhood being overwhelmingly downplayed.

When Bowen presented his (anonymously published) classic paper, "On the Differentiation of Self" (Anonymous, 1972), at a national conference of family researchers and family therapists in Philadelphia, he was not only sharing his twelve-year personal journey toward differentiation from his own family of origin, but was also strikingly differentiating himself from many of his peers in the field

of family therapy. BFST attended to the past as well as the present, to the intrapersonal as well as the interpersonal, and to the affective as well as the cognitive. It was the only couple therapy theory of its day emerging from family therapy that simultaneously addressed the individual, the dyad, and the family of origin. Never one to be concerned with political correctness, Bowen treaded where most feared to go.

*Jay Haley, Power, and the Reification of Systems:* As influential as Jackson, Satir, and Bowen were as marital thinkers and clinicians, no one during the heyday of the family therapy movement had as much influence on the practice of couple therapy as Jay Haley. Indeed, the publication of Haley's early (1963) classic paper, entitled simply, "Marriage Therapy," arguably marked *the* defining moment at which family therapy incorporated and usurped what was left in the stalled-out marriage counseling and psychodynamic marital therapy movements. It was perhaps all the more ironic that this paper appeared in a major psychiatric journal, the *Archives of General Psychiatry*.

Beyond its very substantial content, Haley's (1963) article (and many subsequent publications) challenged virtually every aspect of extant psychodynamic and humanistic therapy principles. It disavowed widespread beliefs about the nature of marital functioning and conflict, what constituted the appropriate focus of therapy, the role of the therapist, and what constituted appropriate therapeutic techniques.

For Haley, the central relational dynamic of marriage involved *power* and *control*. As he put the matter, ". . . the major conflicts in marriage center in the problem of who is to tell whom what to do under what circumstances . . ." (Haley, 1963, p. 227). Problems arose in marriage when the hierarchical structure was unclear, when there was a lack of flexibility, or when the relationship was marked by rigid symmetry or complementarity. When presenting complaints centered explicitly on the marital relationship, control was easily seen by Haley as the focal clinical theme. More subtly, though, Haley also believed that even when the presenting problem was the symptom of one person, power was at issue: the hierarchical incongruity of the symptomatic partner's position was central, in that the symptom bearer was assumed to have gained and maintained an equalization of marital power through his or her difficulties. Symptoms of individuals, then, became ways to define relationships, and they were seen as both metaphors for and diversions from other problems that were too painful for the couple to address explicitly.

In this way, symptoms of individuals in a marriage, as well as straightforwardly relational complaints, were mutually protective (Madanes, 1980), and were significantly seen as serving *functions* for the partners-as-a-dyad. Since symptoms and other problems were seen as functional for the marital unit, resistance to change was seen as almost inevitable, leading Haley (1963) to formulate his "first law of human relations," that is, "when one individual indicates a change in relation to another, the other will respond in such a way as to diminish that change" (p. 234; original emphasis omitted).

Such a view of the almost inherent property of marital (and family) systems to resist change was not limited to the husband-wife interaction. This view necessarily led to the position that the therapist, in his or her attempts to induce change, must often go about this task indirectly. Thus, for Haley (1963), the therapist "may never discuss this conflict (who is to tell whom what to do under what circumstances) explicitly with the couple" (p. 227). Haley (1976) believed that "the therapist should not share his

observations . . . that action could arouse defensiveness . . ." (p. 18). Achieving insight, while not entirely dismissed, was enormously downplayed in importance, in marked contrast to psychodynamic models.

Also viewed negatively by Haley were such commonplace and heretofore unchallenged clinical beliefs as the possible importance of discussing the past ("It is a good idea to avoid the past . . . because marital partners are experts at debating past issues . . . No matter how interested a therapist is in how people got to the point where they are, he should restrain himself from such explorations" (Haley, 1976, p. 164); the importance of making direct requests ("The therapist should *avoid forcing a couple to ask explicitly for what they want from each other* . . . this approach is an abnormal way of communicating," Haley, 1976, p. 166; original emphasis); and the possible usefulness of interpretation (". . . the therapist should not make any interpretation or comment to help the person see the problem differently," Haley, 1976, p. 28). Nor was the expression of feelings, common to other couple treatment methods, valued by Haley ("when a person expresses his emotion in a different way, it means that he is communicating in a different way. In doing so, he forces a different kind of communication from the person responding to him, and this change in turn requires a different way of responding back. When this shift occurs, a system changes because of the change in the communication sequence, but this fact has *nothing to do with expressing or releasing emotions* (in the sense of catharsis)" (Haley, 1976, p. 118; emphasis added). Nor did Haley value expression of feelings for the enhancement of attachment or fostering a sense of security through self-disclosure. Indeed, feeling expression in general was of no priority to Haley (". . . he should not ask how someone feels about something, but should only gather facts and opinions," Haley, 1976, p. 28).

In contrast, Haley's preferred therapeutic interventions emphasized planned, pragmatic, parsimonious, present-focused efforts to disrupt patterns of behavior that appeared to maintain the major problem of the couple. The strategic therapist was very active and saw his or her central role as finding creative ways to modify problem-maintaining partners so that symptoms, or other presenting problems, no longer served their earlier maladaptive purposes. Directives were the most important therapist change-inducing tools. Some directives were straightforward, but Haley also helped to create a rich fund of indirect, and sometimes resistance-oriented paradoxical directives, e.g., reframing, prescribing the symptom, restraining change, and relabeling, for example, "whenever it can be done, the therapist defines the couple as attempting to bring about an amiable closeness, but going about it wrongly, being misunderstood, or being driven by forces beyond their control" (Haley, 1963, p. 226).

Haley's theoretical and technical contributions were enormously influential in the broad field of family therapy and couple therapy. More than any other individual, Haley influenced sizeable portions of at least an entire generation of marital (and family) therapists to see family dynamics ". . . as products of a 'system,' rather than features of persons who share certain qualities because they live together. Thus was born a new creature, 'the family system' " (Nichols & Schwartz, 1998, pp. 60–61). The notion of symptoms serving functions "for the system" was a hallmark of the strategic approach that pervaded clinical discussions, presentations, and practices in the late 60s through the 70s. The anthropomorphizing of the family or couple "system" seemed to "point to an inward, systemic unity of purpose" that rendered 'the whole' not only

more than the sum of its parts . . . [but] somehow *more important than its parts*" (Bogdan, 1984, pp. 19–20). Haley had not heeded the warning of his colleague Jackson (1965a) to "avoid the pitfalls of reification and acknowledge the fictitious nature of all our constructs" (p. 9).

In sum, Haley urged clinicians to avoid discussing the past, resist temptations to instill insight, and downplay couples' direct expression of wishes and feelings. As Framo (1996) would venture three decades after Haley's (1963) concept-shifting marriage therapy article, "I got the impression that Haley wanted to make sure that psychoanalytic thinking be prevented from ruining the newly emerging field of family therapy" (p. 295).

Family therapy had now not merely incorporated, merged with, or absorbed marriage counseling and psychoanalytic couple therapy; it had engulfed, consumed, and devoured them both.

## PHASE IV: REFINEMENT, EXTENSION, DIVERSIFICATION, AND INTEGRATION (1986–present)

Marriage counseling, which had generated no enduring theoretical contributions, and almost entirely lacked a research base, had almost expired until it was legitimized and resuscitated by achieving licensure in the early to mid-1960s. It had accomplished its professional mission. Psychoanalytic marriage therapy was struggling with anxiety over maintaining its conceptual and technical integrity and boundaries, as it walked the fine line between intrapsychic and interpersonal emphases, and seemed to be immobilized by its ambivalence.

From about the mid-1960s until about the early 1980s, there appeared few major conceptual advances in the realm of psychoanalytic/psychodynamic couple therapy, and even the simple frequency of publications on the topic dwindled. Dicks' (1967) classic, *Marital Tensions,* which eventually became the unofficial bible of object relations thinking in couple therapy, was not widely read at first, and was mostly unknown to American clinicians. Despite its ultimate status as a classic (but not Twain's sort of classic), it went out of print only a few years after its initial appearance. Probably, the only other influential conceptual and technical contribution in the psychodynamic realm from the mid-1960s until the mid-1980s was offered in Sager's (1976, 1981; Sager et al., 1971) concept of the "Marriage Contract," which we will comment on later in this section. Framo's (1976, 1981) work on couple groups and combined sessions with family of origin, steeped in object relations theory (Framo, 1965, 1996), was among the most innovative of its time. Unfortunately, because of the essential disavowal of most things psychodynamic by the overwhelmingly systems-oriented family therapy field, Framo's work never has had the full impact on the couple therapy world it otherwise might have.

At the same time, the humanistic-experiential wing of the field had been essentially silenced by Satir's marginalization during the period of family therapy's heyday, not to be heard from substantially again until the late 1980s.

During this period in couple therapy's conceptual history, only a handful of important texts appeared, including two multiauthor books (Paolino & McCrady, 1978; Sholevar, 1981), and two single-author books (Segraves, 1982; Wile, 1981). Emerging integrative (Segraves, 1982) and nontraditional (Wile, 1981) approaches largely stood on their own, lacking any organized following. The two leading edited textbooks of this period, incorporating multiple viewpoints and addressing a variety of central topics (Paolino & McCrady, 1978; Sholevar, 1981) were among the earliest signs that a critical mass of couple-focused psychotherapists was beginning to redevelop. The

first comprehensive assessment of the evidence about couple therapy's effectiveness (Gurman, 1973b) also appeared during this period.

By the mid-1980s, couple therapy had reasserted its existence and established what would become more sustained theory development and empirical research than had been seen in decades. We have identified 1986, the year of publication of Jacobson and Gurman's *Clinical Handbook of Marital Therapy,* as the approximate beginning of couple therapy's fourth, and current, phase. The *Handbooks'* (Gurman & Jacobson, 2002; Jacobson & Gurman, 1986, 1995) widespread readership and utilization seem to have signified couple therapy's highly visible and permanent return to the world of influential approaches to psychotherapy.

## REFINEMENT

The last decade and a half have witnessed the appearance on couple therapy's center stage of three traditions of treatment in particular. In addition to their increasingly solid research base, what is especially compelling about these approaches is their continual modification and conceptual and technical refinement during this period.

### Behavioral Marital Therapy: Expanding Functional Analysis

Behavioral Marital Therapy (BMT), a social learning theory-based approach, was visibly launched by the early works of Stuart (1969, 1980) and Jacobson (Jacobson & Margolin, 1979; Jacobson & Martin, 1976), which were among the most important publications on couple therapy outside mainstream family therapy. BMT, like all behavioral approaches, and more than any other approaches to psychotherapy, attempts to ground its clinical practices in empirical research. To date, BMT is the most intensively and frequently investigated couple therapy method (Halford, 1998).

BMT has gone through four rather distinct phases in its short twenty five-year existence, each characterized by significant modifications and refinements of the underlying treatment model and its application.

The first two phases, which we call "Old BMT," correspond to what Jacobson and Christensen (Christensen, Jacobson, & Babcock, 1995; Jacobson & Christensen, 1996) call "Traditional Behavioral Couple Therapy." This phase is comprised of two subphases: the simple behavior exchange phase, and the skills training phase.

In the *simple behavior exchange phase,* the clinical emphasis was on influencing partners to identify desired changes in each other's overt behavior, and then to exchange these pleasing behaviors (Azrin, Naster, & Jones, 1973; Stuart, 1969) in "tightly structured . . . agreements" (Halford, 1998) based on the marital quid pro quo concept of Jackson (Lederer & Jackson, 1968). This style of contracting was somewhat replaced by "good faith contracts" (Weiss, Birchler, & Vincent, 1974), in which there was not to be the linked, paired exchange of highly specific behaviors, but where exchanges were to be activated unilaterally (and, hopefully, simultaneously). The behavioral exchange aspects of BMT are now generally considered an important but secondary element of social learning-based couple therapy, and with good reason. Early behavioral couple therapists had fundamentally misunderstood the essences of Jackson's quid pro quo by equating it with point-for-point exchange procedures rather than as a broader perspective regarding how marital partners define themselves-in-relationship (Gurman & Knudson, 1978; Segraves, 1982). Even as consummate a scholar as Gottman (1999) has misconstrued the original thrust of the marital

quid pro quo as involving "keep(ing) tabs on positives given and received" (p. 12).

In the *skills training phase,* BMT placed an almost unswerving emphasis on the therapist's teaching couples the communication and problem-solving skills that characterize healthy, satisfying marriages, and the absence of which were assumed to maintain recurrent marital conflict and dissatisfaction. These skills were often taught to couples in rather discrete learning modules, following a "relatively fixed curriculum" (Halford, 1998, p. 615). Interestingly, although the essence of behavior therapy, including BMT, is not the use of specific techniques but the clinical application of the functional analytic method (Kanfer & Phillips, 1970), behavior therapists in this phase seem often to have become so enamored of a learnable, teachable clinical methodology that they often called upon such skills-training components in therapy when they may not have been needed. Ironically, it appears that they often failed to make the important functional analytic distinction between a problem of acquisition (the requisite behaviors have not been learned) and a problem of performance (the behaviors have been learned, are used elsewhere, but appear insufficiently in this relationship).

The second aggregate phase in BMT's evolution, which we call "New BMT," corresponds to Jacobson et al.'s (Christensen et al., 1995; Jacobson & Christensen, 1996) development of "Integrative Behavioral Couple Therapy," but includes other important contributions as well. Jacobson and Christensen's work highlights the *acceptance phase.* The development of methods to increase partners' mutual acceptance (vs. a primary focus on behavior change) was motivated by the need to expand the therapist's intervention repertoire in the face of "the polarization of difficult couples" whose problems were not adequately addressed by traditional skills-training (Cordova, Jacobson, & Christensen, 1998), e.g., in dealing with inherently unresolvable "perpetual issues" (Gottman, 1999), and in the face of accumulating research evidence (Jacobson & Addis, 1993) of BMT's having apparently reached a ceiling in terms of its effectiveness. The addition of acceptance interventions (e.g., "empathic joining," Christensen et al., 1995) not surprisingly appears to increase the odds of favorable clinical outcomes (Cordova et al., 1998) vs. traditional methods. More surprisingly, this shift to acceptance work seems to have signified that behavioral therapists "found that the nomenclature of trait psychology is useful for understanding their clients, just as it is useful to us in understanding others in everyday life" (Hamburg, 1996, p. 56). That is, Jacobson's more recent emphasis on the importance of working with salient couple themes (in behavioral language, response classes) rather than narrowly defined problem events (reminiscent of "old" behavioral exchange interventions), exemplifies this profound shift from a decidedly "state"-oriented treatment philosophy, to a much more balanced "state/trait" attitude.

The most recent phase in BMT's evaluation is the *self-regulation phase,* best exemplified by the work of Halford (1998; Halford, Sanders, & Behrens, 1994). These strategies add to the Old BMT emphasis on changing the partner's behavior the central notion of changing one's own maritally relevant behavior to facilitate increased mutual satisfaction. Such self-regulating or self-control foci might include altering one's response to one's partner's undesired behavior, meeting some unmet needs in other situations, changing one's approach to trying to persuade one's partner to change, etc. Halford (1998) suggests the possibility that "the disappointing long term maintenance of benefits from (BMT) may be attributable to this failure individually to

empower our clients" (pp. 621–622). Certainly, adding a "change thyself" component to traditional interactional change targets renders New BMT systemic, in the sense of attending to multiple levels of relevant human behavior, although still largely not examining some important domains, e.g., family-of-origin influences. (Note also the treatment-relevant role of problematic physiological responses in marital conflict, Gottman, 1999). It is curious and unfortunate that Old BMT approaches did not try to deal with self-change dimensions of couple disharmony of the kinds Halford (1998) has addressed. First, doing so is entirely consistent with the functional analytic approach to clinical problems, the core of all behavior therapy. Moreover, self-control principles and techniques had been written about widely by prominent behavior therapists (e.g., Franks, 1969; Kanfer & Phillips, 1970; Thoreson & Mahoney, 1974; Watson & Tharp, 1972) long before early seminal BMT works (e.g., Jacobson & Margolin, 1979; Stuart, 1980) appeared. Perhaps in an (unconscious?) effort to remain disconnected from the realm of psychodynamics, arising in a time still dominated by psychodynamic theories (if not within family therapy!), Old BMT inadvertently failed to look "inside" marital partners. While Halford (1998) pessimistically concludes that "there is no evidence that we have improved upon the efficacy obtained 20 years ago in [BMT]" (p. 617), it seems likely that the recent additions of both acceptance-enhancing interventions and self-control methods to Old BMT interventions are likely to significantly improve treatment results.

### Emotionally Focused Couple Therapy: Reattachment to the Experiential Tradition

Although not as widely familiar as BMT, Emotionally Focused Couple Therapy (EFT) (Greenberg & Johnson, 1986, 1988; Johnson, 1986, 1996; Johnson & Greenberg, 1995), has also established a strong empirical base (Johnson, Hunsley, Greenberg, & Schindler, 1999; and see below). Of at least equal importance historically, EFT represents the first significant reattachment among marital therapists to the broader marital/family therapy field of the experiential tradition in psychotherapy, exemplified by such contributors as Carl Rogers and Fritz Perls. Of more direct connection to the marital/family field, is the overall philosophical correspondence of EFT values and methods to those of Satir's (1965) humanistic approach discussed earlier.

The fundamental premise behind EFT's theory of adult intimacy and its vicissitudes is that all human beings have a wired-in need for consistent, safe contact with responsive and caring others, i.e., an innate need for relational security. EFT, then, sees marital conflict and harmony as dependent upon the degree to which the marital partners' basic needs for bonding or attachment are satisfied. In this fundamental way, EFT owes part of its conceptual heritage to object relations theory (Scharff & Bagnini, 2002), although its methods differ from those that prize an interpretive therapist stance.

In this vein, and in rather stark contrast to the views of behavioral and strategic couple therapists, EFT sees emotion as the primary organizer of intimate relational experience, influencing significantly both interactional tendencies and patterns, and perceptions and meaning attribution. Thus, Johnson (1986) made the crisp distinction between an emphasis on "bonds vs. bargains" as the bases for models of committed adult relationships, i.e., emotional attachment vs. rational negotiation.

In this light, EFT has the two basic aims of exploring each partner's views of self and other, as organized by their immediate (in-session) affective experience, and helping them to access previously unacknowledged (often to oneself, as well as to one's mate) feelings so they may be expressed directly in the moment of the therapeutic session.

The overall corrective emotional experience sought in EFT is achieved through a mixture of Gestalt, client-centered, and general "systemic" interventions, in which affective immediacy is high. Such experiences, occurring through working with a therapist who herself feels safe to the couple, is assumed to increase mutual empathy, decrease defensiveness, and lead to an increased, but uncoached couple capacity for problem solving. EFT aims to restructure interpersonal patterns to incorporate each partner's needs for experiencing secure attachment. The treatment model itself has been described with unusual clarity (e.g., Johnson & Greenberg, 1995), and includes "cycle de-escalation" (creating a working alliance and delineating core conflict issues; mapping the recurrent problematic interaction patterns; accessing relevant unacknowledged feelings; reframing problems in light of these feelings); "changing interactional positions" (encouraging identification with one's disowned needs; encouraging acceptance of the partner's emotional experience; explicating very specific relationship needs); and "consolidation/integration" (developing new solutions to old problems; consolidating the "new positions" and attachment patterns) (Johnson, 1999).

The effective practice of EFT appears to require a very high level of therapist skill to evoke and contain unexpressed feelings, and a relatively high level of partner-partner trust. EF therapists do not typically explore the past, interpret unconscious motivations, or teach interpersonal skills.

In terms of its technical portfolio, EFT is probably "overweighted" in the priority given to the role of evoking emotion.

Nonetheless, it has accrued substantial research support. What is more, EFT, more than any other couple therapy method of recent times, has reelevated the "self" of each relationship partner to psychological and phenomenological prominence, along with the couple-as-a-system. Ironically, through EFT, the influence of that "naïve and fuzzy thinker" (Nichols & Schwartz, 1998, p. 122), Virginia Satir, has risen again in the marital therapy field. As Schwartz and Johnson (2000) recently noted, "the field is slowly catching up with that 'touchy/feely' visionary, Virginia Satir, and shaking off its no-emotion legacy" (p. 32). EFT has made all the more fitting the comment of the Duhls (1981), "It is hard to kiss a system" (p. 488).

### Insight-Oriented Marital Therapy: Return of the Suppressed

Perhaps even less recognizable than EFT to many readers is the Insight-Oriented Marital Therapy (IOMT) of Snyder (1999; Wills, Faitler, & Snyder, 1987). Largely disseminated through a series of research studies discussing its development and demonstrating its long-term effectiveness (Snyder & Wills, 1989; Snyder, Wills, & Grady-Fletcher, 1991), IOMT, like EFT, provides the most substantial empirical grounding to date for the public reemergence of the suppressed psychodynamic couple therapy methods of the 1960s. Although IOMT is not a psychoanalytic or even a purely object relations approach, it emphasizes relational dispositions of individuals and their associated core (individual) relational themes generated over time in intimate (including family-of-origin) relationships. Its central relational theory base is closer to modern "interpersonal role theory" (Anchin & Kiesler, 1982) and cognitive "schema theory" (Young, 1994), but it is decidedly psychodynamic, and overlaps with models based on attachment theory. Un-

like most traditional BMT, IOMT recognizes as real and significant for marital quality those processes and conflicts that occur within, as well as, between partners, e.g., the frequent contradictions and incongruencies within individuals about their relational needs and expectations (Sager, 1976, 1981). Unlike EFT, one of the IOMT therapist's central technical role requirements is to interpret partners' behavior, feelings, and cognitions, both contemporaneously and genetically (historically). Like earlier psychoanalytic and object relations couple therapy approaches (e.g., Framo, 1965; Skynner, 1976, 1981), IOMT also acknowledges the reality of and clinically addresses collusive relationship elements (Catherall, 1992; Dicks, 1967; Scharff, 1995), or what Snyder (1999) refers to, gently, as "partners' inadvertent maintenance of maladaptive relationship patterns."

IOMT is an overarching framework for organizing therapeutic interventions and the sequencing of their use, and draws upon psychodynamic, experiential, and cognitive and behavioral techniques. Insight, affective immediacy, as well as attribution modification and skill enhancement (though not necessarily through systematic instruction) are all valued in this approach. The main phase of IOMT is called "affective reconstruction," and emphasizes the therapist's interpretation of maladaptive relationship themes in terms of their developmental origins and the connections of those earlier experiences to current relational fears, dilemmas, and interaction styles.

Although IOMT has not developed into a true "school" of therapy and is not widely known outside clinical and family psychology, its central assessment and treatment principles are widely known. That is, IOMT seems to embody a formal explication of many of the implicit principles and practices of the many workaday clinicians who describe themselves as "psychodynamically oriented/eclectic," probably the largest theoretical orientation of marital and family therapists (Rait, 1988). In this sense, the principles of IOMT would probably be conceptually very accessible to numerous marital therapists. Like EFT, IOMT reflects and has contributed to the reemergence of the "self in the system" (M. P. Nichols, 1987). Together, IOMT and EFT remind us of Antonio Ferreira's (1978) comment about family systems, "We had to learn that the family was a system before we could learn that the family does not always act like a system."[4]

## Reemergence of Psychodynamic Couple Therapy

We indicated in the Figure (see p. 204) the public reemergence of the psychoanalytic perspective in the marital field around 1985. This general perspective has been revived in the last decade and a half through three influential pathways. First, as in the development of IOMT, marital treatment researchers have began to make significant contributions to the refinement of technique, e.g., in the construction of treatment manuals that guide practice in outcome studies. The second source of a renewal of interest in psychodynamic elements of marital therapy has been the growing number of integrative couple therapies, to be discussed below.

The third origin of reinvigorated interest in the psychodynamics of couple treatment is to be found among a sizeable handful of clinical theorists (e.g., Bader & Pearson, 1988; Nadelson, 1978; Scharff, 1995; Scharff & Scharff, 1991; Siegel, 1992; Solomon, 1989; Willi, 1982) who have been working independently of one another to clarify psychodynamic (typically, object relations) theory as it applies to

conjoint therapy, and to refine intervention strategies and techniques to achieve the types of changes usually sought in these therapy approaches, e.g., increased individuation, modified and more flexible individual and dyadic defenses, and improvement in capacities for containing and holding difficult emotions. An excellent brief history of the psychoanalytic and object relations theory tradition in couple therapy can be found in Scharff (1995) and in Scharff and Bagnini (2002).

All variant methods of psychodynamic couple therapy attribute central importance to the unconscious communication and behavior-maintaining processes that characterize all intimate relationships, and which are maladaptively rigid in conflict-ridden couples. While these approaches differ in technical particulars, most of them are conceptually indebted to the object relations contributions of Dicks (1967), undoubtedly the seminal thinker in this realm. Among the central concepts in this treatment approach are projective identification, splitting, collusion, holding, and containment (Catherall, 1992). As we previously noted, although most early psychoanalytic couple therapy focused alternately on the psychodynamics of the individual partners, modern object relations couple therapy maintains a balanced focus on the structure of shared, interactional marital defenses, and the joint avoidances they perpetuate (e.g., anxiety about intimacy). Often overlooked in critiques of object relations couple therapy is its fundamental belief in the reparative, healing aims of these shared defenses.

Perhaps psychodynamic elements in couple therapy have gained renewed support in recent years because of the burgeoning development of integrative approaches, which often are as concerned with the intrapersonal as with the interpersonal. Perhaps the rebirth of this interest is partially attributable to the

---

[4] Framo, J. (1978). Personal communication.

broad field of family therapy having firmly established its place in the world of psychotherapy, and thus developing the "institutional security" to become more open to some of the very kinds of clinical views that had served so well as the adversarial foil for the growth of the family therapy movement. Whatever the explanation(s) of the resuscitation of interest in couple psychodynamics, at the birth of this millennium, it appears quite likely that this interest has returned for good.

## EXTENSION

*Treatment of Psychiatric Disorders:* The current phase of couple therapy's history is characterized not only by increasing refinement of clinical treatment approaches, but also by an extension of the purview of marital therapy beyond the treatment of obvious relationship conflict and distress to the treatment of individual psychiatric disorders. Ironically, despite the historically ingrained disdain among many first- and second-generation family therapists toward psychiatric diagnosis, it seems often forgotten that a major impetus for the very beginning of the field was the study of major mental illness (Wynne, 1983). While family, and to a lesser extent marital, therapists have thus shown interest in the systems-oriented treatment of adult psychiatric disorders for some time, recent clinical research excursions into this realm represent the first significant advances on these matters in decades.

An enormous amount of attention has been paid in recent years to studying the role of marital factors in the etiology, maintenance, and diminution of three particular disorders: depression (mostly of women), anxiety (agoraphobia, mostly of women), and alcoholism (mostly of men). To date, the only major method of couple therapy that has been empirically tested in the treatment of these disorders is BMT, or at least couple therapies that emphasize communication training and problem solving. For depression, such couples work has been of a general marital nature, i.e., traditional BMT; for alcoholism, it has usually been a combination of traditional BMT and alcohol consumption-specific response training; and for agoraphobia, either communication training or partner-assisted exposure. Other treatment approaches (e.g., Papp, 2000), not yet empirically tested, focus more on the tracing of intergenerational relational themes and identification of and intervention into constraining gender beliefs and power inequities.

Findings to date suggest that couple therapy may positively affect symptomatic outcomes by increasing the likelihood of initial engagement in treatment and adherence to medication regimens, e.g., disulfiram (Antabuse) (alcoholism), by increasing exposure to anxiety-eliciting stimuli and lowering treatment dropout rates (agoraphobia), and by developing more adaptive responses to drinking episodes. Moreover, only couple therapy appears to help alleviate marital distress often associated with depression, compared to either individual Cognitive or Interpersonal psychotherapy of depression (Beach, Fincham, & Katz, 1998). Given that marital conflict and distress predict relapse for all three of these disorders (Beach et al., 1998; Daiuto, Baucom, Epstein, & Dutton, 1998; Epstein & McCrady, 1998), inclusion of couple interventions seems routinely warranted in most comprehensive treatment plans.

Research to date suggests that couple therapy by itself is not a sufficient intervention for alcoholism (without, e.g., disulfiram) or for agoraphobia (without, e.g., in-vivo exposure), but it may be sufficient for the treatment of depression in married women whose relationships are seriously distressed, especially when the depressed wife is more concerned about the couple's marital problems than about her depression, or when the marital problems seem to have preceded the onset of depressive symptoms. These findings reinforce the clinical salience of the concordance between some adult psychiatric disorders and marital conflict and strongly support couple interventions for "individual" disorders. At the new millennium, couple therapy is extending its effective reach beyond its traditional and more limited role of treating relationship conflict.

*Preventive Interventions:* Interestingly, at the very same time that couple therapy has been extended to the treatment of psychiatric disorders, couple interventions have also seen more application at the opposite end of the clinical continuum. Over the past twenty years, increased interest has developed in distress and divorce prevention programs for couples (Bradbury & Fincham, 1990; Fraenkel et al., 1997; Stanley, Markman, St. Peters, & Leber, 1995). These programs are part of a broader trend toward prevention programs in mental health, and draw on the basic rationale and principles of prevention science (Coie, Watt, West, et al., 1993). Indeed, there are several good arguments for programs targeted to nondistressed couples (primary prevention) or couples showing early signs of difficulty (secondary prevention) to complement the usual range of therapy interventions targeted at distressed couples (tertiary prevention).

First, as we note in an upcoming section, although numerous studies and reviews have established the efficacy and effectiveness of couple therapy overall, many couples who improve in therapy do not move out of the distressed range or maintain their gains long-term (Hahlweg & Markman, 1988; Jacobson & Addis, 1993). Given that many distressed couples wait many years before seeking services, it seems logical to provide happy or only mildly distressed couples with research-based information, skills, and ideas

to help them deal with the inevitable conflicts that surface as people share a life together (Markman, Stanley, & Blumberg, 1994). As noted earlier, marital conflict and disruption are associated with a wide range of mental and physical health problems in both adults and children, and through these effects, have an impact upon the economy because of days lost at work and need for health services (see reviews by Bloom, Asher, & White, 1978; Fraenkel et al., 1997; Gottman, 1994a,b; Grych & Fincham, 1990). Programs designed to help couples maintain "relational wellness" and prevent destructive conflict could thus have wide-ranging public health benefits.

In addition, there is growing evidence that such programs can be efficacious in reaching these preventive goals. In an early meta-analysis of 85 studies of marriage enrichment and preparation programs, Giblin and associates (Giblin, Sprenkle, & Sheehan, 1985) found average effect sizes suggesting that participants improved more than 67% than those in control groups. Bradbury and Fincham (1990) later critiqued this analysis and the component studies—for one thing, most involved only pre- and post-program measures, rather than long-term followup—but concurred that the analysis showed a promising trend in prevention effectiveness, a conclusion originally reached by Gurman and Kniskern (1977), and more recently by Guerney and Maxson (1990).

More solid evidence has emerged from a program of research on the Prevention and Relationship Enhancement Program (PREP), based at the University of Denver (Markman, Floyd, Stanley, & Storaasli, 1988; Markman, Remick, Floyd, et al., 1993). These longitudinal studies have demonstrated that nondistressed premarital couples randomly assigned to a 15-hour PREP course showed significant benefits over control couples up to four years later, including greater relationship and sexual satisfaction, lower problem intensity, greater longevity, and better communication skills. At five-year followup, PREP couples also reported significantly fewer instances of domestic violence than control couples. The program teaches communication and problem-solving skills, how to address differences in core values and expectations, how to identify and work with hidden issues, and how to strengthen fun, friendship, and sensuality in relationships.

Different prevention and enrichment programs draw upon different clinical theories, including cognitive-behavioral, systems, humanistic-experiential, and psychodynamic (Berger & Hannah, 1999). Moreover, some programs, such as Guerney's (1977; Guerney, Brock, & Coufal, 1986) Relationship Enhancement, are applied to both clinical and nonclinical couples. Some focus on skills training (cf. Markman et al., 1994), whereas others feature discussion of partners' responses to self-report inventories that examine expectations and basic values (cf. Olson, 1990). Program lengths vary from one-day workshops to courses held over several months. Formats also vary greatly, from group lectures followed by skill-practice sessions conducted privately with each couple, to more of an encounter group involving interaction among the couples. At this point, research has just begun to compare the effectiveness of the various programs. Studies thus far support the importance of couples learning and practicing communication and problem-solving skills over programs that focus on enrichment and identifying problem areas but do not teach skills (Stanley, Blumberg, & Markman, 1999).

An interesting and lively debate about the need for teaching communication skills recently emerged around findings published by Gottman and colleagues (Gottman, Coan, Carrère, & Swanson,

1998). These authors argued that their data did not support the preventive importance of these Rogerian active listening skills because couples who were satisfied at 6-year followup did not demonstrate behaviors that resembled such skills. Although the details of the debate are more complex than space allows, Stanley, Bradbury, and Markman (2000) countered that Gottman et al. had fallaciously translated their findings into intervention recommendations. Among other points, they noted that the communication skills taught in programs such as PREP are to be used only when couples sense that their usual approach to talking about problems is failing them, and they require more structure in order to create a safe space for dialogue. Although the specific debate about these skills is interesting and important in itself, at a broader level, the debate is a good reminder that while research is critical to the development of the field, care must be taken in the translation and interpretation of research findings for interventive practice.

One of the most interesting aspects of the prevention movement is that, in a way, it represents at least one aspect of the field of couple intervention coming full circle from where it started. As Broderick and Schrader (1981, 1991) have noted, the psychoeducationally oriented "family life education" movement focused largely on couples' preparation for marriage, and actually pre-dated the founding of the marriage counseling field.

Recall that we opened this historical review noting that the bulk of couple counseling was initially conducted by pastoral counselors, other clergy, or other non-mental health professionals and paraprofessionals. Because of the wish to disseminate the program widely and in contexts where nondistressed couples gather to focus on couple and family issues, a number of programs are designed to be delivered by clergy and paraprofessionals within religious institutions. The difference is that, rather than interventions being derived solely from common sense or vague theory, as in the past, the current wave of programs are typically based at least in part upon some of the most rigorous research in the field on variables that discriminate distressed from happy couples or predict from groups of happy couples who become dissatisfied and/or dissolved years later (Gottman, 1994a,b; Gottman et al., 1998; Markman et al., 1988, 1993). In addition, the relative efficacy of different program "deliverers" is now being studied. For instance, the PREP/Denver group is currently conducting a large dissemination study in which premarital couples are randomly assigned to PREP delivered by university-based staff, or by clergy or lay leaders in their own religious settings, or partake of the usual premarital interventions offered in their church or synagogue (Markman, 2000).

Some have raised concerns about the degree to which psychoeducational and prevention programs for couples may become co-opted by conservative religious groups to advance their limited vision of family and family values (Laird, 1999). However, it should be noted that the notion and basic form of programs designed to strengthen relationships and prevent conflict are not by definition tied to such political and social agendas. For instance, with an expanded research agenda that includes more study of variables distinguishing distressed from satisfied gay and lesbian couples and predicting relationship outcomes over time, research-based programs for such couples could be developed and/or expanded (Fraenkel, 1999).

In sum, the development of couple distress prevention programs appears to hold great promise for reducing the likelihood of disruption and distress experienced by a large number of couples over the course of their relationships. As oth-

ers have (Lebow, 1997), we do not believe such programs will ever completely replace the need for tertiary preventive efforts (i.e., treatment). Moreover, as Bray and Jouriles (1995) point out, up to half the couples who are offered PREP and similar programs do not choose to participate, even when such programs are offered at no cost. In addition, in order for such programs to thrive, much work will be needed to shift couples from an attitude of "if it ain't broke, don't fix it" to one of proactive attempts to maintain wellness. The training of therapists would need to broaden as well, such that they see themselves as interventionists with a wide range of "targets," from healthy, happy couples to those needing intensive therapy.

## DIVERSIFICATION

Beginning in the late 1970s to mid-1980s, the field of couple and family therapy was challenged to question many of its fundamental assumptions. The challenge came from three overlapping sources that, in turn, mutually influenced one another: feminism, multiculturalism, and postmodernism. Whereas earlier systemic theories shifted therapists' focus from individuals to dyads, all three threads of this movement toward a more diversified view of couple and family life essentially involved conceptually "stepping back" to view couples one concentric ring wider than the previous close focus on dyadic interchanges. Stepping back in this way forced therapists to examine the impact of broader social beliefs and forces that reached the couple through the channels of gender, race, ethnicity, social class, and sexual orientation, in turn shaped by how these "demographic characteristics" of persons had been construed differently in different historical eras. As Goldner (1985a) states, "Erecting a conceptual boundary around the family was clearly essential for the development of family systems theory, but it also deflected theoretical attention away from an encounter with the ways in which participation in family life is not merely an idiosyncratic accommodation to the 'needs of the family system' but is regulated by social forces operating above and beyond the family's affective field" (p. 33).

*Feminism:* Feminist therapists such as Goldner (1985a,b, 1988), Hare-Mustin (1978, 1987), James and her collaborators (James & McIntyre, 1983; James & MacKinnon, 1990), Libow and colleagues (Avis, 1988, 1989; Libow, Raskin, & Caust, 1982), and the Women's Project (Walters, Carter, Papp, & Silverstein, 1988) argued that how men and women view and act out their roles as partners and parents is tied to historically rooted societal beliefs about gender, power, and intimacy, as well as to how men and women are differentially encouraged to focus on work or home life. Through this lens, fundamental systemic concepts such as complementarity are seen not as inevitable dyadic patterns determined within the cocoon of the relationship by the particular, idiosyncratic match between partners' emotional and behavioral proclivities, but largely as organized along gender lines in accordance with the society's implicit and explicit expectations.

For instance, the long-held academic and popular belief that men are more instrumental (logical, action-oriented) and women more emotional (able to communicate, expressive) by nature and, if anything, become more so as their qualities accentuate one another's in a complementary developmental spiral, is understood from a feminist perspective as social *prescription* masked as scientific *description.* This constructed complementarity is, in turn, rooted in the larger economic and societal forces that emerged from the Industrial Revolution onwards that assigned men to work outside the home and women to work inside the home (Hare-

Mustin, 1978). To fulfill the needs of a modern economy that requires increasingly long hours and, for some, days to months away from home on business trips, the notion that men lacked the emotional capacities necessary for parenting that women had in abundance (and that relative to men, women lacked the analytic, problem-solving acumen of their husbands) was a convenient conceptual artifice evolved to help men and women to adjust to their socially mandated roles. As Goldner (1985a) writes, "marital complementarity must be understood not only as a psychological arrangement between husband and wife but also . . . *structured* into intimate relations by the larger social context" (p. 38; emphasis in original). Goldner goes on to trace the impact of this fundamental, rigid complementarity on the functioning of the couple as a parenting dyad, arguing in this and a later article (1988) that systems thinkers neglected the gender-based hierarchy situated within the generational hierarchy that formed the organizing frame for most family therapy interventions of the time.

Likewise, the systemic project of conceptualizing all problematic couple interactions as being the result of circular patterns was called into sharp question by feminists, who noted how such a formulation laid equal responsibility on both parties for the intimidation, constraint, and battering of women (Avis, 1992; Goldner, 1985a,b, 1998, 1999; Goldner, Penn, Sheinberg, & Walker, 1990). By committing the ultimate systemic sin of violating the premise of circularity by proposing that some patterns are *linear* in causal direction (the violence perpetrated by a man against a woman), the Ackerman Violence Project (Goldner et al., 1990) highlighted that we can choose how and when to apply our theories, and that theories are constructions we use to make sense of events rather than being inherent in phenomena. Moreover, they reminded the field that, perhaps unlike in the nonhuman sciences, the act of theorizing and (therapizing) occurs within a moral context, and that our choice of a theoretical explanation must be determined both by careful observation as well as by moral sensibilities and implications (Goldner, 1985; Hare-Mustin, 1978; Papp, 1988).

In addition to offering a critique of systemic conceptions of couple and family functioning, feminists pointed out the ways in which the process of therapy is guided by gender stereotypes. Hare-Mustin (1978) notes the paternalistic quality of a hierarchical relationship between therapist and clients, and therapists' either unwitting or deliberate reinforcement of sex role-stereotyped behavior as the solution to couple problems. She recommends a variety of approaches to bring a feminist sensibility to conducting therapy. Goldner (1985) notes the paradoxical position of women in couple therapy: on the one hand, as default monitor of the couple's emotional well-being, the wife signals to the husband the need for help, and typically arranges the first appointment. But once in therapy, the wife is simultaneously the key ally of the therapist in keeping the couple coming, yet is often told to back off from critiquing the husband, lest he exercise his ultimate power to discontinue the therapy. Papp (1988, 2000) demonstrates use of a range of established techniques for disrupting constraining gender beliefs.

Interestingly, as with the other developments in couple therapy, feminism emerged as a critique most directly of *family* therapy—questioning assumptions about men and women as they made the transition from partners to parents and struggled with the division of labor between out-of-home work and domesticity (Goldner, 1985). Goldner notes that although there was already a large feminist literature on couplehood in psychoanalysis, sociology, and history, the feminist critique of couples and family therapy emerged only around the time that these (primarily) feminist women writers reached the age of motherhood. Another explanation is that the birth of the first child often dramatically shifts the distribution of household tasks from more to less egalitarian (Hare-Mustin, 1978), revealing more traditional sex-role assumptions in male partners who seemed to espouse feminist values, or revealing the economically structured sexist bind in which only one partner can work and the man can bring in the higher income. Feminist family therapists identified the resulting inseparable, recursive link between the marital and parenting "subsystems," and the ways in which power inequities and unequal distribution of housework and childcare influence a couple's level of intimacy. Research findings from Gottman and colleagues have substantiated the impact of sharing housework, and husbands' willingness to be influenced by their wives, on relationship satisfaction and longevity (Gottman, 1991, 1994a,b; Gottman et al., 1998).

In any case, by "problematizing" the parenting relationship and locating the basis of these problems in the hidden gendered assumptions underlying marriage, feminism played a major role in bringing forth the more direct interest in couple therapy that characterizes the field today. In terms of the theme of diversification, feminism introduced the notion that the two members of a heterosexual couple will likely have systematically different experiences of their relationship based on differential access to power and different expectations regarding intimacy (Walters et al., 1988). With its attention to the extreme (although common) expressions of differential power between men and women in intimidating and violent behavior, feminism also introduced the notion that not all couple problems could be "ground" through the same "mill" of systemic theories and techniques—that different ways of thinking and intervening are needed for different problems.

*Multiculturalism:* Closely accompanying the emergence of the feminist perspective came the beginning of the field's recognition of the diversity in couples' experiences as a function of differences in ethnicity, race, social class, religious affiliation, sexual orientation, age, and geographic locale. With the exception of work in the area of gay and lesbian couples (Laird & Green, 1996; Sanders, 2000; Slater, 1995), as with feminism, the multicultural perspective on couples has been largely hidden within writings on families (e.g., Boyd-Franklin, 1989; Falicov, 1983, 1988, 1995; McGoldrick, 1993; McGoldrick, Pearce, & Giordano, 1982; Pinderhughes, 1989). To date, there are still few writings specifically on couples as affected by these or other sources of diversity (although see recent writings by Black, 2000; Fraenkel & Wilson, 2000; Mohr, 2000; Perel, 2000).

Writings from the multicultural perspective emphasize two main points. First, the norms regarding quality and quantity of intimacy, the distribution of power between partners, the degree of involvement of other persons in the couple's life (friends, other lovers, extended family), and other core aspects of couple life may vary across couples depending on their ethnicity and race, social class, sexual orientation, and other group affiliations. Second, depending on the standing of each group within the larger social context, partners' group affiliations provide them experiences of privilege or oppression, as well as more or less hospitable living conditions, and these affect couple process and satisfaction. Because all couples (and their constituent partners) are "nested" within a complex matrix of these group affiliations (Falicov, 1995), it is important for therapists to explore the sum total of opportunity or deprivations af-

forded each particular couple based on who they are in terms of this level of identity. For instance, Boyd-Franklin (1993) writes, ". . . for poor, inner-city, African-American families, the day-to-day realities of racism, discrimination, classism, poverty, homelessness, violence, crime, and drugs create forces that continually threaten the family's survival" (p. 361).

The advent of the multicultural perspective in couple therapy has wide-ranging implications for theory, practice, and training, many of which are only beginning to be identified (Lazloffy & Hardy, 2000; Markowitz, 1994). As in the response to the challenge posed by feminism, sensitivity to the impact of differences in cultural affiliations and the accompanying oppression/privilege dimensions, requires a focus not only on the experiences, beliefs, and process of the client couple, but also on the cultural affiliations and accompanying experiences, beliefs, and level of privilege/oppression of therapists. The therapist's ethnic, racial, class, and other group affiliations provide potential biases in observing, interacting, and thinking about couples, as well as being stimuli that may affect the formation of the therapeutic alliance. Hardy (1991) and others argue that training institutions need substantial renovation in terms of curricula, clinical practices, and personnel (involving more professionals and students of color) in order to meet the multicultural challenge. Each couple potentially represents a particular, unique combination of group-based characteristics, experiences, and identifications, and many therapists encounter at least some degree of cultural heterogeneity in their work. As a result, the multicultural perspective at times seems to require stepping down from the expert-observing position more characteristic of traditional systems approaches. Such an orientation calls for a more collaborative, ethnographic approach in which the therapist turns to the couple to inform her or him about the values, rules, and other sources of expectation that characterize their culture(s), and within which couple problems and patterns gather their meaning. This flexibility in hierarchy between therapist and couple is especially critical when the therapist's race, educational level, and class, or other group affiliations automatically place him or her in a position of greater power beyond that accrued by being the designated expert in mental health. It should be considered, however, that hierarchy and expertness are not inherently antithetical to collaboration and humility. A therapist can be an expert about human behavior and still learn from his patients. He can collaborate and still function in a mutually agreed upon hierarchical role with greater knowledge-based power and authority.

*Postmodernism:* Over the past decade or so, through the constructivist (Watzlawick, 1984), social constructionist (Anderson & Goolishian, 1988; Hoffman, 1990), narrative (White, 1988; White & Epston, 1991), and solution-oriented theories and approaches that draw upon them, postmodern ideas have had an enormous impact on family therapy. The postmodern critique of positivism (the belief in an objective reality that exists apart from the perceiver and that can be known through scientific study) and its alternative concept of reality as socially constructed and relative to historical and personal contexts has resulted in a number of shifts in the basic assumptions of systemic therapy (Fraenkel, 1997). These include: a shift from the stance of therapist as expert to one of therapist as collaborative investigator (with couples) of the meanings of their problems and the range of their solutions; a shift away from observing behavior, intervening in interaction sequences, and cybernetic/mechanistic systemic explanations (Hoffman, 1990), and toward a focus on how the language cou-

ples use to describe relationship problems constrains their perceived range of possible solutions (Hudson & O'Hanlon, 1992; Zimmerman & Dickerson, 1994). In addition, because of its critique of positivism and concern about the constraining effects of "grand narratives" (descriptions and explanations that apply to large numbers of persons), postmodern therapists emphasize the unique experience and meaning system of each individual, couple, or family over research- or clinically based general descriptions of problems (Fraenkel, 1995). Although not a deliberate aspect of these approaches, some have noted that postmodern therapies seem to involve an increased tendency to work with individuals on their relationship problems, rather than conjointly (cf. Freedman & Combs, 1996; Minuchin, 1998).

A small but excellent literature has amassed from a narrative perspective on couple therapy. The few pieces written (e.g., Freedman & Combs, 1996a,b, 2000; Neal, Zimmerman, & Dickerson, 1999; White, 1986/1987; Zimmerman & Dickerson, 1993a,b, 1994) well capture the use of this perspective and its translation into actual therapy practices. Such practices include helping couples recognize the constraining impact of particular descriptions and beliefs about their problems; separating themselves from these descriptions through tracing their source, typically in beliefs sustained in the dominant culture ("deconstruction"); and finding creative ways to "externalize" (or separate) these problem-saturated narratives from the couple's core identity and develop alternative ones that provide more satisfaction and opportunities for change at the level of action.

Like narrative therapies, solution-focused couple therapies (Hudson & O'Hanlon, 1992; Weiner-Davis, 1992) are based on the notion that the language used to describe problems limits couples' capacity to generate alternatives. These therapies work with couples to locate and build upon exceptions to the usual problem pattern, and use some creative techniques (such as the "miracle question") to assist couples to move away from a focus on present and past problems and toward their vision of a preferred future (see also Furman and Ahola, 1992, for a wide range of creative approaches in their "solution-oriented" approach). However, in contrast to narrative therapies' focus on how the larger society may negatively affect couples' lives through its promulgation of constraining descriptions and beliefs, solution-focused therapies generally focus on the more micro level of the couple's interaction and experience. In this way, they more closely resemble the earlier strategic approach of the Mental Research Institute, with its focus on changing perceptions through reframing and pattern interruption, albeit with a postmodern twist. Solution-focused approaches have also been both praised (by managed care, for one) and criticized for what can seem like a relentless focus on the future and on moving persons to more positive experiences, without making space for clients to talk about and come to terms with the painful events of their pasts (Efron & Veenendaal, 1993). Moreover, postmodern models of couple therapy may at times commit the same type of logical error regarding hierarchy (i.e., therapist-as-expert) as noted above in our consideration of the impact of multiculturalism on couple therapy theory and practice.

Given the current popularity of the solution-oriented approaches, the narrative metaphor, and postmodern ideas more generally, it is likely that much more will emerge on couples therapy from this perspective in the years to come. Yet the postmodern approaches have not developed without criticism—including from feminism and multiculturalism. Like the feminist and multicultural perspectives, some of the postmodern approaches (particularly narrative) emphasize the effects of the larger social context on how couple partners experience their relationship. But whereas the emphasis in postmodern therapies is on constraining descriptions and beliefs imposed by dominant groups over less powerful groups, feminism and multiculturalism also recognize the very real, "objective" oppressive forces in society that affect the lives of women and persons of color. It is around this point that feminism and multiculturalism experience "dilemmas and points of resistance" with some postmodernism (Hare-Mustin & Marecek, 1994), because of the latter's rejection of "grand narratives" or general statements about what is "true." Whatever their differences and overlaps, perhaps the major combined effect of all three perspectives on the theory and practice of couple therapy has been to force the field to recognize the diversity of experiences of couplehood for men versus women, and for persons of different races, ethnicities, classes, sexual orientations, and other sources of meaning and experience, privilege or oppression.

## INTEGRATION

Another major thrust in the development of couple therapy in Phase Four, has been the "quiet revolution" (Lebow, 1997b, p. 1) in the movement toward integrative clinical theory and practice, paralleling related developments in the world of individual psychotherapy (e.g., Norcross & Goldfried, 1992; Stricker & Gold, 1993), and exposing the reality that eclecticism and integration are probably the modal orientations of couple therapists (Rait, 1988). This movement, begun in response to the recognition of common factors that affect treatment outcomes, and the limited evidence of differential effectiveness of various psychotherapies, asserts that a broad base for understanding human behavior is necessary. Integrative treatment approaches allow greater treatment flexibility and increase treatment applicability, therefore potentially leading to more positive outcomes (Gurman, 1981; Lebow, 1984). Although integrative approaches ultimately equip therapists with a wider range of theories and techniques, there are special challenges in both learning and teaching such couple approaches (Fraenkel & Pinsof, 2001).

The three major strategies of integrative model development (Stricker, 1994) are the common factors approach (focusing on elements of therapy found in most treatments), the technical eclecticism approach (combining techniques from more than one treatment model, with one model remaining dominant), and theoretical integration (creating a superordinate framework drawing upon multiple viewpoints). Recently, Fraenkel and Pinsof (2001) have proposed a fourth approach, theoretical eclecticism, which uses multiple theoretical perspectives either simultaneously or sequentially, without integrating the respective theories, yet specifying principles for relating and making decisions about when to use different theories and techniques.

In couple therapy, two major integrative patterns have emerged. The first involves the combining of conjoint couple therapy with other treatment formats and modalities, such as individual therapy, and the other involves the combining, at theoretical or technical levels, existing conceptual models of couple treatment.

*Integration of Marital Therapy Approaches:* Within the integrative approach that emphasizes the combining of treatment formats and modalities, Feldman's (1985, 1992) "Integrative Multilevel Therapy" stands out. While also paying attention to behavioral, psychodynamic, systemic, and biological aspects of couple relationships, Feldman (1979) particularly emphasizes the judicious use of both individual and conjoint sessions, with sequences and balances between the two determined on a case basis. Pinsof's (1983, 1995) "Integrative Problem-Centered Therapy" exemplifies both flexible combinations of intervention methods and formats and the use of an underlying and verifying theoretical framework and specific theoretical principles for relating and making decisions about different theories and techniques. In Pinsof's approach, the therapist combines interventions from disparate therapy traditions by moving from model to model according to a clearly delineated treatment planning decision tree model, e.g., from present-focused approaches such as structural and cognitive-behavioral, to historically focused approaches, such as object relations and Bowenian. His model also allows for the inclusion of biological intervention. Similar to Pinsof's approach, Fraenkel's (1997; Fraenkel & Pinsof, 2001) integrative approach, the "Therapeutic Palette," delineates a set of principles for how to select one theory over another at any particular time.

As Martin (1976, p. 8) emphasized, and was perhaps the earliest marital therapist to do so: "Those who prefer to stress either the intrapersonal or the interpersonal aspects alone . . . limit themselves. The separation . . . is an artificial separation that does not occur in the nature of the human being . . ." (p. 8). The perspective of simultaneously including both the interpersonal and intrapsychic domains of experience has been developed in several theoretically integrative models of the marital relationships and marital therapy. Sager's (1976, 1981) "Marriage Contracts" Model, which addressed "conscious and verbalized" expectations, "conscious but not verbalized," and "beyond awareness" or unconscious "contracts," was grounded in psychoanalytic theory (Sager 1967a,b), but selectively used behavioral exchanges (such as point-for-point quid pro quos) and other assigned out-of-session tasks. W. C. Nichols' (1988) integrative approach is grounded in developmental and object relations theory, yet also calls upon behavioral exchanges, and communication and problem-solving training. Schwartz' (1995) Internal Family Systems Approach also blends recognition of historically based, intrapsychic experience and internalized representations of "parts" of self, and how these influence and are influenced by current interactions.

The early 1980s saw the independent emergence of at least four integrative, interpersonal/intrapersonal models that, unlike the eclectic approaches considered above, were more theoretically integrative in balancing their attention to both psychodynamic and social learning perspectives. Bagarozzi and Giddings (1983) presented a cognitive-attributional analysis of how partners reinforce and punish each other's behavior that conforms to or fails to conform to their inner representational models, and thus engage in a "mutual shaping process" that maintains projection-based collusion. Both conscious and unconscious dimensions of relationships were explored in therapy. These rich conceptual mapping of two distinctly different theoretical orientations, which was both a marital and family treatment model, unfortunately, has not been developed further by the authors.

The marital interaction model of Berman, Lief, and Williams (1981), which evolved into the "Intersystem Model" (Weeks & Hof, 1987) of the PENN Council for Relationships (formerly the Marriage Council of Pennsylvania), brought together into a coherent framework Sager's (1976) blend of contract theory and object relations theory, multigenerational family systems theory, adult developmental theory, systems theory, and social learning theory. The Intersystem Model simultaneously addresses the interlocking individual, interactional (dyadic), and intergenerational systems, and draws upon a wide array of techniques from several therapeutic traditions. The Intersystem Model clearly stands as one of the most ambitious integrative couple therapy models proposed to date.

Two other integrative couple therapy models have a great deal in common, though they were developed independently. Gurman's "Depth-Behavioral" Brief Integrative Marital Therapy (1978, 1981, 1982, 1990, 1992, 2002) and Segraves' "Combined Psychodynamic-Behavioral Approach" (Segraves, 1978, 1982) both attempt to modify couple partners' inner representational models and interpersonal schemas by both direct (e.g., behavioral) and indirect (e.g., interpretive) means. Both authors argue that since people shape (and maintain important aspects of) each other's personalities, couple therapy can lead to individual change, both behaviorally and intrapsychically. In effect, both approaches also agree that directive and behavioral interventions can serve as a powerful means to intrapsychic ends.

*Couple Therapy and Brief Therapy—Integration with the Broader World of Psychotherapy:* In addition to the important recent integration activity within marital therapy per se, significant links to the broader field of psychotherapy have evolved of late. Among the most viable of these links is the connection recently being forged between couple therapy and brief therapy. By "brief therapy," we do not mean any particular couple therapy model, such as the Brief Therapy of the Mental Research Institute (Segal, 1991). Rather, we refer to broad-gauged efforts to keep treatment short-term irrespective of theoretical orientation. These efforts focus on identifying the basic elements of effective brief therapy in order to understand core change mechanisms, and to maximize the development of change-inducing techniques, as has been done in the field of brief individual psychotherapy (Bloom, 1992; Messer & Warren, 1995). The first book-length treatment of various models of short-term couple therapy appeared only recently (Donovan, 1999).

Gurman (2001) has provided an extensive analysis to date of the "essential redundancy" between couple (and family) therapy and brief therapy. He emphasizes (p. 53) that "there has never been a dominant long-term (family) couple treatment method that served as a standard against which other methods came to be compared," as was true of individual therapies. At the same time, he notes that most couple therapy has been brief compared to traditional psychotherapy standards, by default, not by design. Most couple therapy lasts only up to about 15–20 sessions (Doherty & Simmons, 1996; Rait, 1988). Gurman argues that this naturally occurring brief couple therapy is attributable to particular common marital therapist attitudes and values, and to certain technical factors involved in couple therapy. He suggests that couple therapists overwhelmingly accept all of the central treatment values of brief individual therapists (Budman & Gurman, 1985) (e.g., clinical parsimony, a developmental perspective focused on the question, "Why now?"; an emphasis on patient strengths; the importance of change inducement outside of, as well as inside, therapy; and present-centeredness), plus the unique perspective that the partner-partner relationship is potentially more healing than the patient-therapist relationship emphasized in traditional psychotherapy.

Gurman (2001) also elaborates the ways in which the "four central technical factors of brief therapy" are manifest in the majority of couple therapies. First, the meaning and use of time as a therapeutic resource in couple therapy includes engaging a developmental perspective on problem formation and presentation, early therapist intervention, and flexible treatment session length. Second, the therapist-patient (couple) relationship in couple therapy requires a relatively high level of therapist activity, and yet the therapist's interaction with marital partners is less salient than their interaction with each other, so that change in the natural relational context is emphasized. Moreover, among empirically validated couple therapies, therapists accept their roles as experts, and share their expert knowledge with couples collaboratively. Third, treatment techniques in couple therapy tend to include a balanced emphasis on change both in and out of therapy sessions. Finally, the treatment focus, the cornerstone of all brief therapies, regularly is directed toward behavior patterns of the couple that center on the presenting problem, symptom, or dominant theme (e.g., Pinsof, 1995).

In sum, Gurman (2001) argues that most couple therapy is inherently brief because it activates the same dimensions of effective brief therapeutic intervention found in individual psychotherapies, yet, of course, with a particular interactional (or systemic) awareness that is usually far more muted in individual treatment. Gurman's analysis demonstrates and illustrates many of the important ways in which couple therapy and brief individual therapy may be usefully integrated at the conceptual level. Identifying such common ground is likely to benefit synergistically both domains of clinical practice, and the consumers of such services.

*Couple Therapy and Sex Therapy—A Still Unconsummated Relationship:* Paralleling the increasing attention of late to the inclusion of biological factors in treating marital relationships, especially regarding psychiatric disorders (e.g., Pinsof, 1995), some couple therapists (e.g., Schnarch, 1991, 2001; Weeks & Hof, 1987) have advocated for the integration of marital therapy and sex therapy. Indeed, there is even a professional journal, the *Journal of Sexual Marital Therapy,* that has fostered such an integration for many years. And there is good reason to support such a clinical connection. Marriage is the one and virtually only social and familial relationship in which society-at-large deems sexual expression to be appropriate. In addition, as groundbreaking as was the creation of the early field of marriage counseling, that intimate sexual behavior has become an explicit focus for theory, research, and intervention in the second half of the last century, is truly a profound development. Moreover, at a very practical level, it is probably the rare couple therapy case that has not included at least some discussion of sexual matters, if not outright sex therapy intervention.

And yet, the worlds of the "marital" or "couple" therapist and the "sex therapist" seem rarely to intersect. For example, while sexuality is occasionally referenced in clinical writings and workshop presentations (e.g., Pinsof, 1999) on couple therapy, discussion of commonly used principles, methods, and techniques for the treatment of sexual dysfunctions is almost non-existent.

This unfortunate theory vs. practice gulf may be attributable to two particular aspects of the world of the mental health professions. First, as McCarthy (2002) has succinctly explained, "The traditional marital therapy approach was to view sexual dysfunction as symptomatic of an unresolved relationship problem (e.g., poor communication, power imbalances . . . family of origin conflicts"). Sexual dysfunctions have typically been viewed by family and marital therapists not as real problems in their own right, but as indirect, disguised symbolic expressions of another problem, or as an expression of a problem at some other level of relationship organization or structure. As a result, McCarthy (in press) continues, "The marriage therapy field has not given sufficient attention to sexuality and sexual

dysfunction. Few marriage therapy training programs have courses, practice, or internships in which sex therapy is an integral component."

The second force in the mental health professions that has worked against the needed integration of sex therapy and marital therapy involves the pivotal role of behavior therapy. Although some of the most influential early clinical pioneers of sex therapy, such as Helen Singer Kaplan (1974, 1983), had significant psychoanalytic backgrounds, the overwhelming majority of technical innovation and clinical treatment research has come from clinical psychologists, and primarily from psychologist-behavior therapists (e.g., Heiman & LoPiccolo, 1988; Leiblum & Rosen, 1989; McCarthy, 2002; Wincze & Barlow, 1996). Behavior therapy, the clinical foundation of most sex therapy methods, has never occupied a central role in the formal training of marital and family therapists. Ironically, even when behavioral marital therapy is included in the professional training of psychologists (which is not routinely the case), specific training in the treatment of sexual dysfunctions is not common.

Also ironically, at the same time that some marital therapists (e.g., Pinsof, 1995; Schnarch, 1991; Weeks & Hof, 1987) are calling for a more systematic integration of sex therapy and couple therapy, the overall field of sex therapy is shrinking rather than growing (McCarthy, 2002). This appears to be happening for reasons that have nothing to do with the inappropriateness of such integrative urgings, but rather with such real-world considerations as the non-existence of licensing for sex therapists and the vanishing payment for treatment of sexual dysfunction by insurance companies and other health care "providers" such as managed care corporations. If there is to be a substantive and substantial integration of the fields of sex therapy and marital therapy, new leaders must emerge with expertise in both clinical domains, and with a balanced respect for the complementary, and potentially synergistic, attributes of both domains.

## THE BRIEF, BUT SIGNIFICANT, HISTORY OF MARITAL THERAPY RESEARCH

In this modern era of clinical practice, with its manifold pressures for accountability and evidence of efficacy and effectiveness, it may be difficult for non-grayhaired readers to appreciate just how recent the existence of reasonably credible research on couple therapy actually is. In this section, we will survey and summarize what we consider the most significant and robust findings on marital therapy that seem to have at least a modicum of relevance for public health policy, clinical decision-making, or refinement of theories of couple therapy. We will not ourselves exhaustively review existing treatment research as we (ASG) have done in the past (e.g., Gurman, 1973b; Gurman & Kniskern, 1978b, 1981b; Gurman, Kniskern, & Pinsof, 1986), but will draw upon a large body of existing, integrative reviews, both narrative and meta-analytic, both recent and not-so-recent (especially Alexander, Holzworth-Monroe, & Jameson, 1994; Baucom, Shoham, Meuser, et al., 1998; Beach et al., 1998; Bray & Jouriles, 1995; Christensen & Heavey, 1999; Daiuto et al., 1998; Dunn & Schwebel, 1995; Emmelkamp & Gerlsma, 1994; Epstein & McCrady, 1998; Friedlander, Wildman, Heatherington, & Skowson, 1994; Gurman, 1973b; Gurman, 1978; Gurman & Kniskern, 1978, 1981; Gurman, Kniskern, & Pinsof, 1986; Hahlweg & Markman, 1988; Halford, 1998; Jacobson & Addis, 1993; Johnson et al., 1999; Lebow & Gurman, 1995; Pinsof, 1981; Pinsof & Wynne, 1995; Shadish, Montgomery, Wilson, et al., 1993; Shadish, Ragsdale, Glaser, & Montgomery, 1995;

Whisman & Snyder, 1997). Readers who wish to consider methodological issues regarding both research design and measurement might consult Alexander et al. (1994), Baucom and Hoffman (1986), Beach and O'Leary (1985), Christensen and Heavey (1999), Gurman and Kniskern (1978b), Pinsof (1981), Pinsof and Wynne (1995), and Whisman and Snyder (1997).

### Three-Phase History of Marital Therapy Research

There seems to have been three rather distinct phases in the history of couple therapy research. For each of these phases, we will highlight the most clinically relevant findings of the era, comment on emerging concerns or shifts of emphasis from one phase to the next, and occasionally offer some of our own idiosyncratic views on the salient research themes and findings of a particular phase.

*Phase I: A Technique in Search of Some Data (1930–1974):* Just as Manus declared that, as of 1966, marriage counseling was a "technique in search of a theory," so too, it could be said that for more than its first 40 years, marital counseling/therapy was a field in dire need of some data.

In 1957, Mudd published an article on the "knowns and unknowns in marriage counseling research." Since, by anything even crudely approaching modern standards, there was no empirical research in the field (keep in mind that, at that time, the rise of interest in psychotherapy research in clinical psychology and, to a lesser extent, psychiatry, had not yet taken hold), Mudd could do little more than raise questions worthy of study.

In 1970, Olson reported that the handful of marriage counseling research papers were "mostly . . . descriptive in nature" (p. 524), and that the "best" outcome studies were typically reports of one practitioner on a sample of his own treated

cases, using only his own outcome ratings.

Three years later, Goodman (1973) examined all the existing research in the
field (N = 170) published from 1931 to
1968, and containing "some empirical
data" (p. 111). She found that 56% of
these works were based on subjective reports, and only 22% included a "specified
sample" (p. 112), i.e., they were "so poorly
defined . . . as to provide no information
concerning the populations to which the
findings might apply" (p. 113). Goodman
concluded that the "usual standards for
evaluation research could not be applied
to the marriage counseling papers" (p.
113). Moreover, she found that research
was so sparse that "it is not possible to
identify an active research front for the
field" (p. 116). That same year, Gurman
(1973a,b) reviewed the emerging trends
in the literature on research and practice
in marital therapy, and found that while
the overall literature had a very fast
growth rate, only a handful of measure-
ment-based papers touched on matters of
treatment outcome or process.

As Broderick and Schrader (1981)
noted, by the late 1960s, marital therapy
had reached its "zenith" before what, as
we have shown, would turn out to be a
20-year drought. It was now the mid-
1970s, and marital counseling/therapy
had essentially nothing to show for itself
empirically.

*Phase II: Irrational (?) Exuberance
(1975–1992):* The middle to late 1970s
marked a turning point in the research
history of marital (and family) therapy.
For the first time, the field had accumulated a critical mass of empirical studies
of treatment outcomes that seemed to
have implications for clinical practice, at
least at a broad level of guiding some important aspects of treatment planning.
Moreover, several of the key findings
seemed to help the credibility of the field
of couple and family therapy (by now typ-

ically referred to as if they were unitary)
in both professional, psychotherapeutic
circles, and in governmental policy-mak-
ing circles.

A series of research reviews by Gurman
and his colleagues (Gurman, 1971, 1973b;
Gurman & Kniskern, 1978a,b, 1981a;
Gurman, Kniskern, & Pinsof, 1986) set
forth the following major conclusions
about the empirical status of the efficacy
and effectiveness of couple therapy:

1. Nonbehavioral couple therapies produced beneficial outcomes in terms of
marital distress and satisfaction in about
two-thirds of cases.

2. The positive effects of couple therapy
exceeded those of no treatment.

3. Conjoint therapy was more effective
than individual therapy for marital difficulties.

4. These outcomes occurred in treatments of relatively very short duration,
by traditional psychotherapeutic standards, i.e., about 12–20 sessions.

5. Couple therapy was helpful, alone or
in combination with other (e.g., individual) interventions, in the treatment of
certain psychiatric disorders (e.g., depression, alcoholism, anxiety disorders) usually treated in individual psychotherapy.

6. As in individual psychotherapy (of
nonmarital problems), couple therapy at
times (up to 10%) was associated with
individual or relationship deterioration.
Such negative effects were especially associated with a therapist style, early in
therapy, of confronting patients with
highly affective material, while providing
minimal support and structure to treatment.

7. Co-therapy was no more effective
than single therapist treatment.

Although the validity of some of these
conclusions would later be challenged on
occasion (e.g., Bednar, Burlingame, &
Masters, 1988; Raffa, Sypek, & Vogel,
1990; Wells & Gianetti, 1986a,b), an even
more methodologically sophisticated se-

ries of studies of several different types of couple therapy (see below), often analyzed by more powerful (statistical, vs. narrative, or "eye-ball") methods, would corroborate virtually all of Gurman and colleagues' initial assessments. Given couple therapy's decades-long difficulties in establishing its rightful place in the psychotherapy sun, these findings were greeted with both widespread relief and enthusiasm. Although, in the language of recent financial markets, these findings may at times have been "overvalued," particularly by leaders in the field with primary guild interests, they clearly did not generate unwarranted or "irrational" exuberance. Couple therapy, having established its essential helpfulness, could now direct its attention to more refined and focused questions and concerns.

*Phase III: Caution and Extension (1993–present):* By the mid-to-late 1980s, a meaningful corpus of research had began to accrete, studying primarily the three models of couple therapy (Behavioral, Emotionally-Focused, Psychodynamic/Insight-Oriented), which we described as the dominant models in the Fourth Phase of marital therapy's history. But the exuberance of the previous decade's evaluators would soon be toned down by some important warnings and cautionary notes from leaders in the field. Before turning to those considerations, let us establish a baseline for this body of work. Here, we address a series of questions commonly asked of the research literature (e.g., Christensen & Heavey, 1999; Halford, 1998; Lebow & Gurman, 1995; Whisman & Snyder, 1997).

**Does conjoint couple therapy work for relationship problems?** This fundamental question addresses the matter of whether couple therapy, generally speaking, is more helpful than no treatment. Helpfulness, or positivity of outcome, is typically assessed in terms of levels of patient-reported relationship distress or conflict, observational ratings of couple interactions, or couples' global ratings of relationship satisfaction.

Consensus on this question is nearly absolute. For example, as Christensen and Heavey (1999) assert, "The result of dozens of [comparisons vs. no treatment] indicates unequivocally that couple therapy increases satisfaction more than no treatment" (p. 167). Bray and Jouriles (1995) elaborate that positive overall effects of couple therapy have been found by reviewers of varying theoretical orientations, using different analytical methods, based on "dozens of studies" (p. 462). And Lebow and Gurman (1995) conclude that the "unequivocal" (p. 32) overall evidence of helpfulness confirms "the general finding of efficacy found in less rigorous research" (p. 32), as previously alluded from the first wave of research reviews in the field. Moreover, every efficacy study (controlled, randomized clinical trial) of any method of couple therapy investigated to date has found treatment to outperform no treatment.

**How powerful is conjoint couple therapy?** Researchers have addressed this question in several ways. The first way involves the computation of *effect sizes* (a statistical quantification of treatment outcome data across a variety of change measures across studies) that allow inferences about not merely whether treatment has had an effect, but also how large that effect was. The second statistic used to answer this question is a simple descriptive one, i.e., the *rate of improvement,* that is, the percent of couples, "improved," "satisfied," etc., at termination of treatment or at followup, most often based on patients' self-ratings.

Overall, couple therapy research has found effect sizes for the three most commonly studied treatment methods that are considered by statisticians to be "medium" (.50) to "very large" (1.0), with the majority falling in the "large" (.80) category or better. Effect sizes in this range translate to a "percent of couples improved" rate of approximately 60–75% (vs. roughly 35% improved among distressed couples not receiving treatment), almost identical to what Gurman (1973b) reported 28 years ago using the traditional "narrative" approach to evaluating large bodies of research data. These effect sizes and improvement rates approximate or exceed what has typically been found in studies of individual (non-couple-focused) psychotherapies. At the individual level, these findings suggest that, overall, a randomly selected treated couple is better off at the end of therapy than about 70% of untreated couples, i.e., that the chances of improvement hover around seven in ten.

In addition to effect sizes and improvement rates, three other indices of the power of couple therapy have been used: measures of clinical (vs. statistical) significance, assessment of the durability of post-treatment effects, and assessment of possible "negative effects" as a result of treatment.

*Clinically significant change* is said to occur when, say a couple's score on a measure of functioning, changes to such a degree that the post-therapy score moves the couple from within the pre-therapy range of "abnormal" scores to within the post-therapy range of "normal" scores (Jacobson & Truax, 1991). Using such stringent criteria, some data have suggested (Jacobson & Addis, 1993; Shadish et al., 1993) that as few as 35–40% of treated couples may actually move from "distressed" to "nondistressed" levels.

The *durability of change* is also extremely important, of course, because treatment effects that are limited to those that are short-lived may well not justify the costs, of various sorts, involved to produce them. The data on this question are not yet extensive, but suggest the following: there is reason to believe that while

there appears to be only minimal "relapse" at 6-to-9-months post-therapy, a significant portion of couples may relapse (i.e., return to the "distressed" or "unsatisfied" range) between 1 and 4 years after treatment (Hahlweg & Markman, 1988; Jacobson & Addis, 1993; Shadish et al., 1993). Most reports of such data have involved behavioral couple therapy.

At this time, two models of couple therapy have provided data that counter this disquieting trend. Emotionally Focused Therapy appears to maintain, and even improve, its effects at up to 2 years' followup (Johnson et al., 1999), and Insight-Oriented Marital Therapy (Snyder, Wills, & Grady-Fletcher, 1991) has shown very robust effects at 4 years' followup.

Finally, as has been known to be true of individual therapy for a long time (Bergin, 1963), couple therapy is not always either helpful or unhelpful, but may even make matters worse, leading to so-called *negative effects* or *deterioration*. This possibility, which certainly should not be surprising, was first discussed over twenty years ago by Gurman and Kniskern (1978a). Although the matter seems almost never to have been raised again in over two decades of research writing on couple therapy, a recent report by Hahlweg and Klann (1997) of couple therapy in Germany suggests that up to ten percent of treated couples consider themselves worse off after therapy than before. These data correspond very closely to Gurman and Kniskern's much earlier estimation of a negative effect rate of 5–10%.

**What is the relative effectiveness of different couple therapies?** To borrow a borrowed phrase from Luborsky, Singer, and Luborsky's (1975) discussion of the comparative efficacy of individual psychotherapies, "Everybody has won, and all must have prizes" (p. 995). More accurately, all those couple therapies that have been reasonably well put to the empirical test to data have won, i.e., have proven superior to no treatment. These methods are Behavioral (including cognitive-behavioral) Therapy, Emotionally Focused Therapy, and Insight-Oriented Marital Therapy. Thus far, there is no strong evidence that any one of these approaches is more effective than the others, or any other. To date, there have been very few head-to-head comparative studies in clinical trials, so that the occasional differences that have been found may be quite unreliable, and, in any case, have not been replicated.

At the same time, not all influential approaches to systems-oriented therapy even deserve consideration for "prizes" to date for their treatment of couples, e.g., Structural, Strategic, Bowen Family Systems, Solution-Focused, and Narrative methods with couples have essentially never been tested empirically. This fact should certainly not lead us to dismiss outright treatments that have not yet been tested empirically. Nonetheless, the proponents of such untested methods have a collective obligation to provide more than anecdotal evidence of their efficacy and effectiveness.

**What predicts responsiveness to treatment?** To whatever extent a therapy method "is effective," not all of its effectiveness can be attributed to method-based interventions per se, as decades of research in individual therapy have made quite clear (Lambert & Bergin, 1994). In individual therapy, therapy techniques account for far less of the variance in outcome than patient factors and therapist-patient relationship factors. As no one knows better than couple and family therapists, psychotherapeutic change is interactional. Beyond our overall awareness of the general power of any particular approach, it is especially meaningful to clinicians to be able to identify predictors of couples' responsiveness to therapy.

Nontechnique predictors of treatment outcome can be usefully divided into those

that are measurable outside the therapy context (e.g., patient factors, therapist factors), and those that are usually measured in the conduct of treatment itself (Gurman & Razin, 1977). In the "outside" measures, of course, the mechanism of action by which an extratherapy variable exerts its influence may not be immediately obvious.

To date, the body of research on both in-session and out-of-session predictors of outcome is not especially large, and yet, taken as a whole, does seem to create a meaningful picture with potential implications for both treatment planning and treatment monitoring. In Behavioral Marital Therapy (BMT), couples seem to be more likely to benefit from therapy if they are younger, less distressed, less gender-polarized, more emotionally engaged in the relationship, and committed to it. In Emotionally Focused Therapy (EFT), couples more likely to benefit may be older (average 35) and emotionally engaged, whereas neither pre-therapy distress level or sex-role traditionality appear associated with outcome. In Insight-Oriented Marital Therapy (IOMT), lower distress levels, (younger) age, and emotional engagement seem, as in BMT, predictive of change. As for in-session behavior, positive predictors of outcome include active collaboration with the therapy process (BMT), patient alliance with the therapist, especially in terms of the "task" components thereof (EFT), a couple's ability to "soften" their interactions and their level of emotional experiencing (EFT), and a couple's emotional engagement, marked especially by a low frequency of negative nonverbal affective display (IOMT).

While some of these statistical associations may be method-specific (e.g., EFT pushes for emotional experiencing more than BMT), two meaningful patterns may be identified. First, the rich seem to get richer, so to speak, as is often true in individual psychotherapy: couples who are younger, less distressed/dissatisfied, and more emotionally attuned to each other seem most likely to benefit from conjoint therapy. Second, couples who collaborate well with both each other and the therapist, and engage in cooperative, affectively meaningful exchange, seem to do better. This first conclusion may be relevant to the allocation of treatment resources, while the second may offer guideposts to therapists for early in-therapy predictors of outcome that may require their attention. Moreover, these composite findings certainly reinforce the relevance of couple prevention programs.

**Is couple therapy helpful for "individual" problems?** Earlier, we summarized the existing research findings on the treatment role of couple therapy for individual disorders such as depression, substance abuse, and anxiety disorders. It is worth noting here that, consistent with the empirically based conclusion reached fifteen years ago by Gurman et al. (1986), studies in this realm have never fond any evidence that might be construed as supporting the notion that individual symptoms serve relational functions (note the difference between relational functions and relational consequences), an idea strongly advanced by some marital therapists (e.g., Haley, 1976; Madanes, 1980).

*Coda on Couple Therapy Research:* To conclude this section, we will not address the numerous and important methodological and conceptual issues that clearly still need a great deal of the field's attention, such as the choice of criteria to assess change, matters of possible differential effectiveness of different methods with different types of problems (whether defined by interpersonal/dyadic or individual criteria), or considerations of cost-effectiveness as well as clinical effectiveness. Others have done an especially good job of addressing these issues in great detail (e.g., Alexander et al., 1994; John-son & Lebow, 2000; Lebow & Gurman, 1995; Pinsof & Wynne, 1995). Rather, we offer some contextualizing comments on the general thrust of Third Phase couple therapy research.

In the title of this phase of the history of couple therapy research, we chose the word "extension" to refer to the emerging applications of couple therapy methods to problems that are in addition to the traditional bread and butter of marriage counseling/couple therapy practice, i.e., relational distress, conflict, and dissatisfaction. Several reliably diagnosed adult disorders of individuals that, together, account for a large portion of the presenting problems in a general psychotherapy or psychiatric practice, also benefit from couple therapy. These difficulties extract a tremendous toll from those who suffer these disorders, those with whom they have intimate relationships, and contemporary society at large, and the field of couple therapy should be pleased with itself for adding effective treatment procedures for such disabling conditions to the standard regimen of psychiatric and psychological interventions.

At the same time, we would like to offer the view that the field of couple therapy has perhaps responded with greater alarm than is warranted by recent data suggesting that treatment effects may diminish at followup, and that the kinds of changes that are achieved in therapy, while statistically impressive, may not, in truth, be "significant" in clinical terms. We (Gurman, 1978; Gurman & Kniskern, 1978a,b, 1981a,b; Gurman Kniskern, & Pinsof, 1986) certainly have applauded all efforts to improve the efficacy and effectiveness of couple therapy, and frequently have been critical of those in the field who dismiss such concerns (e.g., Gurman, 1983). Nonetheless, we think a few ameliorating observations and reflections on what recent couple therapy research has shown are in order at this point in the field's history.

First, the overall outcomes of couple therapy, whether assessed in controlled "efficacy" studies or in uncontrolled "effectiveness" studies, have not been anything to scoff at. The effect sizes and improvement rates of various couple therapies are virtually indistinguishable from those that have been found for a wide variety of individual psychotherapies for decades (cf. Bergin & Garfield, 1994).

Second, while cost-effectiveness has rarely been addressed directly in empirical studies of couple therapy, we may usefully speculate about at least two manifestations of cost-effective couple therapy benefits. First, in an economic perspective, Pinsof and Wynne (1995) note that a typical course of ten-session couple therapy at $100 per session is far less than the short-term legal costs of divorcing, and still less than the long-term economic costs of divorce. In addition, we note that, by definition, every course of conjoint couple therapy involves two patients/clients (not to mention indirect but likely positive effects on their children), a rather efficient use of psychotherapeutic time, to say the least. If we assume that, in at least most "improved" marital relationships, both partners have contributed to positive change, then the public health value of our work may be said to be greater than that which usually accrues to individual psychotherapy.

Third, while we fully agree that statistically significant outcomes are not an adequate alternative to clinically significant outcomes, we question the adequacy and appropriateness of the criteria used heretofore to establish "clinical significance." Requiring a couple to move into the statistical range of couples who are "nondistressed" or "normal," seems to beg the more relevant clinical issue of whether this particular (set of) change(s) for this particular couple with this particular

problem (cf. Paul, 1967) is clinically, i.e., experientially, significant. A good deal of couple/therapy is crisis intervention, within which changes that in one or two areas that seem "small" to an outsider may greatly enhance a couple's functioning, but not necessarily in ways that are usually measured by researchers, i.e., "normal" "adjustment" scores. Such a requirement would be analogous, in other therapy contexts, to requiring a depressed person to be almost depression-free, or a generally anxious person, almost anxiety-free, in order to be thought of as "significantly improved." Finally, as Lebow and Gurman (1995, p. 33) have noted, "For highly troubled samples, a fifty percent movement . . . into the non-distressed range may constitute effective treatment."

Fourth, we may rightly express concern about the apparently variable durability of couple therapy-induced change. But, rather than talking about the inadequacy of our therapeutic methods, we may also consider that the problem lies in the insufficiency of their application. That is, perhaps we are doing a lot of the right things with couples, but not doing them enough. Bray and Jouriles (1995) have asked whether "it is realistic to expect that one round of therapy is enough to last a lifetime" (p. 470), especially for people with a significant history of relational vulnerability and couples with a long history of high levels of conflict. Certainly, a developmental perspective on couple relationships would suggest that "brief, intermittent" (Cummings & Sayama, 1995) or "time-sensitive" (Budman & Gurman, 1988) treatment is more appropriate, both practically and conceptually, not unlike a sort of infectious disease model of therapy, in which the current intervention is expected to be helpful, but not to preclude all future infections.

Moreover, perhaps our typical therapies are just too brief (cf. Gurman, 2001). Consider that our typical 10–20 therapy hours with couples face the challenge of offsetting and counterbalancing the destructive effects of many years, and possibly thousands of hours, of pain-inducing, distance-generating conflict. That our methods of therapy can yield the kinds of benefits they do in such short order is really quite impressive.

Finally, we may have erred to a degree in still another way in so harshly criticizing the helpfulness of our current couple therapy methods. Perhaps we have expected a good deal more of therapy methods qua techniques than is warranted. Over two decades ago, one of us warned of the dangers of "technolatry" (Gurman & Kniskern, 1978b), the worship of the false god of therapeutic technology. This tendency is very clear in the research literature on couple therapy, notwithstanding the empirical lessons learned in the broader domain of individual psychotherapy research, such as the often-cited and persuasive conclusion that technique factors appear to account for a rather small portion of the variance in treatment outcome, compared to patient factors such as degree of disturbance, therapy expectations, and demographics; therapist factors such as emotional health, credibility, and values; and common factors such as therapist feedback, providing a corrective emotional experience, giving advice, developing a therapeutic alliance, offering reassurance, taking risks, and reality testing (Garfield, 1994; Lambert & Bergin, 1994). This trend may be understandable in light of the fact that the overwhelming majority of couple therapy research has been conducted by behavior therapists. Perhaps BMT's incorporation of "acceptance" methods, and the increasing visibility and influence of research on alternative models of couple therapy, such as those that emphasize affective experience, insight, and the therapeutic relationship, will lead to further exploration of nontechnique factors in couple therapy outcomes.

In conclusion, we are reminded of the advice of the famed statistician Ronald Fisher (1989); "We should use our brains as well as $F$-ratios to draw inferences."[5] Moreover, just as we encourage more acceptance in our couples, perhaps we should aim for more acceptance toward both ourselves as therapists and our therapeutic methods.

## A MILLENNIAL CONCLUSION

The field of couple therapy approaches the millennium with almost a century-long history of fragmented growth and identity diffusion. It also approaches that marker with a more recent history colored by renewed vigor and historically uncharacteristic rigor.

### Four Great Historical Ironies

Rather than prognosticate about the field's future, or attempt to identify priorities for the continuing evolution of psychotherapy with couples, we have chosen to conclude this millennial account by noting four shifts and trends in the field that we think constitute not merely interesting evolutionary directions, but significantly altered shapes the field is taking on. Given couple therapy's history-as-we-have-seen-it, we consider these changes and configurations within the field to reflect profound ironies.

First, the *reinclusion of the individual,* roughly equivalent to what Nichols (1987) called the "self in the system," may be the most far-reaching irony of all. As we have argued, couple therapy nearly died during the pure systems period of usurpation by family therapy. Johnson and Lebow (2000), in their recent decade review of marital therapy, identified the renewal of interest in affect (e.g., in Emotionally Fo-

---

[5] Hendricks, J. (1989). Personal communication.

cused Therapy) as one of the major changes in recent years. We think that this important change reflects a much broader shift of perspective. It seems to express renewed interest in the psychology of the individual, not only in terms of affect, but also in terms of the cognitive-attributional elements of relationships, and even the capacity of individuals to influence relational systems by self-regulation. In this sense, then, we see it as strikingly ironic that while some very influential "systems" therapies almost rang the death knell for couple therapy by largely disavowing the relevance of what occurs "within" people in relationships, it is by the recent radical reinclusion of the individual, by dealing with multiple levels of human experience, that couple therapy has become more genuinely systemic.

Relatedly, the reinclusion of individuals has also included increasing acceptance of *the reality of individual psychiatric/psychological disorders.* Recognition that "systems" therapies such as couple therapy are not universally the treatment of choice for such problems had led to more moderate, realistic, and therefore, acceptable claims regarding the efficacy and applicability of couple therapy. Ironically, then, more muted and cautious claims about the power of such interpersonally oriented treatments has rendered them more, rather than less, credible in the mental health fields in general. This is especially so insofar as these more sober assessments lead naturally to the fostering of integration among intervention methods (e.g., couple therapy plus drug therapy), and among models of couple therapy. Many of the most recent advances in couple therapy have derived from scientific investigation of psychological disorders, mirroring the early history of the broader field of family therapy.

The third irony in the history of couple therapy history involves *the roots of influential couple treatment methods.* Haley

(1984) derisively noted that "there was not a single school of family therapy which had its origin in a marriage counseling group" (p. 6). Conversely, the couple therapy methods, both reparative and preventive, that have contributed the most in the last two decades to our understanding of intimate relationships and their treatment have all derived from traditional theoretical perspectives and therapeutic models. Ironically, then, it has been through extensions of social learning theory, psychodynamic theory, and humanistic/experiential theory, and not "pure" family systems theory, that new conceptual and scientific life has been injected into the field of couple therapy in the current generation.

The fourth, and final irony in the evolution of couple therapy, is the most historically telling. No other collective methods of psychosocial intervention have demonstrated a superior capacity to effect clinically meaningful change in as many spheres of human experience as the couple therapies, and many have not yet even shown a comparable capacity. Ironically, *despite its long history of struggles against marginalization and professional disempowerment, couple therapy at the millennium has emerged as one of the most vibrant forces in the entire domain of family therapy and of psychotherapy-in-general.*

## REFERENCES

Ackerman, N.W. (1970). Family psychotherapy today. *Family Process 9:* 123–126.

Alexander, F. (1968). An empirical study on the differential influence of self-concept on the professional behavior of marriage counselors. Unpublished Doctoral Dissertation, University of Southern California.

Alexander, J.F., Holtzworth-Munroe, A., & Jameson, P. (1994). The process and outcome of marital and family therapy: Research review and evaluation (pp. 595–630). In A.E. Bergin & S.L. Garfield (eds.), *Hand-*

book of psychotherapy and behavior change (4th ed.). New York: John Wiley & Sons.

Anchin, J.C., & Kiesler, D.J. (eds.). (1982). Handbook of interpersonal psychotherapy. New York: Pergamon Press.

Anderson, H., & Goolishian, H.A. (1988). Human systems as linguistic systems: Preliminary and evolving ideas about the implications for clinical theory. Family Process 27: 371–393.

Anonymous (1972). On the differentiation of self (pp. 111–173). In J. Framo (ed.), Family interaction: A dialogue between family researchers and family therapists. New York: Springer Publishing Company.

Avis, J.M. (1988). Deepening awareness: A private study guide to feminism and family therapy. Journal of Psychotherapy and the Family 3: 15–46.

Avis, J.M. (1989). Integrating gender into the family therapy curriculum. Journal of Feminist Family Therapy 1: 3–26.

Avis, J.M. (1992). Where are all the family therapists? Abuse and violence within families and family therapy's response. Journal of Marital and Family Therapy 18: 223–230.

Aylmer, R.C. (1986). Bowen family systems marital therapy (pp. 107–148). In N.S. Jacobson & A.S. Gurman (eds.), Clinical handbook of marital therapy. New York: Guilford Press.

Azrin, N.H., Naster, B.J., & Jones, R. (1973). A rapid learning-based procedure for marital counseling. Behaviour Research and Therapy 11: 365–382.

Bader, E., & Pearson, P.T. (1988). In quest of the mythical mate. New York: Brunner/Mazel.

Bagarozzi, D.A., & Giddings, C.W. (1983). The role of cognitive constructs and attributional processes in family therapy: Integrating intrapersonal, interpersonal, and systems dynamics (pp. 207–219). In L. Wolberg & M. Aronson (eds.), Group and family therapy 1981. New York: Brunner/Mazel.

Barker, R.L. (1984). Treating couples in crisis. New York: The Free Press.

Bateson, G., Jackson, D.D., & Weakland, J.H. (1956). Toward a theory of schizophrenia. Behavioral Science 1: 251–264.

Baucom, D.H., & Hoffman, J.A. (1986). The effectiveness of marital therapy: Current status and application to the clinical setting (pp. 597–620). In N.S. Jacobson & A.S. Gurman (eds.), Clinical handbook of marital therapy. New York: Guilford Press.

Baucom, D.H., Shoham, V., Meuser, K.T., Daiuto, A.D., & Stickle, T.R. (1998). Empirically supported couple and family interventions for marital distress and adult mental health problems. Journal of Consulting and Clinical Psychology 66: 53–88.

Beach, S.R., Fincham, F.D., & Katz, J. (1998). Marital therapy in the treatment of depression: Toward a third generatin of therapy and research. Clinical Psychology Review 18: 635–661.

Beach, S.R.H., & O'Leary, K.D. (1985). Current status of outcome research in marital Therapy (pp. 1035–1072). In L. L'Abate (ed.), The handbook of family psychology and therapy. Homewood IL: Dorsey.

Bednar, R.L., Burlingame, G.M., & Masters, K.S. (1988). Systems of family treatment: Substance or semantics? Annual Review of Psychology 39: 401–434.

Beels, C.C., & Ferber, A. (1969). Family therapy: A view. Family Process 8: 280–318.

Berger, R., & Hannah, M. (1999). Handbook of preventive approaches in couple therapy. New York: Brunner/Mazel.

Bergin, A.E. (1963). The effects of psychotherapy: Negative results revisited. Journal of Counseling Psychology 10: 244–250.

Bergin, A.E., & Garfield, S.L. (eds.). (1994). Handbook of psychotherapy and behavior change: An empirical analysis (4th ed.). New York: John Wiley & Sons.

Berman, E.B., Lief, H., & Williams, A.M. (1981). A model of marital integration (pp. 3–34). In G.P. Sholevar (ed.), The handbook of marriage and marital therapy. New York: Spectrum.

Black, L.W. (2000). Therapy with African American couples (pp. 205–221). In P. Papp (ed.), Couples on the fault line: New directions for therapists. New York: Guilford Press.

Bloom, B. (1992). Planned short-term psychotherapy: A clinical handbook. Boston: Allyn & Bacon.

Bloom, B., Asher, S., & White, S. (1978). Marital disruption as a stressor: A review and analysis. Psychological Bulletin 85: 867–894.

Bogdan, J. (1984). Doctor Pangloss as family therapist. *The Family Therapy Networker* 8(2): 19–20.

Bowen, M. (1976). Principles and techniques of multiple family therapy (pp. 388–404). In P.J. Guerin, Jr. (ed.), *Family therapy: Theory and practice.* New York: Gardner Press.

Bowen, M. (1978). *Family therapy in clinical practice.* New York: Jason Aronson.

Boyd-Franklin, N. (1989). *Black families in therapy: A multisystems approach.* New York: Guilford Press.

Boyd-Franklin, N. (1993). Race, class and poverty (pp. 361–376). In F. Walsh (ed.), *Normal family processes* (2nd ed.). New York: Guilford Press.

Bradbury, T.N., & Fincham, F.D. (1990). Preventing marital dysfunction: Review and analysis (pp. 375–401). In D. Frank, F.D. Fincham, & T.N. Bradbury (eds.), *The psychology of marriage: Basic issues and applications.* New York: Guilford Press.

Bray, J.H., & Jouriles, E.N. (1995). Treatment of marital conflict and prevention of divorce. *Journal of Marital and Family Therapy 21:* 461–473.

Broderick, C.B., & Schrader, S.S. (1981). The history of professional marriage and family therapy (pp. 3–35). In A.S. Gurman & D.P. Kniskern (eds.), *Handbook of family therapy.* New York: Brunner/Mazel.

Broderick, C.B., & Schrader, S.S. (1991). The history of professional marriage and family therapy (pp. 3–40). In A.S. Gurman & D.P. Kniskern (eds.), *Handbook of family therapy* (Vol. 2). New York: Brunner/Mazel.

Budman, S.H., & Gurman, A.S. (1988). *The theory and practice of brief therapy.* New York: Guilford Press.

Burman, B., & Margolin, G. (1992). Analysis of the association between marital relationships and health problems: An interactional perspective. *Psychological Bulletin 112:* 39–63.

Catherall, D.R. (1992). Working with projective identification in couples. *Family Process 31:* 355–367.

Christensen, A., & Heavey, C.L. (1999). Interventions for couples. *Annual Review of Psychology 50:* 165–190.

Christensen, A., Jacobson, N.S., & Babcock, J.C. (1995). Integrative behavioral couple Therapy (pp. 31–64). In N.S. Jacobson & A.S. Gurman (eds.), *Clinical handbook of couple therapy* (2nd ed.). New York: Guilford Press.

Coie, J., Watt, N., West, S., Hawkins, J., Asarnow, J., Markman, H., Ramey, S., Shure, S., & Long, B. (1993). The science of prevention: A conceptual framework and some directions for a national research program. *American Psychologist 48:* 1013–1022.

Cordova, J.V., Jacobson, N.S., & Christensen, A. (1998). Acceptance versus change interventions in behavioral couple therapy: Impact on couples' in-session communication. *Journal of Marital and Family Therapy 24:* 437–455.

Cummings, N., & Sayama, M. (1995). *Focused psychotherapy: A casebook of brief, intermittent psychotherapy throughout the life cycle.* New York: Brunner/Mazel.

Daiuto, A.D., Baucom, D.H., Epstein, N., & Dutton, S.S. (1998). The application of behavioral couples therapy to the assessment and treatment of agoraphobia: Implications of empirical research. *Clinical Psychology Review 18:* 663–687.

Dattilio, F.M., & Bevilacqua, L. (eds.). (2000). *Comparative treatments for relationship dysfunction.* New York: Springer Publishing Company.

Dicks, H.V. (1967). *Marital tensions.* New York: Basic Books.

Doherty, W.J., & Simmons, D.S. (1996). Clinical practice patterns of marriage and family therapists: A national survey of therapists and their clients. *Journal of Marital and Family Therapy 22:* 9–25.

Donovan, J. (ed.). (1999). *Short-term couple therapy.* New York: Guilford Press.

Duhl, B.S., & Duhl, F.J. (1981). Integrative family therapy (pp. 483–513). In A.S. Gurman & D.P. Kniskern (eds.), *Handbook of family therapy.* New York: Brunner/Mazel.

Dunn, R.L., & Schwebel, A.I. (1995). Meta-analytic review of marital therapy outcome research. *Journal of Family Psychology 9:* 58–68.

Efron, D., & Veenendaal, K. (1993). Suppose a miracle doesn't happen: The non-miracle option. *Journal of Systemic Therapies 12:* 11–18.

Emmelkamp, P.M.G., & Gerlsma, C. (1994).

Marital functioning and the anxiety disorders. *Behavior Therapy 25:* 407–429.

Epstein, E.E., & McCrady, B.S. (1998). Behavioral couples treatment of alcohol and drug use disorders: Current status and innovations. *Clinical Psychology Review 18:* 689–711.

Falicov, C.J. (1983). *Cultural perspectives in family therapy.* Rockville, MD: Aspen Systems.

Falicov, C.J. (1988). *Latino families in therapy: A guide to multicultural practice.* New York: Guilford Press.

Falicov, C.J. (1995). Training to think culturally: A multidimensional comparative framework. *Family Process 34:* 373–388.

Feldman, L.B. (1979). Marital conflict and marital intimacy: An integrative psychodynamic-behavioral-systemic model. *Family Process 18:* 69–78.

Feldman, L.B. (1985). Integrative multi-level therapy: A comprehensive interpersonal and intrapsychiatric approach. *Journal of Marital and Family Therapy 11:* 357–372.

Feldman, L.B. (1992). *Integrating individual and family therapy.* New York: Brunner/Mazel.

Floyd, F.J., Markman, H.J., Kelly, S., Blumberg, S.L., & Stanley, S.M. (1995). Preventative intervention and relationship enhancement (pp. 212–226). In N.S. Jacobson & A.S. Gurman (eds.), *Clinical handbook of couple therapy* (2nd ed.), New York: Guilford Press.

Fraenkel, P. (1995). The nomothetic-idiographic debate in family therapy. *Family Process 34:* 113–121.

Fraenkel, P. (1997). Systems approaches to couple therapy (pp. 379–414). In W.K. Halford & H.J. Markman (eds.), *Clinical handbook of marriage and couples interventions.* New York: John Wiley & Sons.

Fraenkel, P. (1999). ". . . and liberty and relationship strengthening programs for all (who want them)." *American Family Therapy Academy Newsletter 78:* 43–45.

Fraenkel, P., Markman, H., & Stanely, S. (1997). The prevention approach to relationship problems. *Sexual and Marital Therapy 12:* 249–258.

Fraenkel, P., & Pinsof, W. (2001). Teaching family therapy-centered integration: Assimilation and beyond. *Journal of Psychotherapy Integration 11:* 59–85.

Fraenkel, P., & Wilson, S. (2000). Clocks, calendars, and couples: Time and the rhythms of relationships (pp. 63–103). In P. Papp (ed.), *Couples on the fault line: New directions for therapists.* New York: Guilford Press.

Framo, J.L. (1965). Rationale and techniques of intensive family therapy (pp. 143–212). In I. Boszormenyi-Nagy & J.L. Framo (eds.), *Intensive family therapy.* New York: Harper & Row.

Framo, J.L. (1976). Family of origin as a therapeutic resource for adults in marital and family therapy: You can and should go home again. *Family Process 15:* 193–210.

Framo, J.L. (1981). The integration of marital therapy with sessions with family of origin (pp. 133–158). In A.S. Gurman & D.P. Kniskern (eds.), *Handbook of family therapy.* New York: Brunner/Mazel.

Framo, J.L. (1989). How AFTA got started. *American Family Therapy Association Newsletter 37:* 10–15.

Framo, J.L. (1996). A personal retrospective of the family therapy field: Then and now. *Journal of Marital and Family Therapy 22:* 289–316.

Franks, C.M. (ed.). (1969). *Behavior therapy: Appraisal and status.* New York: McGraw-Hill.

Freedman, J., & Combs, G. (1996a). Gender stories. *Journal of Systemic Therapies 15*(1): 31–46.

Freedman, J., & Combs, G. (1996b). *Narrative therapy.* New York: W.W. Norton.

Freedman, J., & Combs, G. (2000). Narrative therapy with couples (pp. 342–361). In F.M. Dattilio & L.J. Bevilacqua (eds.), *Comparative treatments for relationship dysfunction.* New York: Springer Publishing Company.

Friedlander, M.L., Wildman, J., Heatherington, L., & Skowson, E.A. (1994). What we do and don't know about the process of family therapy. *Journal of Family Psychology 8:* 390–416.

Friedman, E.H. (1985). *Generation to generation: Family process in church and synagogue.* New York: Guilford Press.

Furman, B., & Ahola, T. (1992). *Solution talk:*

*Hosting therapeutic conversations*. New York: W.W. Norton.

Garfield, S.L. (1994). Research on client variables in psychotherapy (pp. 190–228). In A.E. Bergin & S.L. Garfield (eds.), *Handbook of psychotherapy and behavior change* (4th ed.). New York: John Wiley & Sons.

Gerson, R., Hoffman, S., Sauls, M., & Ulrici, D. (1993). Family-of-origin frames in couples therapy. *Journal of Marital and Family Therapy 19:* 341–354.

Giblin, P., Sprenkle, D.H., & Sheehan, R. (1985). Enrichment outcome research: A meta-analysis of premarital, marital, and family interventions. *Journal of Marital and Family Therapy 11:* 257–271.

Goldner, V. (1985a). Feminism and family therapy. *Family Process 24:* 31–47.

Goldner, V. (1985b). Warning: Family therapy may be hazardous to your health. *The Family Therapy Networker 9*(6): 18–23.

Goldner, V. (1988). Generation and gender: Normative and covert hierarchies. *Family Process 27:* 17–31.

Goldner, V. (1998). The treatment of violence and victimization in intimate relationships. *Family Process 37:* 263–286.

Goldner, V. (1999). Morality and multiplicity: Perspectives on the treatment of violence in intimate life. *Journal of Marital and Family Therapy 25:* 325–336.

Goldner, V., Penn, P., Sheinberg, M., & Walker, G. (1990). Love and violence: Gender paradoxes in volatile attachments. *Family Process 29:* 343–364.

Goodman, E.S. (1973). Marriage counseling as science: Some research considerations. *The Family Coordinator 22:* 111–116.

Gottman, J.M. (1991). Predicting the longitudinal courses of marriage. *Journal of Marital and Family Therapy 17:* 3–7.

Gottman, J.M. (1994a). *What predicts divorce?* Hillsdale NJ: Lawrence Erlbaum Associates.

Gottman, J.M. (1994b). *Why marriages succeed or fail*. New York: Simon and Schuster.

Gottman, J.M. (1999). *The marriage clinic: A scientifically based marital therapy*. New York: W.W. Norton.

Gottman, J.M., Coan, J., Carrère, S., & Swanson, C. (1998). Predicting marital happiness and stability from newlywed interaction. *Journal of Marriage and the Family 60:* 5–22.

Greenberg, L.S., & Johnson, S.M. (1986). Emotionally focused couples therapy (pp. 253–278). In N.S. Jacobson & A.S. Gurman (eds.), *Clinical handbook of marital therapy*. New York: Guilford Press.

Greenberg, L.S., & Johnson, S.M. (1988). *Emotionally focused couple therapy*. New York: Guilford Press.

Greene, B.L. (ed.). (1965a). *The psychotherapies of marital disharmony*. New York: The Free Press.

Greene, B.L. (1965b). Introduction: A multi-operational approach to marital problems (pp. 1–14). In B.L. Greene (ed.), *The psychotherapies of marital disharmony*. New York: The Free Press.

Grych, J., & Fincham, F. (1990). Marital conflict and children's adjustment. *Psychological Bulletin 108:* 267–290.

Guerin, P.J., Jr. (1976). Family therapy: The first twenty five years (pp. 2–22). In P.J. Guerin, Jr. (ed.), *Family therapy and practice*. New York: Gardner Press.

Guerin, P.J., Jr., Fay, L.F., Burden, S.L., & Kautto, J.G. (1987). *The evaluation and treatment of marital conflict: A four-stage approach*. New York: Basic Books.

Guerney, B.G. (1977). *Relationship enhancement*. San Francisco: Jossey-Bass.

Guerney, B., Brock, G., & Coufal, J. (1986). Integrating marital therapy and enrichment: The Relationship Enhancement approach (pp. 151–172). In N.S. Jacobson & A.S. Gurman (eds.), *Clinical handbook of marital therapy*. New York: Guilford Press.

Guerney, B., & Maxson, P. (1990). Marital and family enrichment research: A decade review and look ahead. *Journal of Marriage and the Family 52:* 1127–1135.

Gurin, E., Veroff, J., & Feld, S. (1960). *Americans view their mental health*. New York: Basic Books.

Gurman, A.S. (1971). Group marital therapy: Clinical and empirical implications for outcome research. *International Journal of Group Psychotherapy 21:* 174–189.

Gurman, A.S. (1973a). Marital therapy: Emerging trends in research and practice. *Family Process 12:* 45–54.

Gurman, A.S. (1973b). The effects and effectiveness of marital therapy: A review of outcome research. *Family Process 12:* 145–170.

Gurman, A.S. (1978). Contemporary marital therapies: A critique and comparative analysis of psychoanalytic, behavioral and systems theory approaches (pp. 445–566). In T. Paolino & B. McCrady (eds.), *Marriage and marital therapy.* New York: Brunner/Mazel.

Gurman, A.S. (1979). Dimensions of marital therapy: A comparative analysis. *Journal of Marital and Family Therapy 5:* 5–16.

Gurman, A.S. (1981). Integrative marital therapy: Toward the development of an interpersonal approach (pp. 415–462). In S.H. Budman (ed.), *Forms of brief therapy.* New York: Guilford Press.

Gurman, A.S. (1982). Changing collusive patterns in marital therapy. *American Journal of Family Therapy 10:* 71–73.

Gurman, A.S. (1983). Family therapy research and the "New Epistemology." *Journal of Marital and Family Therapy 9:* 227–234.

Gurman, A.S. (1990). Integrating the life of an integrative family psychologist (pp. 250–266). In F. Kaslow (ed.), *Voices in family psychology* (Vol. 2). Newbury Park CA: Sage Publications.

Gurman, A.S. (1992). Integrative marital therapy: A time-sensitive model for working with couples (pp. 186–203). In S. Budman, M. Hoyt, & S. Friedman (eds.), *The first session in brief therapy.* New York: Guilford Press.

Gurman, A.S. (2001). Brief therapy and family/couple therapy: An essential redundancy. *Clinical Psychology: Science and Practice 8:* 51–65.

Gurman, A.S. (2002). Brief integrative marital therapy: A depth-behavioral approach (pp. 180–220). In A.S. Gurman & N.S. Jacobson (eds.), *Clinical handbook of couple therapy* (3rd ed.). New York: Guilford Press.

Gurman, A.S., & Jacobson, N.S. (1995). Therapy with couples: A coming of age (pp. 1–6). In N.S. Jacobson & A.S. Gurman (eds.), *Clinical handbook of couple therapy* (2nd ed.). New York: Guilford Press.

Gurman, A.S., & Jacobson, N.S. (eds.). (2002). *Clinical handbook of couple therapy* (3rd ed.). New York: Guilford Press.

Gurman, A.S., & Kniskern, D.P. (1977). Enriching research on marital enrichment programs. *Journal of Marriage and Family Counseling 3:* 3–11.

Gurman, A.S., & Kniskern, D.P. (1978a). Deterioration in marital and family therapy: Empirical, clinical and conceptual issues. *Family Process 17:* 3–20.

Gurman, A.S., & Kniskern, D.P. (1978b). Research on marital and family therapy: Progress, perspective, and prospect (pp. 817–901). In S.L. Garfield & A.E. Bergin (eds.), *Handbook of psychotherapy and behavior change* (2nd ed.). New York: John Wiley & Sons.

Gurman, A.S., & Kniskern, D.P. (1979). Marriage therapy and/or family therapy: What's in a name? *American Association for Marriage and Family Therapy Newsletter 10*(3): 1, 5–8.

Gurman, A.S., & Kniskern, D.P. (1981a). Family therapy outcome research: Knowns and unknowns (pp. 742–775). In A.S. Gurman & D.P. Kniskern (eds.), *Handbook of family therapy.* New York: Brunner/Mazel.

Gurman, A.S., & Kniskern, D.P. (eds.). (1981b). *Handbook of family therapy.* New York: Brunner/Mazel.

Gurman, A.S., & Kniskern, D.P. (1986). Commentary: Individual marital therapy—Have reports of your death been somewhat exaggerated? *Family Process 25:* 51–62.

Gurman, A.S., & Kniskern, D.P. (1992). The future of marital and family therapy. *Psychotherapy: Theory, Research, & Practice 29:* 65–71.

Gurman, A.S., Kniskern, D.P., & Pinsof, W.M. (1986). Process and outcome research in family and marital therapy (pp. 565–624). In A. Bergin & S. Garfield (eds.), *Handbook of psychotherapy and behavioral change* (3rd ed.). New York: John Wiley & Sons.

Gurman, A.S., & Knudson, R.M. (1978). Behavioral marriage therapy I: A psychodynamic-systems analysis and critique. *Family Process 17:* 121–138.

Gurman, A.S., & Razin, A.M. (1977). *Effective psychotherapy: A handbook of research.* New York: Pergamon Press.

Hahlweg, K., & Klann, N. (1997). The effectiveness of marital counseling in Germany: A contribution to health services research. *Journal of Family Psychology 11:* 410–421.

Hahlweg, K., & Markman, H.J. (1988). Effectiveness of behavioral marital therapy: Empirical status of behavioral techniques in preventing and alleviating distress. *Journal of Consulting and Clinical Psychology 56:* 440–447.

Haley, J. (1963). Marriage therapy. *Archives of General Psychiatry 8:* 213–234.

Haley, J. (1976). *Problem-solving therapy.* San Francisco: Jossey-Bass.

Haley, J. (1984). Marriage or family therapy. *American Journal of Family Therapy 12:* 3–14.

Halford, W.K. (1998). The ongoing evolution of behavioral couples therapy: Retrospect and prospect. *Clinical Psychology Review 18:* 613–633.

Halford, W.K., & Markman, H.J. (eds.). (1997). *Clinical handbook of marriage and couples intervention.* New York: John Wiley & Sons.

Halford, W.K., Sanders, M.R., & Behrens, B.C. (1994). Self-regulation in behavioral couples therapy. *Behavior Therapy 25:* 431–452.

Hamburg, S. (1996). Review of Jacobson & Gurman's *Clinical handbook of couple therapy* (2$^{nd}$ ed.). *Child and Family Behavior Therapy 18:* 55–60.

Hardy, K.V. (1991). The theoretical myth of sameness: A critical issue in family therapy training and treatment (pp. 74–93). In G.W. Saba, B.M. Karrer, & K.W. Hardy (eds.), *Minorities and family therapy.* New York: Haworth Press.

Hare-Mustin, R.T. (1978). A feminist approach to family therapy. *Family Process 17:* 181–194.

Hare-Mustin, R.T. (1987). The problem of gender in family therapy theory. *Family Process 26:* 15–27.

Hare-Mustin, R.T., & Marecek, J. (1994). Feminism & postmodernism: Dilemmas and points of resistance. *Dulwich Centre Newsletter 4:* 13–19.

Heiman, J., & LoPiccolo, J. (1988). *Becoming orgasmic.* New York: Prentice-Hall.

Hoffman, L. (1990). Constructing realities: An art of lenses. *Family Process 29:* 1–12.

Hudson, P., & O'Hanlon, W.H. (1992). *Rewriting love stories: Brief marital therapy.* New York: W.W. Norton.

Jackson, D.D. (1959). Family interaction, family homeostasis and some implications for conjoint family psychotherapy (pp. 122–

141). In J. Masserman (ed.), *Individual and family dynamics.* New York: Grune & Stratton.

Jackson, D.D. (1965a). Family rules: The marital quid pro quo. *Archives of General Psychiatry 12:* 589–594.

Jackson, D.D. (1965b). The study of the family. *Family Process 4:* 1–20.

Jacobson, N.S., & Addis, M.E. (1993). Research on couples and couples therapy: What do we know? Where are we going? *Journal of Consulting and Clinical Psychology 61:* 85–93.

Jacobson, N.S., & Christensen, A. (1996). *Integrative behavioral couple therapy.* New York: W.W. Norton.

Jacobson, N.S., & Gurman, A.S. (eds.). (1986). *Clinical handbook of marital therapy.* New York: Guilford Press.

Jacobson, N.S., & Gurman, A.S. (eds.). (1995). *Clinical handbook of couple therapy* (2$^{nd}$ ed.). New York: Guilford Press.

Jacobson, N.S., & Margolin, G. (1979). *Marital therapy: Strategies based on social learning and behavior exchange principles.* New York: Brunner/Mazel.

Jacobson, N.S., & Martin, B. (1976). Behavioral marriage therapy: Current status. *Psychological Bulletin 83:* 540–566.

Jacobson, N.S., & Truax, P. (1991). Clinical significance: A statistical approach to defining meaningful change in psychotherapy research. *Journal of Consulting and Clinical Psychology 58:* 12–19.

James, K., & MacKinnon, L. (1990). The "incestuous" family revisited: A critical analysis of family therapy myths. *Journal of Marital and Family Therapy 16:* 71–88.

James, K., & McIntyre, D. (1983). The reproduction of families: The social role of family therapy. *Journal of Marital and Family Therapy 9:* 119–129.

Johnson, S. (1986). Bonds or bargains: Relationship paradigms and their significance for marital therapy. *Journal of Marital and Family Therapy 12:* 259–267.

Johnson, S. (1996). *The practice of emotionally focused marital therapy.* New York: Brunner/Mazel.

Johnson, S.M. (1999). Emotionally focused couple therapy (pp. 13–41). In J. Donovan (ed.), *Short-term couple therapy*. New York: Guilford Press.

Johnson, S.M., & Greenberg, L.S. (1995). The emotionally focused approach to problems in adult attachment (pp. 121–146). In N.S. Jacobson & A.S. Gurman (eds.), *Clinical handbook of couple therapy* (2nd ed.). New York: Guilford Press.

Johnson, S.M., Hunsely, J., Greenberg, L., & Schindler, D. (1999). Emotionally focused couples therapy: Status and challenges. *Clinical Psychology: Science and Practice 6:* 67–79.

Johnson, S., & Lebow, J. (2000). The "coming of age" of couple therapy: A decade review. *Journal of Marital and Family Therapy 26:* 23–38.

Kanfer, F.H., & Phillips, J.S. (1970). *Learning foundations of behavior therapy*. New York: John Wiley & Sons.

Kaplan, H.S. (1974). *The new sex therapy*. New York: Brunner/Mazel.

Kaplan, H.S. (1983). *The evaluation of sexual disorders*. New York: Brunner/Mazel.

Kerr, M., & Bowen, M. (1988). *Family evaluation*. New York: W.W. Norton.

Kiecolt-Glaser, J.K., Fisher, L.D., Ogrocki, P., Stout, J.C., & Speicher, C.E. (1987). Marital quality, marital disruptions and immune function. *Psychosomatic Medicine 49:* 13–34.

L'Abate, L., & McHenry, S. (eds.). (1983). *Handbook of marital interventions*. New York: Grune & Stratton.

Laidlaw, R.W. (1957). The psychiatrist as marriage counselor (pp. 52–61). In C.E. Vincent (ed.), *Readings in marriage counseling*. New York: Crowell.

Laird, J. (1999). The politics of "smart marriage." *American Family Therapy Academy Newsletter 77*(Fall): 43–45.

Laird, J., & Green, R.J. (eds.). (1996). *Lesbians and gays in couples and families: A handbook for therapists*. San Francisco: Jossey-Bass.

Lambert, M.J., & Bergin, A.E. (1994). The effectiveness of psychotherapy (pp. 143–189). In A.E. Bergin & S.L. Garfield (eds.), *Handbook of psychotherapy and behavior change* (4th ed.). New York: John Wiley & Sons.

Lazloffy, T.A., & Hardy, K.V. (2000). Uncommon strategies for a common problem: Ad-dressing racism in family therapy. *Family Process 39:* 35–50.

Lebow, J.L. (1984). On the value of integrating approaches to family therapy. *Journal of Marital and Family Therapy 20:* 127–138.

Lebow, J. (1997). The integrative revolution in couple and family therapy. *Family Process 36:* 1–17.

Lebow, J.L., & Gurman, A.S. (1995). Research assessing couple and family therapy. *Annual Review of Psychology 46:* 27–57.

Lebow, J.L., & Gurman, A.S. (1998). Family systems and family psychology (pp. 473–496). In A.S. Bellak & M. Hersen (eds.), *Comprehensive clinical psychology* (Vol. 1). New York: Pergamon Press.

Lederer, W., & Jackson, D.D. (1968). *The mirages of marriage*. New York: W.W. Norton.

Leiblum, S., & Rosen, R. (eds.). (1989). *Principles and practices of sex therapy* (2nd ed.). New York: Guilford Press.

Leslie, G.R. (1964). Conjoint therapy in marriage counseling. *Journal of Marriage and the Family 26:* 65–71.

Lewis, J.M., & Gossett, J.T. (2000). *Disarming the past: How an intimate relationship can heal old wounds*. Phoenix, AZ: Zeig, Tucker & Co.

Libow, J. A., Raskin, P.A., & Caust, B.L. (1982). Feminist and family systems therapy: Are they irreconcilable? *The American Journal of Family Therapy 10:* 3–12.

Luborsky, L., Singer, B., & Luborsky, L. (1975). Comparative studies of psychotherapies: Is it true that "Everybody has won and all must have prizes?" *Archives of General Psychiatry 32:* 995–1000.

Madanes, C. (1980). Marital therapy when a symptom is presented by a spouse. *International Journal of Family Therapy 2:* 120–136.

Manus, G.I. (1966). Marriage counseling: A technique in search of a theory. *Journal of Marriage and the Family 28:* 449–453.

Markman, H.J. (2000). Personal communication.

Markman, H.J., Floyd, F.J., Stanley, S.M., & Storaasli, R.D. (1988). Prevention of marital distress: A longitudinal investigation. *Journal of Consulting and Clinical Psychology 56:* 210–217.

Markman, H.J., Renick, M.J., Floyd, F.J.,

Stanley, S.M., & Clements, M. (1993). Preventing marital distress through communication and conflict management training: A four and five year follow-up. *Journal of Consulting and Clinical Psychology 62:* 70–77.

Markman, H., Stanley, S., & Blumberg, S.L. (1994). *Fighting for your marriage.* San Francisco: Jossey-Bass.

Markowitz, L.M. (1994). The cross-currents of multiculturalism. *The Family Therapy Networker 18:* 27.

Martin, P.A. (1965). Treatment of marital disharmony by collaborative therapy (pp. 83–102). In B.L. Greene (ed.), *The psychotherapies of marital disharmony.* New York: The Free Press.

Martin, P.A. (1976). *A marital therapy manual.* New York: Brunner/Mazel.

McCarthy, B.W. (2002). Sexuality, sexual dysfunction, and couple therapy (pp. 629–652). In A.S. Gurman & N.S. Jacobson (eds.), *Clinical handbook of couple therapy* (3rd ed.). New York: Guilford Press.

McGoldrick, M. (1993). Ethnicity, cultural diversity, and normality (pp. 331–360). In F. Walsh (ed.), *Normal family processes* (2nd ed.). New York: Guilford Press.

McGoldrick, M., Pearce, J.K., & Giordano, J. (eds.). (1982). *Ethnicity and family therapy.* New York: Guilford Press.

Meissner, W.W. (1978). The conceptualization of marriage and family dynamics from a psychoanalytic perspective (pp. 25–88). In T. Paolino & B. McCrady (eds.), *Marriage and marital therapy.* New York: Brunner/Mazel.

Messer, S.B., & Warren, C.S. (1995). *Models of brief psychodynamic therapy: A comparative approach.* New York: Guilford Press.

Michaelson, R. (1963). An analysis of the changing focus of marriage counseling. Unpublished Doctoral Dissertation, University of Southern California.

Minuchin, S. (1998). Where is the family in narrative family therapy? *Journal of Marital and Family Therapy 24:* 397–403.

Mittelman, B. (1948). The concurrent analysis of married couples. *Psychiatric Quarterly 17:* 182–197.

Mohr, R. (2000). Reflections on Golden Pond (pp. 312–334). In P. Papp (ed.), *Couples on the fault line: New directions for therapists.* New York: Guilford Press.

Mudd, E.H. (1957). Knowns and unknowns in marriage counseling research. *Marriage and Family Living 19:* 75–81.

Nadelson, C.C. (1978). Marital therapy from a psychoanalytic perspective (pp. 89–164). In T. Paolino & B. McCrady (eds.), *Marriage and marital therapy.* New York: Brunner/Mazel.

Neal, J., Zimmerman, J.L., & Dickerson, V.C. (1999). Couples, culture, and discourse: A narrative approach (pp. 360–400). In J. Donovan (ed.), *Short-term couple therapy.* New York: Guilford Press.

Nerin, W.F. (1986). *Family reconstruction: Long day's journey into light.* New York: W.W. Norton.

Nichols, M.P. (1987). *The self in the system.* New York: Brunner/Mazel.

Nichols, M.P., & Schwartz, R.C. (1998). *Family therapy: Concepts and methods.* Boston: Allyn & Bacon.

Nichols, W.C. (1973). The field of marriage counseling: A brief overview. *The Family Coordinator 22:* 3–13.

Nichols, W.C. (1988). *Marital therapy: An integrated approach.* New York: Guilford Press.

Norcross, J.C., & Goldfried, M.R. (eds.). (1992). *Handbook of psychotherapy integration.* New York: Basic Books.

Oberndorf, C.P. (1931). Psychoanalysis of married couples. Paper presented at the American Psychiatric Association.

Oberndorf, C.P. (1934). Folie à deux. *International Journal of Psychoanalysis 15:* 14–24.

Oberndorf, C.P. (1938). Psychoanalysis of married couples. *Psychoanalytic Review 25:* 453–475.

Olson, D.H. (1970). Marital and family therapy: Integrative review and critique. *Journal of Marriage and the Family 32:* 501–538.

Olson, D.H. (1990). Marriage in perspective (pp. 402–419). In F.D. Fincham & T.N. Bradbury (eds.), *The psychology of marriage: Basic issues and applications.* New York: Guilford Press.

Olson, D.H., Russell, R.C.S., & Sprenkle, D.H. (1980). Marital and family therapy: A decade review. *Journal of Marriage and the Family 42:* 973–992.

Olson, D.H.L., & Sprenkle, D.H. (1976). Emerging trends in treating relationships.

*Journal of Marriage and Family Counseling* 2: 317–329.

Paolino, T., & McCrady, B. (eds.). (1978). *Marriage and marital therapy*. New York: Brunner/Mazel.

Papero, D. (1995). Bowen family systems and marriage (pp. 11–30). In N.S. Jacobson & A.S. Gurman (eds.), *Clinical handbook of couple therapy* (2nd ed.). New York: Guilford Press.

Papero, D.V. (2000). Bowen's systems theory (pp. 25–44). In F.M. Dattilio & L.J. Bevilacqua (eds.), *Comparative treatments for relationship dysfunction*. New York: Springer Publishing Company.

Papp, P. (1988). Couples (pp. 200–250). In M. Walters, B. Carter, P. Papp, & O. Silverstein (eds.), *The invisible web: Gender patterns in family relationships*. New York: Guilford Press.

Papp, P. (2000). Gender differences in depression: His or her depression (pp. 130–151). In P. Papp (ed.), *Couples on the fault line: New directions for therapists*. New York: Guilford Press.

Paul, N. (1969). The role of mourning and empathy in conjoint marital therapy (pp. 186–205). In G. Zuk & I. Boszormenyi-Nagy (eds.), *Family therapy and disturbed families*. Palo Alto CA: Science & Behavior Books.

Paul, N., & Paul, B. (1975). *A marital puzzle*. New York: W.W. Norton.

Perel, E. (2000). A tourist's view of marriage: Cross-cultural couples—challenges, choices and implications for therapy (pp. 178–204). In P. Papp (ed.), *Couples on the fault line: New directions for therapists*. New York: Guilford Press.

Pinderhughes, E. (1989). *Understanding race, ethnicity, and power: The key to efficacy in clinical practice*. New York: The Free Press.

Pinsof, W.M. (1981). Family therapy process research (pp. 699–741). In A.S. Gurman & D.P. Kniskern (eds.), *Handbook of family therapy*. New York: Brunner/Mazel.

Pinsof, W.M. (1983). Integrative problem-centered therapy: Toward the synthesis of family and individual psychotherapies. *Journal of Marital and Family Therapy 9*: 19–35.

Pinsof, W.M. (1995). *Integrative problem-centered therapy*. New York: Basic Books.

Pinsof, W.M. (1999). Building love and transforming conflict in couples therapy. Workshop presented at the Annual Conference of the American Association for Marital and Family Therapy, Chicago, October.

Pinsof, W.M., & Wynne, L.C. (1995). The efficacy of marital and family therapy: An empirical overview, conclusions, and recommendations. *Journal of Marital and Family Therapy 21*: 585–613.

Pittman, F. (1989). Remembering Virginia. *The Family Therapy Networker 13*(1): 34–35.

Raffa, H., Sypek, J., & Vogel, W. (1990). Commentary on reviews of "outcome" studies of family and marital psychotherapy. *Contemporary Family Therapy 12*: 65–73.

Rait, D. (1988). Survey results. *The Family Therapy Networker 12*(1): 52–56.

Roberto-Forman, L. (2002). Transgenerational marriage therapy (pp. 118–147). In A.S. Gurman & N.S. Jacobson (eds.), *Clinical handbook of couple therapy*. New York: Guilford Press.

Sager, C.J. (1966). The development of marriage therapy: An historical review. *American Journal of Orthopsychiatry 36*: 458–467.

Sager, C.J. (1967a). The conjoint session in marriage therapy. *American Journal of Psychoanalysis 27*: 139–146.

Sager, C.J. (1967b). Transference in conjoint treatment of married couples. *Archives of General Psychiatry 16*: 185–193.

Sager, C.J. (1976). *Marriage contracts and couple therapy*. New York: Brunner/Mazel.

Sager, C.J. (1981). Couples therapy and marriage contracts (pp. 85–130). In A.S. Gurman & D.P. Kniskern (eds.), *Handbook of family therapy*. New York: Brunner/Mazel.

Sager, C.J., Kaplan, H.S., Gundlach, R.H., Kremer, M., Lenz, R., & Royce, J.R. (1971). The marriage contract. *Family Process 10*: 311–326.

Sander, F.M. (1979). *Individual and family therapy: Toward an integration*. New York: Jason Aronson.

Sanders, G. (2000). Men together: Working with gay couples in contemporary times (pp. 222–256). In P. Papp (ed.), *Couples on the fault line: New directions for therapists*. New York: Guilford Press.

Satir, V. (1964). *Conjoint family therapy.* Palo Alto: Science and Behavior Books.

Satir, V.M. (1965). Conjoint marital therapy (pp. 121–133). In B.L. Greene (ed.), *The psychotherapies of marital disharmony.* New York: The Free Press.

Satir, V. (1972). *Peoplemaking.* Palo Alto, CA: Science and Behavior Books.

Scharff, J.S. (1995). Psychoanalytic marital therapy (pp. 164–193). In N.S. Jacobson & A.S. Gurman (eds.), *Clinical handbook of couple therapy* (2$^{nd}$ ed.). New York: Guilford Press.

Scharff, J.S., & Bagnini, C. (2002). Object relations couple therapy (pp. 59–85). In A.S. Gurman & N.S. Jacobson (eds.), *Clinical handbook of couple therapy* (3$^{rd}$ ed.). New York: Guilford Press.

Scharff, D.E., & Scharff, J.S. (1991). *Object relations couple therapy.* New York: Jason Aronson.

Schnarch, D. (1991). *Constructing the sexual crucible.* New York: W.W. Norton.

Schnarch, D. (2001). The therapist in the crucible: Early developments in a new paradigm of sexual and marital therapy (pp. 43–56). In S. McDaniel, D. Lusterman, & C. Philpot (eds.), *Casebook for integrating family therapy.* Washington DC: American Psychological Association.

Schwartz, R.C. (1995). *Internal family systems therapy.* New York: Guilford Press.

Schwartz, R.C., & Johnson, S.M. (2000). Commentary: Does couple and family therapy have emotional intelligence? *Family Process 39:* 29–33.

Segal, L. (1991). Brief therapy: The MRI approach (pp. 171–199). In A.S. Gurman & D.P. Kniskern (eds.), *Handbook of family therapy* (Vol. 2). New York: Brunner/Mazel.

Segraves, R.T. (1978). Conjoint marital therapy: A cognitive behavioral model. *Archives of General Psychiatry 35:* 450–455.

Segraves, R.T. (1982). *Marital therapy: A combined psychodynamic behavioral approach.* New York: Plenum Press.

Shadish, W.R., Montgomery, L.M., Wilson, P., Wilson, M.R., Bright, I., & Okwumabua, T. (1993). Effects of family and marital psychotherapies: A meta-analysis. *Journal of Consulting and Clinical Psychology 61:* 992–1002.

Shadish, W.R., Ragsdale, R., Glaser, R.R., & Montgomery, L.M. (1995). The efficacy and effectiveness of marital and family therapy: A perspective from meta-analysis. *Journal of Marital and Family Therapy 21:* 345–360.

Shields, C.G., Wynne, L.C., McDaniel, S.H., & Gawinski, B.A. (1994). The marginalization of family therapy: A historical and continuing problem. *Journal of Marital and Family Therapy 20:* 117–138.

Sholevar, G.P. (ed.). (1981). *The handbook of marriage and marital therapy.* New York: Spectrum.

Siegel, J. (1992). *Repairing intimacy: An object relations approach to couples therapy.* Northvale NJ: Jason Aronson.

Simmons, D.S., & Doherty, W.J. (1995). Defining who we are and what we do: Clinical practice patterns of marriage and family therapists in Minnesota. *Journal of Marital and Family Therapy 21:* 3–16.

Skynner, A.C.R. (1976). *Systems of family and marital psychotherapy.* New York: Brunner/Mazel.

Skynner, A.C.R. (1980). Recent developments in marital therapy. *Journal of Family Therapy 2:* 271–296.

Skynner, A.C.R. (1981). An open-systems, group analytic approach to family therapy (pp. 39–84). In A.S. Gurman & D.P. Kniskern (eds.), *Handbook of family therapy.* New York: Brunner/Mazel.

Slater, S. (1995). Persistent stressors in lesbian couples' lives (pp. 37–62). In *The lesbian family life cycle.* New York: The Free Press.

Snyder, D.K. (1999). Affective reconstruction in the context of a pluralistic approach to couple therapy. *Clinical Psychology: Science and Practice 6:* 348–365.

Snyder, D.K., & Wills, R.M. (1989). Behavioral versus insight-oriented marital therapy: Effects on individual and interspousal functioning. *Journal of Consulting and Clinical Psychology 57:* 39–46.

Snyder, D.K., Wills, R.M., & Grady-Fletcher, A. (1991). Long-term effectiveness of behavioral versus insight-oriented marital therapy: A four-year follow-up study. *Journal of Consulting and Clinical Psychology 59:* 138–144.

Solomon, M.F. (1989). *Narcissism and intimacy.* New York: W.W. Norton.

Sprenkle, D.H., & Storm, C.L. (1983). Divorce therapy outcome research: A substantive and methodological review. *Journal of Marital and Family Therapy 9:* 239–258.

Stanley, S.M., Blumberg, S.L., & Markman, H.J. (1999). Helping couples fight for their marriages: The PREP approach (pp. 74–89). In R. Berger & M. Hannah (eds.), *Handbook of preventive approaches in couple therapy.* New York: Brunner/Mazel.

Stanley, S.M., Bradbury, T.N., & Markman, H.J. (2000). Structural flaws in the bridge from basic research on marriage to interventions for couples. *Journal of Marriage and the Family 62:* 256–264.

Stanley, S.M., Markman, H.J., St. Peters, M., & Leber, D. (1995). Strengthening marriages and preventing divorce: New directions in prevention research. *Family Relations 44:* 392–401.

Stricker, G. (1994). Reflections on psychotherapy integration. *Clinical Psychology: Science and Practice 1:* 3–12.

Stricker, G., & Gold, J.R. (eds.). (1993). *Comprehensive handbook of psychotherapy integration.* New York: Plenum Press.

Stuart, R.B. (1969). Operant-interpersonal treatment of marital discord. *Journal of Consulting and Clinical Psychology 33:* 675–682.

Stuart, R.B. (1980). *Helping couples change: A social learning approach to marital therapy.* New York: Guilford Press.

Thoreson, C.E., & Mahoney, M.J. (eds.). (1974). *Behavioral self-control.* New York: Holt, Rinehart & Winston.

Walters, M., Carter, B., Papp, P., & Silverstein, O. (1988). *The invisible web: Gender patterns in family relationships.* New York: Guilford Press.

Watson, A.S. (1963). The conjoint psychotherapy of married partners. *American Journal of Orthopsychiatry 33:* 912–922.

Watson, D.C., & Tharp, R.G. (1972). *Self-directed behavior: Self-modification for personal adjustment.* Monterey CA: Brooks/Cole.

Watzlawick, P. (ed.). (1984). *The invented reality: How do we know what we believe we know?* New York: W.W. Norton.

Weeks, G., & Hof, L. (1987). *Integrating sex and marital therapy.* New York: Brunner/Mazel.

Weiner-Davis, M. (1992). *Divorce-busting.* New York: Summit Books.

Weiss, R.L., Birchler, G.R., & Vincent, J.P. (1974). Contractual models for negotiation training in dyads. *Journal of Marriage and Family 36:* 321–330.

Wells, R.A., & Gianetti, V.J. (1986a). Individual marital therapy: A critical reappraisal. *Family Process 25:* 43–51.

Wells, R.A., & Gianetti, V.J. (1986b). Rejoinder: Whither marital therapy? *Family Process 25:* 62–65.

Whisman, M.A., Dixon, A.E., & Johnson, B. (1997). Therapists' perspectives of couple problems and treatment issues in couple therapy. *Journal of Family Psychology 11:* 361–366.

Whisman, M.A., & Snyder, D.K. (1997). Evaluating and improving the efficacy of conjoint couple therapy (pp. 679–693). In W.K. Halford & H.J. Markman (eds.), *Handbook of marriage and couples intervention.* New York: John Wiley & Sons.

White, M. (1986/1987). Couple therapy: 'Urgency for sameness or appreciation of difference.' *Dulwich Centre Review/Summer:* 11–13.

White, M. (1988). The externalizing of the problem and the re-authoring of lives and relationships. *Dulwich Centre Newsletter/Summer:* 3–21.

White, M. (1991). Deconstruction and therapy. *Dulwich Centre Newsletter 3:* 21–40.

White, M., & Epston, D. (1990). *Narrative means to therapeutic ends.* New York: W.W. Norton.

Wile, D.B. (1981). *Couples therapy: A nontraditional approach.* New York: John Wiley & Sons.

Willi, J. (1982). *Couples in collusion.* Claremont CA: Hunter, House.

Wills, R.M., Faitler, S.L., & Snyder, D.K. (1987). Distinctiveness of behavioral versus insight-oriented marital therapy: An empirical analysis. *Journal of Consulting and Clinical Psychology 55:* 685–690.

Wincze, J., & Barlow, D. (1996). *Enhancing sexuality: Client workbook.* New York: Gray Wind Publications.

Wynne, L.C. (1983). Family research and family therapy: A reunion? *Journal of Marital and Family Therapy 9:* 113–117.

Young, J.E. (1994). *Cognitive therapy for personality disorders: A schema-focused approach.* Sarasota FL: Professional Resource Press.

Zimmerman, J.L., & Dickerson, V.C. (1993a). Bringing forth the restraining influence of pattern in couples therapy (pp. 194–215). In S. Gilligan & R. Price (eds.), *Therapeutic conversations.* New York: W.W. Norton.

Zimmerman, J.L., & Dickerson, V.C. (1993b). Separating couples from restraining patterns and the relationship discourse that supports them. *Journal of Marital and Family Therapy 19:* 403–413.

Zimmerman, J.L., & Dickerson, V.C. (1994). Using a narrative metaphor: Implications for theory and clinical practice. *Family Process 33:* 233–245.

Manuscript received August 16, 2000; final revision submitted January 7, 2002; accepted January 10, 2002.

# Marriage in the 20th Century: A Feminist Perspective

*A defining feature of the 20th century in Western civilization was a profound change in the roles women play in both private and public life. The field of couple therapy was influenced by that change and, to a limited extent, participated in it. I will argue that the field has avoided fully embracing the principles of feminism that generated the social changes in gender and marital roles, settling instead for a more token acknowledgment that gender means* something, *without wanting to specify what that* something is. *In responding to the other articles in this issue, I make the case that the connection between gender and power in marriage needs to be more fully integrated, in the theory, research, and treatment of couples.*

*Fam Proc 41:261–268, 2002*

CREATURES of habit and routine that we are, it is occasionally useful to take a step back and try to get a broader view of things. The three major articles written for this issue attempt to provide that broader view to the topics of marriage, marital research and couple therapy. In doing so, the authors have exam-

ined a wealth of scholarship. They have discerned patterns and trends in what has been deemed real, meaningful, and desirable about couple relationships. Some of their conclusions are compelling; others are provocative. The ideas presented in this issue will certainly stimulate conversations among colleagues about future directions in couple therapy and research on couples, which was surely the central goal of the Editor for this special issue of the journal.

However, even broad views can miss important elements of a gestalt. As postmodernism argues, we see only what we are prepared to believe. I read these three articles prepared to believe most of what the authors had to say, but because of my own point of view within the field, I was also prepared to see things that the authors either did not see, or saw quite differently. Regarding the meaning of gender in couple relationships, particularly the linkage between power and gender, I think these articles demonstrate two kinds of errors. The first error, demonstrated by Gurman and Fraenkel, is to acknowledge that gender is relevant, but then to move rapidly from defining and exploring the problem to declaring it solved. The second error, demonstrated in the article by Gottman and Notarius, and in the one by Pinsof, is to see elements of the problem without fully recognizing it as a significant and coherent issue.

## GENDER AND COUPLE THERAPY

Gurman and Fraenkel define the current period (1986–present) of couple therapy as one of "Refinement, Extension, Diversification and Integration" (p. 220), noting that the synergistic forces of feminism, multiculturalism and postmodernism forced both theorists and practitioners of couple therapy to recognize the importance of context in determining what is believed to be real or true. Unfortunately, with respect to feminism, their article demonstrates little acknowledgment of either the refinement, extension, or integration of feminist thinking into couple therapy. The impact of feminism on the field has itself gone through several stages, only one of which is thoroughly addressed by Gurman and Fraenkel. The feminist *critique* of couple and family therapy was but the first stage of incorporating gender as a major organizing construct in the field. This stage can be traced back to the late 1970s (fully a decade after the current women's movement began to challenge the meanings ascribed to gender in the broader culture) when Hare-Mustin (1978) first called family and couple therapists to account for being essentially conservative and homeostatic regarding the roles of women within marriage. Since then, the incorporation of gender into couple therapy has followed the same interwoven processes that resulted in gender becoming a major focus of change in society as a whole: critique, advocacy, resistance, reformation.

By the early 1980s the feminist critique was appearing in workshops on the programs of national conferences, and some senior women in the field organized the Women's Project in Family Therapy (Walters, Carter, Papp & Silverstein, 1988). During the mid-1980s, two important invitational conferences were held in Connecticut (known as the Stonehenge conferences after the Inn where they took place). These conferences brought together a diverse group of 60 or so women family therapists who had begun to think, write, teach, and practice about how gender influenced the behavior of their clients, the way they construed clients' problems, and the very practice of couple therapy. The reformation of couple therapy had begun.

Feminists began not only to critique but to advocate—for gender-focused courses in training curricula, for a feminist-oriented journal of family and couple therapy, for inclusion of gender as a category of social analysis as meaningful as the category of generation (Goldner, 1988). Like all social revolutions, the transformation that feminists were advocating for the field was not universally applauded. From the beginning of the critique there was resistance, which took the form of assertions that to apply feminist principles to the practice of couple therapy was itself a form of sexism and, further, that it was a violation of the ideal of therapeutic neutrality. Carefully and persistently feminists challenged the premise that therapeutic neutrality was possible, making the case that neutrality is implicitly supportive of the status quo, which in a sexist society, means that neutrality is an inherently pro-sexist position (Hare-Mustin, 1980). A number of authors drew attention to the issue of wife battering as an example of a situation in which therapeutic neutrality could be particularly devastating, leaving a battered woman to draw the conclusion that she was as responsible for her victimization as her partner (Almeida, 1993; Bograd, 1984). Slowly, the zeitgeist of the field began to change, and by the late 1980s, family therapists were generally accepting the idea that gender ought to be considered as a factor in trying to understand the constraints that prevent couples from solving their problems.

In the past decade or so, the writing about gender and couple therapy has shifted away from critique and toward the specification of exactly how gender influences the ways that men and women experience their problems and conceptualize their appropriate roles within their relationships. What began as a critique evolved into an exploration of how feminist principles could be applied to the theories and practices of couple therapy. This has proved to be a complex and arduous process. Feminists could easily agree that women are disadvantaged by the structure of heterosexual marriage, and that couple therapy has done little to address that disadvantage; but specifying how to redress gender inequities in marriage and other committed relationships has proven to be a thornier problem, about which there is still no universal agreement. Nonetheless, a fair number of writers have been offering suggestions about how to apply feminist principles to the practices of couple therapy in order to transform those relationships rather than just help them to fit better into the prevailing paradigm of marriage (for example, Goodrich, 1991; Goodrich, Rampage, Ellman & Halstead, 1988; Knudson-Martin & Mahoney, 1996, 1998; Larson, Hammond, & Harper, 1998; Rabin, 1996; Rampage, 1995, 1998).

As an intellectual project in family and couple therapy, feminist revisionism in the past decade has lost the momentum described by Sprenkle (1990) in his review of family therapy in the 1980s. Several factors have contributed to this. A number of early voices have left the field, retired, or moved on to other projects. Practitioners who were never comfortable with close scrutiny of gender as a therapeutic variable have been eager to define the problem as solved. Therapists, as well as clients, have been willing to accept the tiniest token of change—he talks to her for a few minutes a day, she opens her own checking account—as an adequate response to gender inequities in marriage. Gender has been subsumed under the larger umbrella of diversity. The economics of the field have pushed practitioners in the direction of concrete, behavioral solutions to only those problems that can easily be described on a symptom checklist. Finally, couple therapy has not been immune from the backlash against feminism that Susan Faludi (1991) documented in other domains of society.

## Feminism versus Genderism

Current discourse in couple therapy has largely replaced feminism with a less politically charged interest in gender effects (Philpot & Brooks, 1995; Snyder, 1992). As a consequence of this transformation, participation has expanded from a small group composed almost entirely of female feminists to include both men and women, many of whom would not characterize themselves as feminist, but are nonetheless interested in the ways that gender influences how clients construe their problems, and how they enact solutions to those problems. The broadening base of therapists interested in gender issues has had multiple effects. On the one hand, it has legitimized gender as a clinical issue. It would be difficult in the year 2002 to find a therapist willing to assert that gender has *no* impact in psychotherapy. On the other hand, the broader acceptance of gender as a legitimate variable in therapy has considerably diluted the original focus of the critique, i.e. that heterosexual marriage is a relationship in which power counts heavily, and in which power is most often distributed unevenly, in a way that favors husbands over wives. Many of the practitioners who currently write about gender prefer to identify themselves as "non-sexist" or "gender sensitive" rather than feminist. In general terms, these labels seem to indicate a belief that gender has *some* consequence in male-female relationships, but also an unwillingness to view such relationships as having significant power dimensions. Consequently, gender issues in couple therapy, though more widely accepted as relevant, have often been removed from the political or power context in which feminists placed them.

This state of affairs falls considerably short of where feminists were hoping couple therapy would be at the start of the new millennium, and certainly far from the integration that Gurman and Fraenkel so optimistically report. If gender differences do not reflect an underlying social construct, such as power, then they must be either coincidental, biologically determined, or a matter of personal preference. None of these hypotheses explain why large numbers of *women,* but very few men, have been persistently, passionately, urgently pressing for changes in these arrangements for the past four decades. Women have pressed for the change because women have borne the weight of the inequities woven into the very fabric of heterosexual marriage. Shifting the burdens of marriage into something more closely resembling parity is what feminism is about, and that task is far from accomplished. Without an analysis of power at its very core, "gender-sensitive" or "non-sexist" therapy is mere pretense or (worse yet) trite, essentialist pap on the order of *Men are from Mars— Women are from Venus* (Gray, 1994).

## RESEARCH FINDINGS ON GENDER AND COUPLES

Gottman and Notarius describe in great detail (perhaps too great to be appreciated by the nonresearcher) the vast array of research studies that have investigated a myriad of questions about how marriage works and why it so often does not. The work of couple therapists has been greatly enhanced in the last decade by the availability of research data describing in considerable detail what kinds of couple transactions are associated with greater satisfaction in the relationship and, conversely, what kinds of transactions lead to deterioration and divorce.

While actually referencing many studies that have found gender differences to be relevant, Gottman and Notarius offer no general hypothesis about what it is *about* gender that is relevant for marital satisfaction. The fact that gender differences identified by research do not support the existence of completely universal and non-overlapping categories of maleness and femaleness in the way Parsons (and others) imagined, does not mean that *no* gender differences exist, or that what differences do exist are arbitrary or meaningless. Gender identity (as contrasted to biologically determined sexual identity) may be socially constructed, but that does not mean that it is trivial or ephemeral. Instead, it may mean that our understanding of gender needs to be refined by addressing more subtle questions, such as "What are the conditions under which couples manifest behaviors, cognitions, and affect that are associated with stereotypic gender roles?" and, "What are the relative costs for men and women who conform to those roles?"

Actually, the gender-related findings noted by Gottman and Notarius *do* seem to fall into a coherent pattern. The findings include the following: "balance in husband-wife power was related to marital quality" (p. 174); "egalitarian couples had the highest . . . marital satisfaction" (p. 174); "men display a more coercive style in resolving marital conflict, while women display a more affiliative style" (p. 174); "the escalation sequence of men rejecting influence from their wives predicted subsequent divorce" (p. 175); "Across couple types, marital satisfaction was associated with interactions confirming equality between partners" (p. 176); "there is a precipitous drop in marital quality within one year after the birth of the first child; people revert to stereotypic gender roles; ... fathers withdraw into work; and marital conversation and sex sharply decrease" (p. 172); "There is extensive literature that indicates, for men, marriage offers health-buffering effects ... and that women are more likely to experience health-related problems if the marriage is distressed" (p. 189); "The power dimension of violence suggests a systematic use of violence to intimidate and control the abused wife" (p. 101); "husbands who had less power were more physically abusive toward their wives" (p. 101). A reasonable conclusion to draw from these findings is that marriages in which the principle of equality between partners animates their everyday transactions are more satisfying (and less dangerous) than relationships in which partners struggle for power, or in which too much control is vested in one person.

Furthermore, equality cannot be taken for granted. Even those young couples who establish routines that equitably distribute the burdens and rewards of being in a committed relationship find that the arrival of children creates formidable pressures to fall back into more stereotypic, and far less satisfying patterns. That this pressure is related to gender is strongly suggested by research finding that long-term gay and lesbian relationships are less marked by traditional gender roles than heterosexual couples (Cardell, Finn, & Maracek, 1981; Harry, 1984).

### THE FUTURE OF MARRIAGE AND OTHER PAIR-BONDS

In his article, Pinsof suggests that merely trying to perfect our methods of couple therapy in the hope that this will somehow improve the sturdiness of the institution of marriage is tantamount to changing the arrangement of deck chairs on the Titanic—an intervention doomed to fail, because it is aimed at the wrong problem. Certainly there is room for improvement in how we help couples solve their problems. But Pinsof says that it is society's very definition of marriage (and our implicit support for that definition) that constrains us from more effective interventions. He points out a host of emerging realities about couple relationships. Most of us are all too familiar with the statistics he cites about the divorce rate in this country hovering at 50%. But not only are couples ending their marriages in higher frequencies than ever, in increasing numbers they are also entering into coupled relationships that exist outside the structure of traditional marriage. Young couples who cohabitate prior to marrying; older couples who cohabitate rather than marry and give up Social Security benefits; gay, lesbian, and transgendered couples who are restricted from marrying by archaic and discriminatory state laws—these and other groups form an increasing proportion of the people in this society who choose to affiliate as couples, but are not legally married. Furthermore, a significant number of children will be born to or adopted by such couples, and their lives will be deeply impacted by the success their parents have in maintaining a viable and stable relationship. Instead of decrying these various forms of coupling for undermining marriage as an institution, Pinsof invites us to recognize that they represent legitimate variations of pair-bonding, and to think of how we as therapists can support and strengthen the relationships that they encompass.

Expanding the definition of what constitutes "legitimate" coupling—rather than trying to get couples to fit themselves into the one constraining and archaic form available—has great merit. If couples are choosing not to marry, or not to stay married, we should consider the possibility that it is the institution, rather than the people, that needs to be changed. Certainly making it possible for gay couples who *want* to marry to do so would be a simple and straightforward social intervention that would end a legal unfairness that impairs the ability of gay couples to form stable unions and provide the security of two legal parents for their children.

But more is needed than merely an expansion of the definitions of who can marry and what constitutes "legitimate" coupling. In analyzing the reasons for the rapid increase in the divorce rate during the third quarter of the 20th century, Pinsof cites correlational data linking escalating divorce rates, greater availability of effective contraceptives, and increased participation in the paid work force by women. He stops short, however, of following these data to their most obvious conclusion: having once achieved control over their own reproduction, and freedom from economic dependence on their husbands, many, many women concluded that there was not a good enough reason left to stay married. The increase in the divorce rate has largely been driven by women who refuse to stay in marriages they regard as oppressive, in which they carry more of the burden but receive less of the benefit than their husbands.

The divorce rate rose at the end of the last century at precisely the same time that women's expectations for their own lives rose. This general rise in expectations has had profound implications for what women want of their partners. As women have come to expect themselves to manage both paid work and family work they expect their husbands, in turn, to increase their participation in both the routine tasks of family and home, and the emotional tasks of maintaining a close and satisfying partner relationship. In other words, women have been hoping to change the very institution of marriage. It may be, in large part, this very hope that accounts for the continued popularity of

marriage in the face of the bleak statistics about divorce. Had these hopes been entirely disappointed, the divorce rate would still be climbing. But slowly, unevenly, and sometimes reluctantly many men *have* adapted their expectations of marriage to be more compatible with the changes women have made in their lives. Many husbands have learned to provide practical care to their own offspring, to change diapers, and to juggle work and doctor's visits when children are sick. To a considerably smaller extent, they have agreed to do housework. They do accept that marriage to a woman who assumes she is your equal partner means having to collaborate on almost every decision you make, from whether to take a job in a different city to whose turn it is to do dishes.

Taking a historical view of even a few hundred years makes it apparent that the institution of marriage has undergone more change in the past 40 years than in the previous millennium. Even now, the changes are more informal than formal, and they are far from universal. The fact that these changes have been disruptive, that there has been resistance, and that some marriages have not had the resilience to survive, does not prove that the changes have been bad. In general, the most oppressive constraints of marriage (inflexible gender-determined roles, unequal distribution of privilege and responsibilities) have yielded somewhat to the wider trends toward democracy, equality, fairness, and flexibility taking place on every level of this society. Still, in many marriages (particularly once children arrive, thus accounting for lower rates of marital satisfaction from that point on), these changes are more theoretical than practiced. Until the normative practices of marriage consistently support the goal of maximizing *both* partners' satisfaction through collaboration and cooperation, the divorce rate is unlikely to abate significantly.

## CONCLUSION

There is no reason to suppose that we are now situated at the endpoint in the evolution of couple relationships, couple therapy, or research on couples. Therefore we must be circumspect in asserting what we believe to be true, knowing that our understanding is as informed by the context of our times, as have all the understandings handed down to us. The authors of these three articles have provided a useful guide to comprehending how we have come to know what we know about couple therapy and research on marriage. They point us to a number of possible changes in what we might deem to be true about these topics in the future.

One change that feminists are still hoping to achieve is to define explicitly marriage and other adult pair-bonding relationships as relationships of *equals*. Were family therapy fully to embrace this goal, then we would routinely help couples recognize and untangle the conundrums they create whenever the balance of that equality is disturbed. We would challenge every assertion of privilege based on gender.

Thanks largely to the success of the movement toward gender equality in this society, those obstacles to true equality in partner relationships that yet remain are often subtle, sometimes even unintended. They exist not so much in the explicit beliefs that couples have about fairness and equality, but because the vast majority of adults in this society believe in these principles as a matter of course. Rather, the obstacles to gender equality that remain are mostly hidden in the assumptions our clients make about themselves and each other, and implicit in the habits of behavior in which they engage without reflection. Therefore, our work must deconstruct the biases of those assumptions,

and invite reflection on the unintended consequences of behavioral habits that are inconsistent with the values of respect, fairness, and equality. We must accept as axiomatic that gender and power remain closely linked, and be attentive to even the smallest transaction between the men and women we see in couple therapy if it links privilege and gender.

We do not, any of us, have the luxury of standing outside the social transformation taking place around the meaning of gender. As therapists we too make assumptions and have habits informed by gender, and those assumptions and habits come with us into the consultation room. It is incumbent on us, because of the unique role we play in the lives of the couples we see as clients, to examine those assumptions carefully, to consider the implications of those habits rather than consoling ourselves that they are coincidental or inconsequential. The more *our* assumptions and practices are consistent with the very same values of respect, fairness and equality that we seek to promote in the relationships of our clients, the more likely it is that we will be truly useful to them.

## REFERENCES

Almeida, R. (1993). Unexamined assumptions and service delivery systems: Feminist theory and racial exclusions. *Journal of Feminist Family Therapy 5:* 3–23.

Bograd, M. (1984). Family systems approaches to wife battering: A feminist critique. *American Journal of Orthopsychiatry 54:* 558–568.

Cardell, M., Finn, S., & Maracek, J. (1981). Sex-role identity, sex-role behavior, and satisfaction in heterosexual, lesbian and male gay couples. *Psychology of Women Quarterly 5:* 488–494.

Faludi, S. (1991). *Backlash: The undeclared war against American women.* New York: Crown Publishing.

Goldner, V. (1988). Generation and gender:

Normative and covert hierarchies. *Family Process 27:* 17–31.

Goodrich, T.J. (1991). *Women and power: Perspectives for family therapy.* New York: W.W. Norton.

Goodrich, T.J., Rampage, C., Ellman, B., & Halstead, K. (1988). *Feminist family therapy: A casebook.* New York: W.W. Norton.

Gottman, J.M., & Notarius, C.I. (2002). Marital research in the 20th century, and a research agenda for the 21st century. *Family Process 41:* 159–197.

Gray, J. (1994). *Men are from Mars—Women are from Venus.* New York: Harper-Collins.

Gurman, A.S. & Fraenkel, P. (2002). A history of couple therapy: A millennial review. *Family Process 41:* 199–260.

Hare-Mustin, R.T. (1978). A feminist approach to family therapy. *Family Process 17:* 181–194.

Hare-Mustin, R.T. (1980). Family therapy may be dangerous to your health. *Professional Psychology 11:* 935–938.

Harry, J. (1984). *Gay couples.* New York: Praeger Publishers.

Knudson-Martin, C., & Mahoney, A.R. (1996). Gender dilemma and myth in the construction of marital bargains: Issues for marital therapy. *Family Process 35:* 137–153.

Knudson-Martin, C., & Mahoney, A.R. (1998). Language and processes in the construction of equality in new marriages. *Family Relations 47:* 81–91.

Larson, J., Hammond, C., & Harper, J. (1998). Perceived equity and intimacy in marriage. *Journal of Marital and Family Therapy 24:* 487–506.

Philpot, C., & Brooks, G. (1995). Inter-gender communication and gender-sensitive family therapy (pp. 303–325). In R. Mikesell, D. Lusterman, & S. McDaniels (eds.), *Integrating family therapy: Handbook of family psychology and systems theory.* Washington DC: American Psychological Association.

Pinsof, W.M. (2002). The death of "Till death us do part": The transformation of pair-bonding in the 20th century in Western civilization. *Family Process 41:* 135–157.

Rabin, C. (1996). *Equal partners, good friends: Empowering couples through therapy.* London: Routledge.

Rampage, C. (1995). Gendered aspects of marital therapy (pp. 261–273). In N. S. Jacobson & A. S. Gurman (eds.), *Clinical handbook of couple therapy* (2nd ed.). New York: Guilford Press.

Rampage, C. (1998). Feminist couple therapy (pp. 353–370). In F. Dattilio (ed.), *Case studies in couple and family therapy.* New York: Guilford Press.

Snyder, M. (1992). A gender-informed model of couple and family therapy: Relationship enhancement therapy. *Contemporary Family Therapy 14:* 15–31.

Sprenkle, D. (1990). Continuity and change. *Journal of Marital and Family Therapy 16:* 337–340.

Walters, M., Carter, B., Papp, P., & Silverstein, O. (1988). *The invisible web: Gender patterns in family relationships.* New York: Guilford Press.

# African American Marriage in the 20th Century*

ELAINE B. PINDERHUGHES, MSW†

*It is not possible to understand African American marriages fully without attention to the social, economic, racial, and historical factors that have stressed male–female relationships beyond those stresses experienced by majority couples. I propose that the societal projection process (Bowen, 1978) has entrapped African Americans in ways that have continually and severely strained their marital and couple relationships. These experiences, and the ways in which African Americans have responded to them, have created a vulnerability that is compounded by societal shifts and changes, and is manifest in the precipitous decline of marriages at a rate higher than that found in all other racial groups in the U.S. I will examine the state of African American marriages in this cultural context, with specific attention to the effects of the unequal sex ratio, socioeconomic conditions, and overstressed male–female relationships. I will then discuss implications and offer suggestions for therapists who work with this population.*

*Fam Proc 41:269–282, 2002*

* I thank William Pinsof for his editorial feedback on this article, and Kate Silfen for her research assistance.

† Professor-Emerita, McGuinn Hall, Boston College Graduate School of Social Work, Chestnut Hill, Boston MA 02467; e-mail: elaine.pinderhughes@bc/edu

THERE is an old joke which says that African Americans are the only immigrants who were heavily recruited to come to this country, had escorts for the trip, and jobs awaiting. Throughout their history in the U.S., the circumstances and consequences of their unique arrival and subsequent treatment profoundly influenced every aspect of their life, especially marriage. The conditions under which they were forced to live have exerted an ongoing and unrelenting disruption of their efforts to build cohesive families within stable marriages. In the continuing absence of environmental supports, their struggles against these undermining influences have left African American marriages fragile and extremely vulnerable to societal shifts and changes (Lawson & Thompson, 1994; Staples, 1981; Tucker & Mitchell-Kernan, 1995).

Only since the 1960s, however, have scholars been concerned about the rising divorce, decreasing marriage, and relatively high male–female relationship instability rates among African Americans. As noted by Pinsof, (2002a,b), the factors responsible for rising divorce rates in the U.S. and elsewhere—namely, the increased human lifespan, the transformation of women's roles, and the shift in values and beliefs about marriage and divorce—have also further weakened marital stability among African Americans. For example, divorce among African Americans has been consistently higher

269

than that for other groups—their divorce rate is twice that for whites (Tucker & Mitchell-Kernan, 1995).

At the same time, the decline in marriages has been even higher, prompting some experts to express fear for the survival of African American families. In 1960, 78% of African American households included a married couple; this rate deceased to 64% in 1970; and by the late 1980s, only 48% of African American households included both a husband and a wife. This downward trend continued, reaching a low of 39% by 1993 (Billingsley & Morrison-Rodriguez, 1998). According to the U.S. Bureau of Census, in 2000, 16% of African American males were married, as compared to 60% of whites; 37% of African American females were married (nearly twice as many unmarried) as compared to 57% of white females.

What accounts for these shifts and for the differences between African Americans and whites? And what is the significance of these shifts for the male–female relationships between African Americans? I will argue that contextual conditions and the societal role of African Americans have been responsible for the problems that threaten marital occurrence, quality, and stability. The conditions include the restriction of economic opportunities, the discrediting of African American identities, and the use of social practices and policies that have legitimized inequality (Billinsley & Morrison-Rodriguez, 1998; Lawson & Thompson, 1994).

### Role of African Americans in the U.S.

Elsewhere I have used Bowen's (1978) theory of the societal projection process to explain the purpose served by the peculiar role African Americans have occupied within the U.S. social system, and to examine the systemic effects for couple and family functioning (Pinderhughes, 1988, 1999). This conceptualization suggests that, just as the scapegoat in the family projection process stabilizes a family, the scapegoat role of African Americans has served as a larger system stabilizer, reducing tension and anxiety for others in the system. Their anxiety-relieving and tension-reducing function for American society has been maintained by stereotypes and social structures, customs (racism and discrimination), laws, and policies that have restricted opportunities, lifestyles, and life choices. Orlando Patterson (1998) quotes Ralph Ellison (1953) to underscore the purpose of this sociocultural role:

> We see that the Negro stereotype is really an image of the unorganized, irrational forces of American life, forces through which, by projecting them in forms of images of an easily dominated minority, the white individual seeks to be at home in the vast, unknown world of America. [p. 41]

Cornel West (1993) also addressed this issue: "Slavery and racial caste have served as the floor upon which white class, ethnic and gender struggles could be diffused and diverted." [p. 156]

As receptacles for anxiety, conflict, confusion, and contradiction within the social system, African Americans have been required to live with multiple and ongoing stresses, and their family and couple functioning have become highly vulnerable. The adaptations they have made in coping with this societal role have become a part of their culture and, as such, these adaptations have both facilitated and undermined marriage. The decline of the African American marriage will be examined in this context.

### Significance of Slavery

Franklin (1967), Frazier (1966), and Patterson (1998) contend that slavery was the initial factor that sabotaged African American marriages: slaves were forbidden by law to marry in some states, and other states seriously circumscribed their freedom to do so. Furthermore, any emotional bonds that slaves sought to create were substantially undermined by the prevailing beliefs and social structures that reified the inferiority of African Americans: males were regarded as oversexed, promiscuous, and incapable of marital commitment; slave sales separated families and disrupted relationships, and females were sexually exploited (Furstenberg, Hershberg, & Modell, 1978; Jordan, 1971; Stampp, 1956).

African-American males were invisible, except when perceived as aggressive and out of control—a perception that persists today (Boyd-Franklin & Franklin, 1999). In my study of slave documents, I discovered that just as African Americans were not considered to be fully human (see the three-fifths clause in the Constitution**), slave fathers of children were not named or listed in birth records. Only the slave mother's name and the name of the mother's owner were recorded. I concluded that this practice

... reflects the long-standing tendency in this country to nullify and neglect maleness in African-American families. For all intents and purposes, the African-American male was a zero—he did not exist. [Pinderhughes, 1999, p. 187]

Stevenson (1995) suggests that

... the slaveowner routinely identified the child's parentage solely with the mother, often denying any acknowledgement of the father's role—biologically, emotionally, socially, or materially. [p. 38]

---

** The three-fifths compromise in the Constitution states that, in counting the population, five slaves should be considered equal to three persons (Article 1, Section 2, *The Constitution of the United States of America.*)

My research in Nigeria in 1974, on group-bonding patterns among the Yoruba (one of the tribes from which a large number of slaves had been taken), confirmed that illegitimacy and one-parent families were patterns that developed after their arrival in the U.S. Our research team found *no* illegitimacy among the traditional tribe members: if a man impregnated a woman, he married her (Pinderhughes, 1978). Although this custom was facilitated by the practice of polygamy, it also meant that, for those natives being taken from Africa, *every mother had a husband and every child had a legal father* (Pinderhughes, 1999). Patterson comments that the most devastating impact of the "holocaust of slavery" was "the ethnocidal assault on gender roles, especially those of father and husband, leaving deep scars in the relations between Afro-American men and women" (1998, p. 25).

After slavery, the stability of the African American family continued to be assaulted by a number of forces that threatened their roles as husbands and wives: for example, the disorganization of the post-Civil War plantation economy, during which there were frequent separations from and desertions by spouses; ongoing economic exploitation; disenfranchisement (maintained by lynching); and other structural inequities affecting employment, housing, and health (Lawson & Thompson, 1994; Pinkney, 1993). Despite the legacy of slavery and post-war instability, African American couples were tenacious and resilient enough to be able to marry and maintain their relationships. In 1880, 80% of African American families included a husband and wife (Billingsley, 1992). But, even though the majority had married and created stable families as soon as they could, the legacies discussed above left marriages and families vulnerable to the assault of massive stresses in the last half of the 20th century.

## Northward Migration and Subsequent Deindustrialization

The northward migration of African Americans began in the early 1900s and continued into the 1960s. Large numbers left the rural South for work in the urban areas of the North and West. A blue-collar middle class with some economic stability emerged, but there also was ongoing economic inequity, high unemployment and underemployment, poor healthcare, and discrimination in housing and education. These factors, along with an erosion of the extended family because of the migration, meant that African American couples continued to be under siege (Lawson & Thompson, 1994). But a majority of African Americans married and stayed married until the 1960s.

With the disappearance of stable employment and blue-collar jobs in urban centers after 1960, this component of the African American middle class was decimated. The shift to a technological economy radically changed the choices and chances for many African American males. High levels of poverty, crime, drug abuse, and incarceration followed (Wilson, 1987). Billingsley and Morrison-Rodriguez (1998) describe how

> . . . the technological changes and the related shift in the number and type of available jobs; changing social mores; and punitive, oppressive and ineffective social policies at the highest levels of government . . . may accomplish what slavery could not—the destruction of the African-American family. [p. 33]

The fragility of African American marriages, derived from their legacies and societal role, are associated with a number of problems that affect male/female relationships. In 1990, African Americans constituted 12% of the U.S. population, but their men made up 47% of the prison population and 28.8% of males in psychiatric hospitals. Fifty-four percent of their children lived in one-parent families, and these children constituted 50% of all children awaiting adoption (Kroll, 1993). Today, African Americans suffer disproportionately and have higher morbidity from stress diseases (high blood pressure, heart disease, and diabetes), and even much higher rates of cancer and HIV-AIDS. In 1996, 41% of childbirth deaths and 30% of the infant mortality rate were African Americans (Black, 1999; Tucker & Mitchell-Kernan, 1995). Byrd and Clayton (2001) claim that since they arrived as slaves, "they have had the worst health care, the worst health status, and the worst health outcome of any racial or ethnic group in the United States" (p. 33).

## The Effects on Marriage

What do these conditions have to do with the state of marriage among African Americans? Why are so many more African American men in prison? Why are so many more children growing up without their fathers in the home? Why are so many more children without a father or mother and in need of a new family? Why are African Americans suffering from poverty and serious health problems in higher numbers? Are these conditions symptomatic of the state of African American marriage, or is the state of African American marriage symptomatic of these conditions? I believe that these conditions constitute causes *and* effects of problems in African American marriages and in the overall relationships between men and women. They are the result of entrapment in the societal projection process and having to live with constant conflict, confusion, and contradiction while trapped within a system that undermines functional roles.

Currently, African Americans must cope, as must everyone in the U.S., with profound societal changes; the technological revolution; the acceptance of premarital sexual activity, premarital births, and tolerance for fathers who fail in their parental responsibilities; lengthened childhood; increased educational expectations; more consumer-driven, individualistic and materialistic values; and deemphasis of the value of social responsibility and sacrifice (Billingsley & Morrison-Rodriguez, 1998). In the wake of historical and current forces, the state of African American marriage is regarded as grim and expected to get worse. While research shows that African Americans value marriage, they are marrying less. When they do marry, they separate or divorce, and are more disinclined to remarry after divorce (Lawson & Thompson, 1994; Patterson, 1998).

## Structural Factors and Marital Decline

Broader structural factors influence African American family life than the family structure itself (Tucker & Mitchell-Kernan, 1995). Researchers are currently engaged in investigating two structural factors that impact marriage occurrence, stability, and quality among African Americans: the unequal sex ratio and socioeconomic conditions, in both of which the societal role is operative.

### The Unequal Sex Ratio

The concept of unequal sex ratio suggests that there are a smaller number of marriageable men than there are marriageable women. In 1985, according to the Wilson-Nickerman Male Marriage Pool Index, there were 73 African American males for every 100 females in the general population. However, among marriageable (i.e., employed) males there were 43 males to 100 females. This compared unfavorably with 93 males to 100 females in general white population, and

with 63 marriageable males to 100 females (Darity & Myers, 1995). In 1991, there were more unmarried white males than females under age 40, while the African American ratio was 77 unmarried men to 100 women under age 40. The reduction of African American men suitable and ready for marriage derives from multiple factors: higher death rates from disease, poor healthcare, and violent crime eliminate large numbers of them from the marriage pool; high rates of drug and alcohol abuse, gang activity, and incarceration further reduce the number of desirable males available for marriage. As a result, there has also been a decrease in the number of married women, a higher number of nonmarital births, and a higher percentage of children living in one-parent households.

### Socioeconomic Conditions

A number of socioeconomic factors also fuel the decline of African American marriages. As discussed above, unemployment and underemployment seriously jeopardize the ability of men to support a household. African American men who have stable employment are twice as likely to marry as men who do not. Increasing economic marginality make men unattractive as husbands, while the men are also less interested in or reluctant to marry because of constraints upon their role as providers (Darity & Myers, 1995; Tucker & Mitchell-Kernan, 1995; Wilson, 1987). The confluence of economic issues and marital decline "results in institutionalizing a majority among African-American men, creating greater marital instability [for them] than probably at any other time in our history" (Myers, 1995, p. 222). The sex ratio conditions impact African American marital behavior five times more than whites, while employment has an effect that is twenty times greater (Tucker & Mitchell-Kernan, 1995).

The decline in marriage is also connected to the increased income of African American women and their greater likelihood of completing training and/or education compared to African American men. At the highest occupational levels, African American women surpass men. Among administrative and managerial workers, there are now 127 African American women to 100 men; among professionals, there are 151 women to 100 men. For whites, there are 64 female managerial workers and 95 professional workers for every 100 white men. Patterson (1998) suggests that these gender disparities may be generated by the racial attitudes of whites since African American women have always been more acceptable to them than are the men. "Greater fear of Afro-American men, induced by racist sexual attitudes, and greater familiarity with Afro-American women in the course of growing up made it easier for Afro-American women to find jobs in clerical, and later in professional, Euro-American settings" (p. 22).

In 1977, African American males were twice as likely to receive professional degrees compared to women. Ten years later, women had taken the lead and the gap is still widening. Patterson (1998) believes that African American women will soon surpass men in median incomes. These women are now even less inclined to marry for economic security. Their relative economic independence, however, is not new. It has its roots in the historical tendency of southern families to educate the female child in preference to the male—a strategy to keep her out of domestic service and away from possible sexual exploitation by the white employer (Staples, 1981). Also, the historically greater availability of employment for African American women (though usually low-paying) as compared to men has given women a significant economic role and more power in the home than that enjoyed by white women. African American women now have significantly greater income and education relative to their husbands than do white wives (Orbuch, Veroff, & Hunter (1998).

## Male–Female Relationships

More debate, pain, anger, anxiety, and conflict have been generated by the topic of male–female relationships than by any other issue in the African American community (Boyd-Franklin & Franklin, 1999). The disastrous state of relations between spouses is regarded as a crisis; their relationships in general are weak, fractured, chaotic, hostile, and embattled. The strong ties generally heralded in African American families are not between spouses or lovers but between blood and adopted kin. This negative state of their gender relations is a major source of the wider problems of African Americans and the main means of the group's victimization of itself (Patterson, 1998).

Stereotypes of African American men play a powerful role in maintaining their status in the social system and, therefore play a part in the problems between men and women. The responses that men have to being treated as invisible (except when perceived as threatening, challenging, or dangerous), and the responses of women to the expectation that they should compensate for social injuries, become sources for tension between partners. Stereotypes of men as irresponsible, undependable, abusive, and exploitative, or of women as evil, domineering, and suspicious, filter into the expectations that each partner has of the other and become the source for marital problems. Work must be done to avoid internalizing stereotypes because translating them into expectations of self or spouse often become the basis of severe relationship conflicts (Black, 1999; Boyd-Franklin & Franklin, 1999; Pinderhughes, 1988).

Power in male–female relationships is another central factor in African American marriages (Hatchett, Veroff, & Douvan, 1995). Power in the home becomes a complex and nodal issue for couples, especially for the male. Dissonance for each spouse occurs from living in the larger society where men are supposed to have more power, but the power is is denied because of race. Men and women become more vulnerable to channeling their frustration from this dissonance into marital conflict (MacAdoo, 1991; Tucker & Mitchell-Kernan, 1995). Higher educational levels, increased income, and greater power in the home for women, coupled with the absence of guidelines for marital behavior (slavery had destroyed African cultural practices), compounding the confusion over gender relations and decision making. The current value placed on egalitarianism in husband–wife roles in today's culture, does not diminish the gender/power issue for African Americans. In fact, it may compound conflicts and magnify the male's ingrained sensitivity to threats to his manhood and power. Research findings suggest that African American men highly value the traditional sex-role power distribution and male authority more than than either African American women, white men, or white women.

African American men are also less likely than white men to view the traditional division of household chores as unfair to their wives or partners (Hatchett et al., 1995; McLloyd, Cauce, Tacheuchi, & Wilson, 2000; Taylor, Tucker, & Mitchell-Kernan, 1998). While this finding may seem contradictory to African American males' expressed approval of equity in power relations (Orbuch et al., 1998; Patterson, 1998), it makes sense in the context of their societal role. Men wish to have a compensatory sense of power in the home. A wife's demand for flexibility in assignment of tasks—which is needed

for adaptive functioning of dual-career families—may compromise a husband's feelings of masculinity if he also feels powerless in other contexts. Tucker and Mitchell-Kernan (1995) warn that this issue can be pivotal in putting African American marriages at risk.

Marital instability, tension, and conflict can also be fueled by "economic anxiety" or "provider role anxiety," that is, concern about the ability to provide for one's family (Hatchett et al., 1995). For "men of color," success in the role of provider is "of major psychological significance" (McLloyd et al., 2000). Provider-role anxiety is heightened if a men has to struggle against the persistent stereotypes of himself as an unreliable family person and provider. It is even more heightened when financial conflicts occur in relation to providing for one's children. Financial insecurity is an abiding anxiety for African American males in particular, even when, and perhaps especially when their incomes rise. Moving out of marriages when the anxiety feels unbearable may be an escape from feelings of failure and an effort to (re)establish a sense of competency.

Gender issues also contribute to marital instability because of the tendency of African Americans to protect their sons in ways they do not protect their daughters. The need to compensate for the greater psychological risks to which males are exposed sets up distorted expectations for them, which then alienates female children in ways that later contribute to problems in marital intimacy (Boyd-Franklin & Franklin, 1999). The necessary adaptations they make to their systemic role can compound the marital problems.

Studying the expectations couples have about marriage offers insight into the fact that African Americans are increasingly making decisions not to marry or, if married, to divorce. These attitudes can shed light on the differences that exist between partners. Differences in expectations and perceptions are a major issue in any relationship, and the societal role of African Americans that embodies so much confusion and contradiction compounds these differences for couples. Researchers have found a variety of gender differences in African American couples' expectations and attitudes toward marriage. Women look for financial security whereas men expect companionship. Married women are considerably less sexually and emotionally satisfied than are men. Men have lower expectations of marriage than women. Vast differences exist between men and women about values regarding sexual morality, preferences in sexual practices, level of sexual activity, and attitudes toward fidelity. Hatchett et al., 1995; Patterson, 1998; South, 1993).

The rates of infidelity of African American men constitutes a prime factor in marital instability and rising divorce. They exhibit infidelity at a rate higher than other groups, and are nearly twice as likely to be unfaithful as white men. However, African American women will not accept infidelity and are far less forgiving than white women (Patterson, 1998). Male infidelity may be connected to the unequal sex ratio in that the overabundance of desirable women makes it easier for men to avoid a committed relationship (Lawson & Thompson, 1994). When men are scarce, they have more potential partners, are more reluctant to enter into long-term relationships, have less need to compromise, and can attract women without offering many incentives for women to accept them (Kiecolt & Fossett, 1995). One can speculate that the societal projection process has pushed African American women to be sensitive about their womanliness, just as it has caused African American men to be sensitive about their manhood. Stereotypes of African American women as unattractive, bossy, castrating, evil, and mean,

threatens their sense of themselves and may cause them to experience infidelity as the ultimate in powerlessness.

## Protective Factors in Marriage

One wonders how any African American marriages are able to survive given the odds against their doing so. Many theories have been generated about factors that enable couples to achieve stable marriages. Researchers are beginning to identify protective factors that support marriage and enhance marital satisfaction. Orbuch and his colleagues (1998) suggest how wives have successfully managed their husbands' sensitivity to power threats. In stable marriages, African American and white wives were supportive in different ways: white wives were cooperative, offering an overt compliance to their husbands; African American wives were collaborative and there was a meshing of ways of interaction. The collaborative style that was observed reflected the significance and value placed by African American men on women's independence and strength and their preference for an equal partner rather than a submissive, cooperative one since their families' survival often depends upon two active partners. It was concluded that the nurturance African American men need has to be *more subtle* than that offered to white men because of the issue of power vulnerability (Orbuch et al., 1998).

Compatibility for African American couples was characterized by openness to new experience, and by more separation and autonomy than for white couples, which was seen to be consistent with wives' greater power and the norm of independence for women. Collaboration rather than cooperation in decision making, and "friendship" as well as partnership were identified as characteristics of African American stable marriages and satisfied spouses (Carolan & Allen, 1999). A study of long-term married couples

(MacKey & O'Brien, 1998) found more conflict in the early years and the use of more confrontational styles to manage conflict in the later years among African American couples than among either white or Mexican couples. They concluded that the types of conflict that all couples face today in negotiating marital roles when there are few available models, may be similar to those reported by African Americans in the study. More studies of long-term, successfully married African American couples may inform our understanding of how all couples negotiate roles and marital conflicts under stress.

Researchers are also studying mediating factors such as neighborhood and family network support, communalism and spirituality/religion, factors that have long been noted as moderators of the stresses of being African American has on marital stability. Findings are beginning to indicate that these forces can function as supports and moderating forces, but they also can be stress reinforcers. For example, although strong kinship network ties facilitate greater potential access to needed support, they also embody a greater risk of unwanted interference (Tucker & Mitchell-Kernan, 1995).

### The Societal Project Process Role

This role is the nodal issue. Network supports and connectedness to community and extended families are nonexistent for many African Americans, especially men, many of whom remain extremely isolated. Increasing rates of suicide, high-risk behavior, crime, drug abuse and addiction stem from isolation. Hypothesizing that the responses of African Americans to their plight have now become internalized, Patterson (1998) argues that centuries of unrelieved oppression and economic discrimination have resulted in cultural patterns (attitudes and behavior, particularly of men) that now

obviate the need for them (p. 166). In other words, the societal projection process has operated such that African Americans themselves are helping to create these disastrous outcomes.

In my opinion there is some truth in the assertion that the societal projection process is at work here. African Americans' responses to the stresses of their social roles have undermined their marital roles. Their efforts to manage these stresses push the flexibility, mutuality, and adaptive compensation that denote healthy family and couple functioning to exaggerated and destructive levels. Hard work can slip into driven dedication; being strong and tough can become domination and abuse of power; flexibility can lead to disorganization and inconsistency; and caution can slip into immobilization, passivity, or withdrawal under extreme stress. Thus African Americans are confronted with this dilemma: to maintain healthy family and couple functioning, they must manage the anger and frustration stemming from their societal role, such that the vulnerability and mutuality so necessary for intimacy are not destroyed by the invincible stance and readiness to struggle that are needed to cope with that role. They must maintain intimate relationships in the face of ongoing, disruptive circumstances that demand very different behaviors. They must not channel their anger and frustration into their bodies or discharge their feelings onto mates or children. Males have especially to guard against using domination in their relationships as a compensation for social injustice. This requires a state of *carefully regulated flexibility and vigilance.* The current condition of African American male–female relationships indicates the Herculean nature of that task. Any solutions to the decline of African American marriage must take into account this stress dilemma.

## COUPLE THERAPY

Couple therapy, like all therapy, has little power to make the larger social system changes that are needed to extract African American couples from their social projection process role. Yet the issues requiring such urgently needed changes are operative in African American clients' problems. Perhaps it is because of our impotence in changing context that the field of family therapy has, until recently, marginalized its significance of context. Literature, theory, and practice have been based on this omission, ignoring the role of the interactive process of race, gender, and class in the problems African American couples bring to therapy, and minimizing the importance of context in the therapeutic process as well as in the measurement of outcomes. Differences are a major issue in all relationships, but they are magnified by contextual dynamics for African Americans. The interaction of race, gender, and class in the problem of African American couples compounds the likelihood that the partners' differences in values and perspectives will be many and deeply rooted. As noted above, such issues as finances, power, partnership, nurturing, and companionship are particularly contextually loaded.

Therapists must be prepared to help couples crystallize their thinking about these differences and how their expectations of one another have been shaped by their social roles and identities in terms of race, gender, and class. Understanding the multiply contextual nature of their problems can help them to find solutions and improve their ways of coping. However, because a noncontextual, Eurocentric perspective has dominated the field, and because most therapists are beneficiaries of a process that victimizes their clients and is part of their problems, therapists have been poorly trained and minimally motivated to pay attention to these complex issues (Hardy & Laszloffy, 1999). Moreover, therapists' societal role has blinded them to their handicap, limiting their capacity to think critically and contextually about the couple's problem.

Therapists have insisted that a philosophical shift is needed in the field to enable a reexamination of its most basic assumptions. Such a shift would increase the likelihood that therapists will be trained to overcome their entrapment; take responsibility for personal biases and behaviors based on that role; become comfortable with the issues of race, class, and gender; and be able to use a broader perspective that respects the multifactorial and transactional nature of their clients' problems. This is a tall order: such shifts would be profound and there is a great resistance to them (Almeida, Woods, Messineo, & Font, 1999; Hardy & Laszloffy, 1999). There is some indication, however, that a beginning is underway because of the attention now being paid to postmodern theory and narrative concepts. Couple therapy based on these ways of thinking will help couples clarify perceptions and beliefs about their experience and problems, understand the sources that are often connected with socialization and dominant societal messages, and develop alternative perspectives that will facilitate more harmonious behaviors and improved relationships. The therapist's stance, as collaborator and learner, can itself be therapeutic since it empowers clients whose life experiences may have led them to expect much less. Because of the strong emphasis on communalism and spirituality among African Americans, encouraging couples to connect with resources such as support groups, advocacy and religious organizations can help satisfy those needs.

Therapists working with African American couples must be careful not to allow the necessary focus on context to reinforce partners' inclinations to avoid responsibility for their behavior by blaming either the system or one another. Therapists must be vigilant about not overfocusing or inappropriately focusing on context to the exclusion of individual or family factors. Some therapists are now suggesting that how couples cope behaviorally, emotionally, and cognitively with specific acts of discrimination—with institutionalized injustice and a range of oppressive behaviors and attitudes—should be assessed and, with appropriate timing, can become a focus in the therapy (Boyd-Franklin & Franklin, 1999; Carolan & Allen, 1999; Green, 1999). All therapists, of whatever color, need to learn to make these conceptual shifts since personal experiences may result in an oversensitivity that leads therapists either to avoid or to overfocus on them.

### Policy

As Pinsof (2002b) suggests, the increase in divorce and the decline in marriages may not reverse. Therefore, programs should be established to support people's pair-bonding choices, and attention must be given to designing programs for African Americans according to their specific needs. I have repeatedly indicated that the situation of African Americans has differed drastically from that of the general population. Policies that address the decline of marriages will likely be insufficient. The future for African Americans may well portend even fewer marriages, more divorces, more single-parent families, and a higher rate of poverty. But the issue of single-parent families deserves closer scrutiny. Pinsof (2002b) notes that a substantial proportion of one-parent families of all ethnic backgrounds have fathers with varying degrees of involvement. For some, their involvement may differ little from that of two-parent families. A number of nonmarital families are functional and represent a reasonable lifestyle choice. Moreover, not all single-

parent families live in poverty. In Denmark and Sweden, 50% of births are to unmarried couples, and the families are thriving. But, the strong institutional and neighborhood support in these countries contribute to positive outcomes.

In the U.S., however, nearly 64% of African American children live in poverty (U.S. Bureau of Census, 1998), and they are at risk for severe problem behaviors related to drug use and crime. Father absence coupled with lack of supervision of the children predisposes them to delinquency. Mothers are often overwhelmed, unskilled, and may lack nurturing supports that would help them to function as effective parents. Abuse and neglect of the children, drug abuse and abuse by their boyfriends, as well as abuse of the children by stepfathers are all too frequent consequences (Billingsley & Morrison-Rodriguez, 1998). Economic issues underlie these scenarios and are cause and consequence of marital decline.

The societal projection process is also heavily implicated, as is the current absence of the national will to undo, if not indict, its destructiveness. To correct this situation would require policies mandating massive social programs and citizen action to combat poverty, racism, crime, drug usage, and disease. Billingsley and Morrison-Rodriguez (1998) recommend that the Black Church, which played a leadership role during slavery and the Civil Rights Movement, mount a spiritual and political campaign to save African American families. Tucker and Mitchell Kernan (1995) suggest that economic inequity and high male mortality and undesirability become prime targets for policy changes. Danziger (1995) advocates renewed efforts to stem unwanted pregnancies by promoting self-sufficiency among males and females: for example, through paid apprenticeships, national service, or other training or work opportunities. Drastic changes are also needed in educational systems and programs that teach healthy family relationships, parenting skills, and provide information about rights advocacy. Prevention programs, as described by Gurman and Fraenkel (2002), must also be expanded.

## CONCLUSION

In the increasingly unstable sociopolitical climate of the new millennium, with its shifting values and social roles, changing family relationships, and fears about survival for self, let alone for one's family, African American families are more in peril than ever before. They must change their self-crippling responses to their societal predicaments. Patterson (1998) points out that men must change their

> ... gender attitudes, their sexual morality, their low opinion of marriage and their chronic infidelity in marriages and cohabiting unions. [p. 164]

But we will be irresponsible if we make such a demand without simultaneously extricating African Americans from their destructive societal process role. This means that White America must find other ways to manage its anxiety and reduce its tension. Otherwise, changes such as those recommended above will be only palliative Band-Aids. Improvement in problems will be only temporary, and the next major societal shift will imperil African Americans again, perhaps this time making their invisibility a physical reality.

## REFERENCES

Almeida, R., Woods, R., Messineo, T., & Font, R. (1999). The cultural context: An overview (pp. 414–431). In M. McGoldrick (ed.), Re-visioning family therapy: Race, culture and gender in clinical practice. New York: Guilford Press.

Billingsley, A. (1992). Climbing Jacob's ladder: The enduring legacy of African-American families. New York: Simon and Schuster.

Billingsley, A., & Morrison-Rodriguez, B. (1998). The black family in the 21st century and the church as an action system: A macro-perspective. Journal of Human Behavior in the Social Environment 1(2/3):31–47. [New York: Haworth Press]

Black, L. W. (1999). Therapy with African-Americans (pp. 205–221). In P. Papp (ed.), Couples on the fault line. New York: Guilford Press.

Boyd-Franklin, N., & Franklin, A.J. (1999). African American couples in therapy (pp. 268–281). In M. McGoldrick (ed.), Re-visioning family therapy: Race, culture and gender in clinical practice. New York: Guilford Press.

Bowen, M. (1978). Family therapy in clinical practice. Northvale NJ: Jason Aronson.

Byrd, W., & Clayton, L. (eds.). (2001). An American health dilemma: A medical history of African-Americans and the problem of race. New York: Routledge.

Carolan, M., & Allen, K. (1999). Commitments and constraints to intimacy for African-American couples at midlife. Journal of Family Issues 20(1):5–24.

Darity, W., & Myers, S. (1995). Family structure and the marginalization of black men: Policy implications (pp. 263–308). In M. Tucker & C. Mitchell-Kernan (eds.), The decline of marriage among African-Americans. New York: Russell Sage.

Danziger, S. (1995). Commentary (pp. 96–102). In M. Tucker & C. Mitchell-Kernan (eds.), The decline of marriage among African-Americans. New York: Russell Sage.

Ellison, R. (1953). Twentieth century fiction and the black mask of humanity. Shadow and act. New York: Vintage Press.

Franklin, J.H. (1967). From slavery to freedom. New York: Alfred A, Knopf.

Frazier, E. (1966). The Negro family in the United States. Chicago: University of Chicago Press.

Furstenberg, F., Hershberg, T., & Modell, J. (1978). The origins of the female headed black family: The impact of the urban experience (pp. 43–57). In R. Staples (ed.), The *black family: Essays and studies* (2nd ed.). Belmont CA: Wadsworth.

Green, R.-J. (1999). Race and the field of family therapy (pp. 93–110). In M. McGoldrick (ed.), *Re-visioning family therapy: Race, culture and gender in clinical practice.* New York: Guilford Press.

Gurman, A.S., & Fraenkel, P. (2002). The history of couple therapy: A millennial review. *Family Process 41:*199–260.

Hacker, A. (1992). *Two nations: Black and white: Separate, hostile and unequal.* New York: Ballantine Books.

Hardy, K., & Laszloffy, T. (1999). The dynamics of a pro-racist ideology: Implications for family therapy (pp. 118–168). In M. McGoldrick (ed.), *Re-visioning family therapy: Race, culture and gender in clinical practice.* New York: Guilford Press.

Hatchett, S., Veroff, J., & Douvan, E. (1995). Marital stability and marriage among black and white couples in early marriage (pp. 177–211), In M. Tucker & C. Mitchell-Kernan (eds.), *The decline of marriage among African-Americans.* New York: Russell Sage.

Jordan, W. (1971). *White over black attitude toward the Negro, 1550–1812.* Baltimore MD: Penguin.

Kiecolt, K. & Fossett, M. (1995). Male availability and marriage among African-Americans (pp. 121–135). In M. Tucker & C. Mitchell-Kernan (eds.), *The decline of marriage among African-Americans.* New York: Russell Sage.

Kroll, J. (1993). *North American Council on Adoptable Children.* St. Paul MN.

Lawson, E. & Thompson, A. (1994). Historical and social correlates of African-American divorce: Review of the literature and implications for research. *The Western Journal of Black Studies 18*(2):91–103.

MacAdoo, H. (ed.). (1991). *Family ethnicity strength in diversity.* Newbury Park CA: Sage Publications.

Mackey, R., & O'Brien, B. (1998). Marital conflict management: Gender and ethnic differences, *Social Work 43*(2):128–143.

McLloyd, V., Cauce, A., Tacheuchi, D., & Wilson, L. (2000). Marital processes and parental socialization in families of color: A decade review of research. *Journal of Marriage and the Family 62:*1–27.

Myers, H. (1995). Commentary (pp. 219–228). In M. Tucker and C. Mitchell-Kernan (eds.), *The decline of marriage among African-Americans.* New York: Russell Sage.

Orbuch, T.L., Veroff, J., & Hunter, A. (1998). Black couples, white couples: The early years of marriage (pp. 23–43). In E.M. Hetherington (ed.), *Coping with divorce, single parenting, and remarriage: A risk and resiliency perspective.* Mahwah NJ: Lawrence Erlbaum Associates.

Patterson, O. (1998). *Rituals of blood: Consequences of slavery in two American centuries.* New York: Basic Books.

Pinderhughes, E.B. (1978). Affiliativeness in Western Nigeria social organization: Toward an understanding of modern, Black American lives (pp. 212–221). *The Ninth Congress of the National Association of Social Workers.* New York: National Association of Black Social Workers.

Pinderhughes, E.B. (1988). Treatment with middle class black families: A systemic perspective (pp. 215–236). In J. Coner-Edwards & J. Spurlock (eds.), *Black families in crisis.* New York: Brunner-Mazel.

Pinderhughes, E.B. (1999). Black genealogy revisited: Restorying an African American family (pp. 179–199). In M. McGoldrick (ed.), *Race, culture and gender in clinical practice.* New York: Guilford Press.

Pinkney, A. (1993). *Black Americans* (4th ed.). Englewood Cliffs NJ: Prentice-Hall.

Pinsof, W.M. (2002a). Introduction to the special issue on marriage in the 20th century in Western civilization: Trends, research, therapy, and perspectives. *Family Process 41:*133–134.

Pinsof, W.M. (2002b). The death of "Till death us do part": The transformation of pairbonding in the 20th century. *Family Process 41:*135–157.

South, S. (1993). Racial differences and the desire to marry. *Journal of Marriage and the Family 53:*357–370.

Stampp, K. (1956). *The peculiar institution.* New York: Alfred A. Knopf.

Staples, R. (1981). Race and marital status: An overview (pp. 173–176). In H. MacAdoo (ed.), *Black families.* Newbury Park CA: Sage Publications.

Stevenson, B. (1995). Family structure in co-
lonial anti-bellum Virginia: Amending the
revisionist perspective (pp. 27–58). In M.
Tucker & C. Mitchell-Kernan (eds.), *The decline of marriage among African-Americans.*
New York: Russell Sage.

Taylor, R., Tucker, M., & Mitchell-Kernan, C.
(1998). Ethnic variation in perceptions of
men's provider role. *Psychology of Women
Quarterly 23:*741–761.

Tucker, M., & Mitchell-Kernan (1995). Trends
in African American family formation: A
theoretical overview (pp. 8–26). In M.
Tucker C. & Mitchell-Kernan (eds.), *The decline of marriage among African-Americans.*
New York: Russell Sage.

West, C. (1993). *Race matters.* Boston MA:
Beacon Press.

Wilson, W. (1987). *The truly disadvantaged:
The inner city, the underclass, and public
policy.* Chicago: University of Chicago Press.

Manuscript received April 19, 2002; accepted
April 23, 2002.